hud

Fulles 4⁵⁰

The Egyptian Army in Politics

The Egyptian Army
in Politics

P. J. Vatikiotis

PATTERN FOR NEW NATIONS?

INDIANA UNIVERSITY PRESS
BLOOMINGTON

Contents

Preface   vii
Introduction   xi

Part I   Background Considerations

1. The Rise of a Military Establishment in Modern
   Egypt   3
2. Egyptian Politics, 1923–1952: Prelude to
   Revolution   21
3. The Free Officers Group   44

   *Part II   The Transformation of the Military Group into
   a Ruling Elite*

4. Early Consolidation of Power   71
5. The Search for a New National Myth: The National Union
   Scheme   97
6. Formation of the United Arab Republic and Its Executive
   Structure   140

   Part III   Theoretical Considerations

7. Problems of Political Leadership: Islam, Nationalism, and
   Arabism   189
8. The Army Officer Corps and the Pyramid of Power   211

9. The Army in Politics: Conclusions   238
   Postscript   260
   Bibliographical Note   262
   Notes   281
   Index   294

Preface

THE STUDY of the Middle East by a Middle Easterner is not always satisfactory. Moreover, while I was eager to utilize the suggestions put forth by various students of methodology, I found that this was not always feasible. I have deliberately avoided as much as possible the use of non-Arab or Western interpretations of the regime in the United Arab Republic. I have been more interested in finding out local understanding, assessment, and appreciation of the system, from which to proceed with my own analysis. Much of the information contained in this book is therefore from Egyptian, Syrian, and other Arab sources. The sifting and interpretation of this information is unavoidably colored by my experience in Egypt between the years 1944 and 1949, and in Palestine before that, as well as by my more recent visit to these countries from August 1958 to June 1959.

This book was begun in the autumn of 1959 and the first draft was completed in July 1960. The factual record, and the analysis derived from it, are based mainly on events through 1959, with some revision for those of 1960.

Certain general hypotheses about the political system in the U.A.R. are presented in this book. They may be relevant also to the political experience of other Arab countries in the Middle East. But they should not be regarded as precise or final conclusions, for no definite patterns of political behavior have as yet crystallized in any of the Arab countries. Rather they are probings into the uncertainties of one of the Arab political communities whose final character has yet to emerge. While there are behavioral patterns in Egypt that are similar to those in other societies, it is often difficult to elicit from them generalizations that are meaningful to the study of politics. There is still a great deal we do not know about the Middle East; and it needs to be learned, described, and argued before it can be elevated into theoretical propositions, let alone conclusive formulations. Much of the empirical evidence necessary to support our assumptions and hypotheses is not readily available in systematic fashion; often it is inaccessible to us. If one bears in mind, moreover, that vast and complex external forces often tend to determine the internal political developments of smaller nations the task of the analyst becomes more difficult.

It is not the purpose of the book to apologize for or to castigate army rule in the U.A.R. Much of what these pages contain may sound critical of President Nasser's regime. This, I dare say, to my sensitive Egyptian and Syrian friends, is unavoidable in scholarship. To some of my co-Westerners whose lofty faith in the universalism of the democratic creed and system may find my occasional pessimism on this score irritating and inexcusable, I beg the chance to disagree and challenge the validity of their assumptions.

The issue of the army and politics in the United Arab Republic, or in other Middle Eastern countries where the military has been a vital political force, will perhaps engage students of that area for a long time to come. The present work, written rather early, must therefore be considered as a preliminary attempt at understanding the conditions that brought military groups into political eminence in the Middle East, and the early evolution of their political behavior. Whatever future patterns are suggested in this work may well be proved wrong at a later date. Indeed, it is difficult and dangerous to write about the political role of a group or an elite which could suddenly be displaced by another totally different group. Whether to write in the present or past tense is a choice those who are concerned with stable political systems rarely have to make. Nothing, therefore, that is postulated here should be considered as final or irrevocable.

Those who have helped with this study are embarrassingly many. Numerous individuals in the United States, United Kingdom, and United Arab Republic have given their time and assistance. It is not possible to mention all of them. But they all have my thanks and gratitude. The gracious hospitality and incomparable humor of Egyptian officials and private citizens who listened patiently to my questions deserve special mention.

Several senior colleagues and friends have contributed to the improvement of the manuscript by reading portions of it. Of these I should like to mention Sir Hamilton Gibb of Harvard University for his detailed criticism of the historical presentation; Mr. Richard H. Nolte, Director of the Institute of Current World Affairs, for patiently indicating linguistic and stylistic problems, as well as for challenging some of the conclusions.

I am indebted to Professor Bernard Lewis of the School of Oriental and African Studies, University of London, for his encouragement and advice while preparing this book; to Professor Majid Khadduri of the Johns Hopkins University for the patience he has exhibited in my training since 1951; and to Professor William D. Schorger, University of Michigan, whose wise counsel, intuitive grasp of Middle Eastern problems, and stimulating companionship in both Cairo and Ann Arbor have been educational and gratifying. To Professors William J. Siffin and Edward H. Buehrig, my colleagues at Indiana University, I am grateful for their editorial assistance.

The manuscript assumed its final form through the patient and able efforts of Mrs. Betty J. T. Drenkhahn and of Miss Miriam S. Farley of the Indiana University Press. I am also grateful to Mrs. Elaine Phillips for her assistance in the typing of the manuscript.

Finally, it is a pleasure to express my gratitude for the generous assistance of the Indiana University Graduate School Council in preparing the manuscript for press; the Social Science Division of the Rockefeller Foundation for its support of the writing of the manuscript; and the Committee on the Near and Middle East of the Social Science Research Council of New York for their generous grant enabling me to conduct field research in the Middle East. None of these individuals or institutions are, of course, responsible for the findings, opinions, or conclusions in the book. For these, I am solely responsible.

P. J. VATIKIOTIS

Bloomington, Indiana
January 1961

Introduction

AN ARMY-SUPPORTED REGIME rules the United Arab Republic today. It is generally well known why the army in countries such as Egypt, Syria, and Iraq has overthrown past ruling groups. Plausible explanations of this phenomenon have been offered frequently since 1949. What has not been attempted so far is a study of the army in the Near East as a political group with interests of its own, with its own understanding of what constitutes the national interest, and with a particular view of its own role as the leader of national resurgence.

Traditional Islam divided the servants of the ruling institution into two major categories: the "people of the pen" (*ahl al-qalam*) and the "people of the sword" (*ahl al-saif*). A military organization of regular troops or mercenary soldiers was usually identified with the ruling class. Both Abbasids in Baghdad (750–1258) and Fatimids in Cairo (963–1170), for instance, depended largely on military leaders for administration and for the execution of public policy. Indeed, generals were often designated as ministers, governors of provinces, and ambassadors. The Ottoman Empire (1453–1918), lacking popular support, used a strong standing army to maintain order over vast imperial domains extending from the Balkans in southeastern Europe to Egypt, North Africa, and the Indian Ocean. Throughout the Middle East, and especially in the Arab countries, it left a legacy of authoritarian government. In these countries policy is still made largely by the sanction of organized force rather than debate.

In the twentieth century the new nation-states in the Middle East, immediately upon achieving independence, proceeded to build and equip modern armies, for a strong national army is the supreme symbol of independence and sovereignty. In the Arab countries, moreover, between the two World Wars, most standing armies were primarily an extension of police security forces, used to maintain internal order and the *status quo*. They were the antidote of the ruler to the frequently erupting mob.

In their attempt to build modern armies, the Arab countries in the Middle East introduced Western technology. But Western technology was not simultaneously extended to other social institutions. Consequently, the army not only became the technologically most advanced institution in the Arab world, but also acquired a special role in the political evolution of these countries. Army officers became conscious of their access to physical force, and of their importance, as a highly organized and stable group, in spearheading national movements.

There are complicating factors in the study of the role of the army in Middle Eastern politics. How do we explain the transformation of the military in general and the army in particular from a praetorian guard in the service of a ruling group or dynasty to an *avant-garde* leading national revolutions? The score or so of military coups d'état in Middle Eastern countries have occurred in large measure as a result of the lack of organized political expression on a mass scale. More often than not they involved a small coterie of officers and tended to develop into strong-man dictatorships. This phenomenon is not without precedent in Islamic history. One recalls, for example, Fatimid agitation in Syria, Iraq, and Persia, and the Bassassiri coup d'état in Baghdad in the eleventh century.

A second complicating factor concerns the question of class.

Is the army in the Arab countries a professional class or group? Without indulging in sociological distinctions between "class" and "group," the author suggests that the army in the Arab states is not necessarily a class in the socio-economic sense, sharing similar social backgrounds and economic interests. It may not be even a professional group in the sense of the German, British, or American regular army officer class. Rather the Army Officer Corps represents the most cohesive elite of younger enthusiasts linked together by vague nationalist aspirations and by concern for the social and economic frustrations of their fellow citizens. They do share, though—especially today—a common educational background: secondary school, military academy, and some even staff college. Their hatred for professional politicians of the "old school" is complemented by their sympathy for their politically impotent countrymen. Army officers in many Middle Eastern states think of themselves as saviors and regenerators of national existence. This self-image also serves as a strong political symbol that is invoked constantly by military rulers when they accede to political power, in order to legitimize their authority. But army officers reject the slow-moving machinery of representative political institutions, which, in their view, are impediments to quick regeneration. They favor so-called direct populistic and authoritarian regimes: what they sometimes refer to as "plebiscitary democracies."

Although Egypt, Syria, Iraq, and Jordan are militarily weak countries, army groups are strong factors in their domestic politics. In these countries the army today not only rules, but resolves practically all political conflicts on a national level. It is the instrument of political change and the manipulator of political ideology and orientation. In Egypt the army has provided the core of political leadership since 1952; in Syria it has allied itself since 1954 with new political groups actively calling for Arab unity and greater independence from the West. In Iraq the army has provided the nucleus of political leadership since 1922, has been resolving power conflicts since 1935, and eventually seized power for itself in 1958. In Jordan the army has provided the major source of support for the ruling monarch.

Once in power, army officers have tried to influence and regiment society through formal mass movements of the "national front" variety. The Arab Liberation movement of Shishakli in Syria in 1952 and the National Union in the U.A.R. today are good examples of this pattern. The military regime in Egypt has tried to build a monolithic party structure that would permeate the countryside. Whatever its methods, this may have been a shrewd move, for the army is as yet the only group in Arab politics which seemingly appreciates the significance of expanding its political constituency outside the urban centers. The army may yet prove to be the catalytic agent for transforming the age-old society in the Arab countries into a modern homogeneous political culture.

This study also considers the professed goals and aspirations of the army group as the leader of Arab national endeavor. Apart from other sources, there are now available written documents and political treatises by army officers in positions of authority as well as by participating civilians. Such writings are basically oriented toward the task of creating a modern Arab society and a modern Arab state. The members of this society are not to be bound together by the traditional bonds of religion, communalism, or sectarianism, but by the single bond of nationality. Such is the prescribed objective, and it requires the formulation of a public philosophy as well as good organization. Although political authority has theoretically been vested in the people, political influence must come not from the traditional sources—monarchs, landowners, and men of religion—but from the new groups of educated and professional citizens. These will constitute the new ruling class.

In the resurgent Arab society, the army, especially the Officer Corps, acquires the role of an elite that is leading the nation toward these prescribed objectives. This elite has both a political and a social task to perform. The most prolific writer among the Egyptian revolutionary officers, Anwar es-Sadat, has often talked of the "spiritual consequences of the battle." He has even indulged in the role of political philosopher, constructing a theory for the new Egyptian politics, as well as the politics of the Arab world. He epitomizes the assumption by the army of the role of national political leader in his famous statement: "The enemies of the Egyptian Revolution used to rule the people through the Armed Forces. Then suddenly, the Armed Forces rebelled against these enemies [of the people] as soon as they acquired new leadership."[1]

In explaining to the public what the "revolution" means the Army Officer Corps, acting as a political leader, faces the difficult task of constructing a new national myth, to supersede an older one, as a means of legitimizing its authority. Whether couched in terms of "Arabism," "nationalism," "historical prowess and glory," "antagonism to the West," "identification of the enemy," or "positive neutralism," this task involves the relation of the Officer Corps as a controlling political group to the total cultural, religious, and social structure of Egypt and Syria.

Throughout this book it is suggested that the military power elite, in Egypt at least, has chosen since July 1952 to play the role of innovator, seeking to transform Egypt and Syria from a traditional agricultural society to a modern industrial one; to be the supreme educator of Egyptian society; and to act as the benevolent father guiding a traditionally divided and fragmented people to greater political cohesion and achievement.

In studying the role of the army officer in Arab politics, one is confronted by a multiplicity of problems and difficulties. The available material, such as the writings by military men mentioned above, provides some basis for an investigation of the role of the army in the evolution of political ideology. Such works, however, tell us little about the internal structure, organization, and functioning of an army elite as a political group. Enunciations of social and economic policy by military leaders of the U.A.R. do not give many clues to the kind of alignments made by the army group with other groups. Access to data on these questions is difficult and often impossible under present conditions.

The research student is thus left with three possible lines of investigation. First, he may embark upon a historical study of the occasions in the past when the army has taken an active role in politics. Such occasions are numerous in the brief history of independent Arab states, and the longer history of the Ottoman state. Second, he may attempt an intensive analysis of situations where a group of army officers has gained political power and control. Depending on the findings of these two approaches, a third approach becomes possible: the study of army officers who achieve political power as a political interest group. Since a variety of Middle Eastern countries have recently experienced the interference of the army in their domestic politics, comparison becomes possible.

All three approaches have been attempted here. Chapter 1 is a brief historical consideration of the military establishment in Egypt. Chapters 2 and 3 analyze the political forces and conditions that led to the rise of a political movement among a particular group of army officers in Egypt, and its eventual access to power. Chapters 4 and 5 make certain propositions regarding the transformation of a military group into a political ruling elite. Variations and patterns in the political orientation of army officers are formulated and analyzed in the discussion of the formation of the United Arab Republic and its executive structure in Chapter 6. The relation between the army officers in power and national desires, political orientation, and the Arab political community is examined in Chapters 5, 6, and 7. Chapter 8 analyzes the relation between the ruling Army Officer Corps and the structure of power. The concluding chapter attempts the formulation of some general hypotheses regarding the total role of the military in Arab politics.

Note on Transliteration of Arabic Terms and Names

Diacritical marks for the *ain* (') and *hamza* (') in Arabic are used only where absolutely necessary to avoid misreading of Arabic book titles, terms, and names. Names and terms that are common in English spelling are rendered in the most simplified phonetic way. Names of well-known personalities in the U.A.R. and the Arab world are spelled closest to the way they have appeared in newspapers and other sources.

Part I
Background Considerations

1. The Rise of a Military Establishment in Modern Egypt

THE MODERN Egyptian military establishment dates from the founding of a semi-independent state by Muhammad Ali (1805–49), an Albanian army officer in the service of the Ottoman Sultan. He came to Egypt with the Turkish troops sent to expel the French forces remaining after Napoleon had returned to France in 1799. He led a successful military mutiny against the Turkish Governor, who was left helpless once British allied troops had evacuated the country. Then he embarked upon a series of shrewd power moves culminating ten years later in the final overthrow of the surviving Mameluke Beys, who had ruled Egypt ever since the sixteenth century.

During a reign of forty-three years, Muhammad Ali built, with the help of foreign advisors and technicians, a modern army and navy. Employing his armed forces almost continuously (1811–39), he crushed the Wahhabi rebellions in Arabia, invaded Syria, and moved as far north as southern Turkey to challenge the authority of his own master, the Ottoman Sultan in Istanbul. One would assume that such extended military experience provided Egypt with a strong military tradition, for the successor Khedives of Egypt, Said, Ismail, and Tewfiq, maintained a well-equipped and trained army. But the native Egyptian, until the 1930's, had never identified this military establishment with national strength or fulfillment. There are serious reasons for this, going further back in history than the nineteenth century.

From Pharaonic times, Egypt has experienced a series of military conquests culminating in foreign colonization and political domination. As successors to Alexander the Great, the Ptolemies founded in Egypt a dynasty foreign to the land and its people. Their armies consisted mainly of foreign regulars and mercenary troops, but they never included any great number of Egyptians. The same was true of their successors, the Romans. What is interesting, however, is that a similar situation prevailed after the Arabization and Islamization of the Nile Valley.

Of the various caliphates, petty dynasties, and Mameluke satrapies between 640 and 1805, none ever encouraged or required native Egyptians to serve in their military forces. Saladin, the hero of Arab-Islamic unity in the twelfth century, never permitted Egyptians to serve in his armed forces. Turks and Kurds formed the core of his army, while Maghribis (North Africans) operated his navy.

Until the nineteenth century the army of Egypt was structured and organized according to the Seljuk Turkish principle of military feudalism. Mercenary troops formed a military caste accepting fiefs of land in return for service. Consequently, there was never really a national army, only professional mercenaries. The fiefs, being hereditary, tended to make still tighter this military caste of Turks, Kurds, and Circassians. At the height of its success, Fatimid military power, for instance, depended mainly on the services of Turks, Berbers, Nubians, and Armenians. Native Egyptians were never allowed to develop a tradition of military service or officer training, since neither was open to them.

General conscription of the native population was unknown. Even under Muhammad Ali, the enterprising new viceroy of Egypt, the armed forces included very few Egyptians beyond enlisted ranks and low-grade commissioned officers. Senior or staff officers were mainly recruited from Albanian, Circassian, and Turkish elements residing in Egypt. These represented the new aristocracy of the ruling class. Other foreign officers who had highly specialized and technical services to offer the Viceroy in building a modern army were imported from Europe.

Muhammad Ali considered the possession of a strong army and navy a more important base for the establishment of his new Egyptian state than the native population of peasant farmers he found there. The view that all other reforms in agriculture, industry, education, and administration were devices to serve and maintain this strong army is not an exaggerated one. Inevitably, however, this new army became the means for the introduction of Egyptian society into the modern age.

The Mameluke princes who ruled Egypt when Muhammad Ali arrived had no regular army but, instead, irregular troops directly loyal to the prince so long as he was able to promote their interests and welfare. Muhammad Ali's first task in Egypt, therefore, was the organization of a modern regular army. But his first attempts in this direction in 1815 almost cost him his life, for the conglomeration of Albanians, Circassians, and Turks making up the Mameluke armies saw an end to their privileged position if the Viceroy's plan were to succeed. Gradually, he was able, by scattering and dispersing these irregular forces away from the capital, to neutralize their influence.

In 1820 Muhammad Ali opened the first military Officers' School in Aswan. Its location in a remote part of Upper Egypt, away from the intrigues of Cairo, is interesting. Under the direction of the French Colonel Sèves (Suleiman Pasha al-Faransawi), the school trained the first crop of 500 officers chosen from Muhammad Ali's personal slaves (*mamalik*). The problem of discipline, indispensable to military training, was crucial at the beginning, for Mameluke slaves were not accustomed to modern organization.

A serious obstacle to the raising of a modern army was the question of conscription and recruitment. Once he had turned his back on the irregular and mixed Mameluke elements, Muhammad Ali had no choice but to recruit or conscript local Egyptians. This proved most difficult. At first he was not anxious to flood his army ranks with Albanians and Turks, although later his Officer Corps was largely Turkish and Albanian. At the same time he was dubious about confronting the Egyptian population with conscription because he feared disaffection and possible rebellion. Muhammad Ali may also have felt that conscription would remove Egyptian agricultural hands from the land, thus affecting agricultural productivity. These and other considerations urged Muhammad Ali to conquer Sennar and Kordofan in the Sudan, with the hope of providing the bulk of recruits from the population of these two provinces. Some 20,000 men were recruited into the army from Sennar and Kordofan. Major difficulties presented by these new Sudanese troops were the effects of climatic changes upon them and the strain of modern military training. Indeed, they did not meet the military standards that the Viceroy expected. The only alternative left open to him was to recruit native Egyptians.

In 1823 the first Egyptians were recruited into Muhammad Ali's modern army and commanded by the first batch of Mameluke cadets from the Aswan Officers School. Many of these cadets received further training at a new General Staff and Command School in Khanka. By 1825, Muhammad Ali had the nucleus of a modern army and the minimum number of training centers for it. But the recruitment and conscription of native Egyptians was not quietly accepted by the whole population. There were outbursts of violence in protest against the system as early as 1825.

Undoubtedly the Viceroy anticipated such a reaction, for Egyptians were not well disposed toward any kind of military service. Under Mameluke rule they were exempt from military service. The *fellah* or peasant, on the land, welcomed relief from such a burden. It was therefore inevitable that he should oppose conscription later. Muhammad Ali's methods of forcefully leading peasants into army training camps were not inducive to their acquiescence. The effects of this negative attitude of the Egyptians toward military service may be observed in our day. *Fellah,* city-dweller, educated, and rich all detest having to serve in the armed forces. Thus it was not until 1947 that the first modern military selective service law in Egypt was passed. But it has been rigidly applied only since 1955, when the Nasser government promulgated a revised act.

Abder Rahman al-Rafii, the Egyptian historian of Muhammad Ali, argues in *Asr Muhammad Ali* (The Age of Muhammad Ali) that the Viceroy was unable to build a modern army without resorting to Egyptian elements. He overlooks the fact that the Officer Corps remained largely Albanian, Macedonian, Turkish, and Circassian. It represented a privileged foreign class permanently settled in Egypt but closely allied with the ruling family of the Viceroy. Nor does he remark on the perpetuation of a system whereby policy decisions continued to be made by what was in effect a military governor supported by a strong army. This pattern in Egypt throughout her history is worth noting. Saladin's Consultative Assembly, for instance, was composed primarily of Kurdish and Turkish princes, all of whom were related to him in one way or another. These were at the same time his military leaders. Not a single Egyptian participated in this Assembly or shared in army leadership. Having conquered Egypt by the sword, Saladin considered the country his feudal domain to be apportioned among his military chiefs, who were also his relatives. Egyptians were encouraged to stick to the land. The British occupation of Egypt in 1882 reasserted this pattern by the presence of British troops and their influence on policy-making until 1952. The same was true in Syria under the French Mandate, as well as during the wartime British occupation of Syria and Lebanon (1941–45). It is also applicable to Iraq between 1920 and 1954 and to Jordan until 1956.

Under Muhammad Ali's successor, Abbas, the political-military status of army officers was reinstated. Lacking the ability, intelligence, and strong personality of his grandfather, Abbas permitted the influx of thousands of Albanians into positions of influence in the army and a deterioration of the relations between this group and the Egyptian population. Said Pasha, who succeeded Abbas, felt that the power of the Albanian officers in the army could be curbed by admitting native Egyptians to the ranks of commissioned officers. He made military service compulsory for all and encouraged Egyptians to join the army with the new prospect of achieving officer grades. In contrast to his father's policy of drafting the poorer elements of the population for indefinite periods, Said limited the period of service to one year but made it applicable to all classes of society. He cleverly required the sons of town and village mayors (*sheikhs* and *umdas*) to serve by sending them to military preparatory schools and, from there, to cadet officer schools. It was during Said's reign as *wali*, or viceroy, of Egypt that the first nucleus of Egyptian army officers was created.

The "maligned" Khedive Ismail, who ruled Egypt from 1863 to 1879, further increased the number of Egyptian army officers. Anxious to Europeanize Egypt quickly, Ismail paid much attention to the education and training of his army. Besides the various military training missions he sent abroad to France and England, Khedive Ismail founded most of the military schools and academies now existing in Abbassieh, bordering the western desert near Cairo. Infantry, cavalry, and artillery schools as well as a Staff College were all concentrated in Abbassieh. A Chief of Staff's department was established for the first time with the help of the famous American Colonel Stone. In addition to his attention to military training and various officers' schools, Ismail spent much of his borrowed money on the institution of an army publicity department. Two publications by Egyptian officers, the

Egyptian Army Staff Newspaper and *Egyptian Military Journal,* first appeared in 1873.

The Khedive's efforts had a definite impact on the Egyptian army officer. For the first time he began to acquire professional identity and a certain amount of pride. In contrast to the morale of the Egyptian officer during the period 1920–45, his predecessor had the added benefit of genuine battle experience in the African campaigns in the Sudan and Ethiopia.

The above brief exposition of the rise and development of the Egyptian army provides the background for an examination of the first major role of the army officer in Egyptian politics. When Khedive Ismail succeeded Said Pasha as *wali* (viceroy) of Egypt in 1863, there was no legislative or consultative assembly in which the public was represented. Aspiring to rid himself completely of Ottoman tutelage, Ismail established by decree in 1866 a Consultative Assembly of Representatives. This Assembly did not have actual power in matters of legislation but merely expressed its views and gave advisory opinions regarding certain matters brought before the Khedive. The election of 75 representatives for a period of three years was restricted to the village *umdas* or mayors, provincial *sheikhs,* and the notables of Cairo, Alexandria, and Damietta. It met for no longer than two months each year.

Although one may consider the Consultative Assembly of Representatives as the first attempt at representative government in modern Egypt, it is obvious that its creation was willed by the ruler. There was no public demand for its institution. Its merely advisory capacity and actual control by the Khedive further limited any benefit in political education for the masses, since they were not permitted to participate in its election or establishment. The rights of nomination, election, and membership were confined to a very small class. Nevertheless, it was a beginning in an electoral process and the extension of the franchise. A fairly numerous class of merchants and artisans was, however, denied participation or representation in this incipient consultative legislative body.

Nor were the fast-increasing numbers among the educated considered. Mass media such as the press were lacking to nurture the public's awareness of the importance of representation in the country's political process and institutions.

The Assembly held three sessions between 1866 and 1873. The financial predicament in which the "modernizing" Khedive Ismail continued to find himself was one reason for its suppression in 1874. The privileged class represented in the Assembly finally objected to the Khedive's persistent demands for increased funds and his search for loans from Europe because they were excluded from the private financial transactions between him and his foreign creditors.

The threat of imminent bankruptcy and serious concern over the ruler's suicidal policies led to opposition when the Assembly reconvened in 1876. Movements were organized against the ruler, who by now had pawned off the country to foreign creditors. These creditors were by 1879 beginning to press their governments to protect their investments, or loans, to the ruler of Egypt. Representatives of these creditors appointed by their governments, England, France, and Italy, were given control over all of Egypt's finances. Ismail was deposed in 1879 and exiled to Italy—a sad end for the modernizer of Egypt, but a fair price for his impatience.

Financial bankruptcy brought European influence and control into the country for the second time since the Napoleonic invasion in 1798. Popular resentment of increased taxation and rigid financial control increased to the point of starting a movement against the ruling family, now identified with foreign powers.

In the meantime, a new force appeared in the Islamic community calling for the recrudescence of Islam to contain the deep incursions of European power into the Islamic world. Jamal al-Din al-Afghani represented this pan-Islamic reaction to Europe, and his presence in Egypt from 1871 to 1879 had a profound effect on the religious leaders as well as on the rising educated class of civilians and army officers. His attractive and versatile teaching won him many disciples, among them the famous reformer Sheikh Muhammad Abdou. Afghani encouraged the incipient Egyptian press to deal with the basic political, economic, and social problems of the country, and to call public attention to the injustices and excesses of the ruling class, headed by the Khedive. His active career as political agitator in Egypt caused the authorities to expel him from the country in 1879, but the effects of his revolutionary teaching were plainly left behind.

It is popular among students of modern Egyptian history to consider the Orabi Revolt in 1881 the first nationalist popular movement in Egypt led by army officers. But the first intervention of the military in the political affairs of modern Egypt came two years before that. The Anglo-French Commission of Inquiry on Egyptian finances had reported in 1878 the need for a ministry with two foreign advisor-controllers to supervise Egypt's financial policies. In August 1878 Nubar Pasha (an Armenian) formed such a cabinet. Besides the two foreign advisor-controllers in the Ministries of Finance (Sir Rivers Wilson) and Public Works (M. de Blignières), other foreigners were appointed to responsible administrative positions in various departments of the government on the premise that they would scrutinize the financial operations of the country.

The last session of the Legislative Council during Khedive Ismail's reign reconvened in January 1879. It objected to the introduction of direct foreign supervision in the cabinet, as well as to the ultimate control foreign representatives exercised over financial policies. Members of the Council were joined in their opposition stand by sectors of the public and by the Khedive himself, who was anxious to rally public support against foreign control.

When public income had first to meet the obligations of Egypt toward its creditors, salaries to civil servants and members of the armed forces were not paid regularly. The civil servants objected to such arrears as well as to the new positions of authority handed over to foreign administrators. The government was eventually able to pay salary arrears to civil servants but found it necessary to retire some 2,500 Egyptian army officers from active service. The attempt to cut down the number of officers because of financial difficulties was based on the assumption that the bulk of public revenue had been assigned to meeting the obligations incurred by the Khedive. But there was also the fear that the army was the only national organization that could effectively combat an increase in foreign influence.

The government unwisely recalled 2,500 officers to Cairo as a prelude to retirement, a dangerous move as it concentrated a large number of disgruntled army officers in the capital. It also coincided with the return of the *mahmal* (the Holy Carpet sent traditionally by Egypt to Mecca every year to cover the Kaaba) from the pilgrimage, a time of high religious emotions. Headed by Lieutenant Colonel Latif Bey Salim, a Military Academy instructor, the officers demonstrated before the Ministry of Finance on February 18, 1879, demanding their rights. The *Official Gazette* of Egypt for February 23, 1879 (No. 799) reports that, seeing Nubar in his carriage, the demonstrators proceeded to inflict physical harm on him and his advisor, Sir Rivers Wilson. Only the personal intervention of the Khedive, who was obviously pleased at his increased popularity, vis-à-vis the government, stopped the demonstrating officers.[1]

Despite the fall of Nubar's ministry, the veto power of foreign advisors was established. Soon thereafter, in April 1879, the Legislative Assembly was dissolved, the Khedive Ismail was deposed in June, and a dictatorial regime headed by the Khedive Tewfiq was inaugurated, mainly through the support of the foreign powers. The brief army movement, however, does represent the first serious attempt by army officers in Egypt to influence policy and exert political authority. It is significant that, although they requested the support of the Assembly, the latter did not respond effectively. Instead, disappointed at its impotence, the Assembly was prompted to found the National Society, known later as the National party. What is important is that these officers were young Egyptians, from the lower commissioned ranks, as distinguished from the Turkish and Circassian staff officers. Their precipitous but short-lived action was identified with a rising tide of nationalist demands against khedivial authority and a mounting resentment against foreign influence. To this extent the army officers in Egypt at the time could claim a share in the movement for national self-determination.

When Khedive Tewfiq succeeded the deposed Ismail, the country was smarting under heavy taxation, foreign financial supervision, and what amounted virtually to Anglo-French political control. The brief experimentation with representative institutions under Ismail whetted Egyptian national appetite enough to make the aspiration for constitutionalism a major motive for national agitation. Such political orientation was encouraged by the Sherif Pasha Government of July 1879. Considered by now the architect of constitutional government in Egypt, Sherif Pasha recruited into his Cabinet leading figures in the national movement, among them Mahmud Sami Pasha Barudi, Mustafa Fahmi Pasha, and Murad Hilmi Pasha. Expectations for better government and a decrease in foreign influence and control were, moreover, heightened by the Khedive's public announcement that khedivial government should be consultative and constitutional, that its leaders should be responsible, and that the Assembly of Notables would be consulted in the matter of finances and legislation.[2] This was interpreted by the Egyptians as meaning that the Khedive accepted the constitutional system and wished to work for its effectiveness.

Having prepared a report on the drafting of a new constitution, Sherif Pasha tendered his resignation. British and French representatives were not too comfortable about Sherif's constitutional plans; they preferred the concentration of power in the person of the Khedive, who would be more amenable to their control. In the meantime, the Assembly of Representatives was suspended indefinitely until the Khedive could look into the new constitutional plan and proposed electoral law of Sherif Pasha. When the latter pressed the Khedive to promulgate both proposals, Tewfiq refused to act on the ground that such measures would not meet with the approval of the British and French consular representatives. Shortly thereafter, in September 1879, the Khedive entrusted the formation of a government to Riyad Pasha, who was inclined toward absolute rule at the expense of constitutional experiments.

One may date the beginning of national agitation against Tewfiq's absolutism from his appointment of Riyad Pasha to head the government. Sherif Pasha was already identified in the minds of members of the now defunct National Assembly, as well as army officers, as the leader of the national constitutional movement. They saw in Riyad a return to absolute rule, increased foreign domination, and a curtailment of their ambition for a greater share in power. And, indeed, Riyad embarked upon a policy of persecuting all opposition among army officers, the emerging Egyptian press, and the National party. He was not inclined to take seriously the demands of the latter organization regarding financial policy. Furthermore, Riyad proceeded to retire as many army officers from active duty as were necessary to ease the budgetary burden.

It was not unlikely, therefore, that a growing feeling of national interest distinct from and contrary to the interests of the ruling Khedive should seek expression through some movement of national magnitude. The army had once before (1879) attempted to impress its demands upon the ruler by a show of force. A precedent was readily available for use in a national crisis.

Egyptian historians at least have tried to portray the Orabi Revolt of 1881–82 as a "national revolution" in which, in addition to the army, all sections of the Egyptian population participated. They argue that, although precipitated by specific demands of the military, the revolt had deep roots in the deteriorating economic-political situation. Undoubtedly, the strengthening of absolute rule in the hands of the Khedive Tewfiq and his first minister, Riyad Pasha, was ultimately reflected in general policy. One of the earliest organizations to be affected was the army. Osman Pasha Rifqi, the Circassian chief of staff, was obviously partial to Circassian, Turkish, and Albanian army officers and constantly sought to concentrate military authority in their hands. Promotion therefore came easily to these elements, at the expense of native Egyptian officers.

In July 1880 the Khedive decreed a new law for military service. A four-year term of service was required, after which the conscript returned to his village, carrying a reserve obligation extending to five years. He attended two months of training in a provincial center in each of these years and then reverted to a territorial reserve status for another six years. In effect, this law extended military service to a total of fifteen years.

Led by Colonel Ahmad Orabi Pasha, Egyptian officers objected to the new law on the ground that it lessened the chances of Egyptian recruits for promotion to commissioned grades while on active duty. Four years was considered too short a period in which to acquire the necessary academic and practical training for promotion to officer grade. Since the law precluded the commissioning of Egyptians from the reserve or territorial status grades, it was in their view a serious and final obstacle to the growth of an Egyptian Officers Corps. They further objected to the transfer of Egyptian officers from command positions to administrative duty in the Ministry of War.

At a meeting of Egyptian line officers at his home on the night of January 16, 1881, Orabi Pasha drafted a series of demands against the government, on the assumption that opposition to the new decrees pertaining to the army was imperative. These demands allegedly sought to bring the strength of the army up to the 18,000 permissible by the *firman*, and to constitute an Assembly of Representatives (or

Chamber of Deputies) in accordance with the Khedive's promises upon his accession to power a year earlier.[3] There is some
controversy over whether or not the officers' manifesto included a demand for the removal of Osman Pasha Rifqi. Most
historians, including Wilfrid Scawen Blunt in *Secret History
of the English Occupation of Egypt*,[4] agree that this first meeting under Orabi's leadership was confined to a discussion of
the aim of removing Osman Rifqi from his position as Minister of War. Conceivably the officers did elect Orabi as their
leader to represent their general grievances and demands to
the authorities; for on the following day Colonels Orabi, Ali
Fahmi, and Abdel Al Hilmi appeared at the Ministry of the
Interior to present the manifesto to Prime Minister Riyad
Pasha. Abder Rahman al-Rafii argues in *al-Thawra al-urabiyya*
(The Orabi Revolt) that this manifesto probably did not include demands for the election of a Chamber of Deputies and
the reform of legislation pertaining to the military establishment. It probably confined itself to a direct request for the
removal of Osman Rifqi.

Be that as it may, the demands were rejected and all three
leaders just mentioned were brought to courts-martial by the
end of January 1881. At this point direct command of line
troops by these officers appeared decisive: their troops moved
in force to seek the release of their commanders. The immediate effect of this forceful interference was the removal of
Osman Rifqi and his replacement in the Ministry of War by
Mahmud Sami Pasha Barudi, who was presumably sympathetic
to the Orabi group. The officers quickly followed up this
interference by drafting a list of demands, the most important
being: the raising of officer salaries, legislation to put criteria
for promotion on a sound basis, and the promulgation of
uniform rules for pension, retirement, and compensation.
Most of these were complied with by the Khedive by decree
between February and April 1881, and a special commission
was appointed to study the reform of legislation directly affecting the armed forces.

It was most unlikely that both the Khedive and his Circassion-Turkish officers would acquiesce in strengthening the political influence of Egyptian elements inside and outside the army. Pressure from the non-Egyptian officers upon the Khedive to curtail the influence of what they referred to as "peasant officers" was supplemented by their fostering of anti-Orabi movements among Sudanese and other officers in the army. The Orabi forces, on the other hand, sensing imminent danger to their position, multiplied their demands on authority and clamored for an increase in army strength, as well as for the institution of a Legislative Assembly to which the Cabinet would be responsible. They hoped that an increase in army strength would bring in more Egyptian elements and therefore widen the base of their support against the Circassian-Turkish group. They also believed that a Legislative Assembly would be responsible for the approval of the national budget and sympathetic toward the Egyptian officers' cause.

By the summer of 1881 the Khedive in conjunction with his first minister, Riyad Pasha, decided to break the nationalist military party of Orabi. Suddenly he dismissed the popular Minister of War, Sami Pasha Barudi, and replaced him by his own brother-in-law, Daoud Pasha Yeken. At the same time Tewfiq tried skillfully to disperse pro-Orabi troops far and wide in the Delta, away from the capital. At this point, on September 9, 1881, Orabi's forces surrounded Abdin Palace to protest the Khedive's policy. Their demands this time, too, included the dismissal of the Cabinet, convocation of the Chamber of Notables, and the increase of army strength. The Khedive yielded by dismissing Riyad's ministry and asking Sherif Pasha to form a new government. Sherif hesitated at first, but at the insistence of Orabi accepted, including in his cabinet Sami Pasha Barudi as Minister of War once again. The Sherif Government proceeded to hold elections for a new Legislative Chamber, which met in December 1881. The newly-drafted constitution was officially presented to the Assembly for discussion and adoption in January 1882.

Developments tended to strengthen the position of the

Orabi-led military party and to curtail the Khedive's absolute rule. Local Turks in Egypt were now in danger of losing their landed wealth and privileged political position. They hoped for some kind of European intervention against Orabi. Meanwhile the Orabi forces were getting impatient with the Sherif Pasha government in spite of Orabi's appointment as Under-secretary of State for War. On January 7, 1881, an Anglo-French note assuring the Khedive of full support against dissident forces in the country was delivered in Cairo, on the pretext that creditor countries would not permit the Assembly to vote on the Egyptian budget. This, in their view, was clearly a matter for the foreign controllers. Sherif Pasha then resigned, and Sami Pasha Barudi formed a new government with Orabi as Minister of War. The leader of the military party had now acceded to a position of legitimate political power, in spite of the fact that he had compromised his nationalist position by acquiescing to the Anglo-French note!

Orabi's drift from his previous alignment with Sherif Pasha contributed to his political failure later. He promoted himself as well as his cohorts, Ali Fahmi, Abdel Al Hilmi, and Tulba Ismet, to the rank of general officer. On February 8, 1882, he and the Prime Minister forced Khedive Tewfiq to proclaim the new constitution by decree. The Khedive now clearly saw that an alliance between Orabi officers and the Legislative Assembly could have disastrous results for him and the Turkish ruling caste around him. Lacking the means to crush Orabi alone, Tewfiq now realized that only outside intervention could help him destroy the military party.

The Powers had already lodged a strong protest with the Khedive against the formation of the Barudi Government. Their objection made it clear to the Legislative Assembly that they would not tolerate the ascendancy of a national movement aimed at curtailing the Khedive's authority. This protest, however, aided Orabi to achieve a measure of cooperation between his military party and civilian notables.

By April 1882 the Barudi Cabinet clashed violently with

the Khedive over the court-martial punishment of conspiring officers in the army. In May the rift between Tewfiq and his ministers was so serious that the Powers saw their chance to intervene. On May 25, 1882, a joint Anglo-French note demanding the resignation of the Barudi ministry, the exile of Orabi, and the transfer inland of both Ali Fahmi and Abdel Al Hilmi was handed to the Khedive. The ministers rejected the note and resigned in protest. Riots in Alexandria during June 1882 led eventually to the British bombardment of the city and ultimate occupation of the entire country. Orabi's movement had come to an end.

"Of a remarkable intuitive intelligence, and a sincere, halting eloquence, his education has been of the simplest"—so writes Desmond Stewart of Orabi Pasha in the July 1958 issue of the *Middle East Forum.*[5] This is too romantic an assessment as well as a misleading, though enthusiastic, evaluation of the Egyptian colonel. Ahmad Orabi was born in March 1841 at Rizna in the Sharqiyya province, near the city of Zaqaziq. His father was the *sheikh el-balad* or village headman, who claimed his descent from a pure Arab Bedouin tribe that had settled in Egypt from Iraq. It seems that young Orabi received his first lessons from a Copt named Mikhail Ghattas, a moneychanger by profession. From there he went to Cairo, where he spent four years at the Azhar. At age thirteen, in compliance with Said Pasha's decree requiring sons of village *sheikhs* and *umdas* to enter military training, Orabi went to a military preparatory school. By 1858, at seventeen, he was commissioned a lieutenant, rising fast thereafter to captain and major in 1859, lieutenant colonel and colonel in 1860.

Orabi could not claim an outstanding background or a brilliant military career. He came from an economically humble milieu, acquired a minimum of formal education, and did not display extraordinary intelligence. Egyptian historians inform us that he became close to the ruler, Said Pasha, and was consequently given administrative assignments of varying impor-

tance, including his appointment to accompany the *wali,* or
viceroy, to Istanbul in 1861 as his aide-de-camp.

It would be unfair to minimize the effect of Orabi's rebellion on the growing momentum of the Egyptian movement
toward national emancipation in the late nineteenth and early
twentieth centuries. It would be gross historical negligence,
however, to gloss over the limitations of Orabi and his movement. In many respects the movement was largely inspired and
conducted by Orabi himself. But it did not necessarily have
a major appeal to all Egyptian army officers, let alone large
sections of the Egyptian public. The final rift between Orabi
and the accepted leader of constitutional government in Egypt,
Sherif Pasha, betrays the shortcomings and, in many ways,
dishonesty of Orabi's motives. Sherif was dropped for the price
of a cabinet portfolio in February 1882. In another sense,
Orabi's major co-workers were Ali Fahmi and Abdel Al Hilmi,
together with the troops these officers commanded at the time,
but not much else. Nor was enthusiasm among the members
of the Legislative Assembly for Orabi's movement spontaneous
or intensive.

More precisely and, therefore, fairly the Orabi Revolt was
first nurtured in Orabi's discontent and frustration with failure to achieve higher status in the military hierarchy. His
Bedouin Arab origin and identification with the native Egyptian in distinction to the Turkish aristocratic caste of officers
was fortuitously in his favor where mass appeal was needed.
His immediate aims, however, were practical and even material—more promotions and more pay for Egyptian army
officers. His greater aspiration was briefly realized when he
became Minister of War. To view, therefore, the Orabi revolt
as marking the beginning of modern Egyptian national agitation is to exaggerate its importance and achievement, as well
as to belittle the national currents already developing in the
country independently of this brief struggle between an army
officer and a weak ruler.

2. Egyptian Politics, 1923–1952: Prelude to Revolution

THE ORABI REVOLT foreshadowed, however imperfectly, the role of the native military establishment in the political development of Egypt, which was to reach its climax in the officers' junta of 1952. Between 1882 and 1923, however, the Egyptian military forces came under direct and rigid British control, and were able to play little part in the political struggle against the British occupation. In this period political leadership was assumed by civilian elements, that is, landowners and the rising professional groups: lawyers, doctors, civil servants, teachers, and students, educated largely in Britain, France, and Germany. These elements now claimed to speak for the Egyptian masses, and like Colonel Orabi Pasha they identified themselves with the native peasants, as distinguished from the ruling class of Turkish, Circassian, and Albanian aristocrats allied with the throne. Saad Zaghloul in 1919 was closer to the Egyptian *fellah* than his immediate predecessor as leader of the national struggle, the polished French-trained lawyer, Mustafa Kamil (d. 1908), or the Bedouin Orabi in 1881.

World War I, which imposed a British protectorate over Egypt, also brought with it relative prosperity. The favorable economic climate encouraged industrial development, and

21

during the 1920's spinning, weaving, tobacco, and sugar-refining plants were established. The growth of industry led to the beginnings of a new business class in a country whose wealth had previously been based entirely upon agriculture. Landed aristocrats now found themselves in company with rising industrial magnates, while men of property, whatever its source, faced an underprivileged group which included not only peasant farmers and agricultural laborers, but a growing class of industrial workers.

Throughout the vicissitudes of Egyptian history since the Islamic conquest of the country in the seventh century, a common feature has been that the ruling group and the institutions of government were essentially of foreign origin. King Farouq was as much a foreigner as his ancestor Muhammad Ali, or the famous warrior Saladin, or the conqueror Napoleon, or the British proconsul, Lord Cromer. The emergence of native political leadership dates back only about forty years.

Under the conditions prevailing in 1919 Saad Zaghloul could hardly command an army as did Muhammad Ali or Saladin in an earlier period. His major political weapon was the Egyptian masses, through whom alone could the awakened, but inexperienced, native leadership achieve emancipation from foreign rule, and win political power. Skillful manipulation of the masses under Zaghloul's leadership led to the famous British Declaration of February 1922, making Egypt an independent kingdom. This event established the leadership of the new national bourgeoisie represented by Zaghloul's Wafd group, who now found themselves in opposition not only to the British Residency but also to the Palace. The year 1922 thus marked the emergence of a native political elite asserting its claims against a foreign dynasty unwilling to relinquish the prerogatives of absolute rule, and against a British power determined to maintain its privileged position in the Middle East. In the same period, similar events were taking place in other Arab countries.

The gathering revolutionary forces in Egypt and elsewhere

had two major objectives: independence from foreign control, and establishment of their own authority by setting up representative institutions in place of an autocratic dynasty that recognized no popular rights. But although it was able to enlist mass support, the nationalist party in Egypt had a very narrow base. During the period of Zaghloul's ascendancy (1919–27) its nucleus consisted largely of landowners, prosperous lawyers, businessmen, and conservative religious leaders. So long as the struggle to achieve national aspirations was focused against the foreigner, these leaders could unite the nation under their own banner. This temporary unity concealed a sharp conflict of interests between the aristocratic and reactionary leadership and the masses who followed them; but for twenty-five years the leadership was able to manipulate the masses to achieve its own political ends.

So long as Zaghloul led the nationalist forces in Egypt, the Wafd presented a united front in its demands against Britain. As the popular nationalist party, it could count on the support of peasants, city and town masses, small entrepreneurs, students, and most of the civil servants. Great numbers of the latter group followed the Wafd because the party, whenever it came into power, rigidly enforced a spoils system. On his death in 1927, Zaghloul's successors continued to enjoy a similar popularity but were soon faced with serious splits in their own ranks.

The first ten years' experience under the constitution of 1923 traumatized political life in Egypt. During this period participation in politics was confined to Wafd party heads, power cliques, such as the one attached to the Palace, and large numbers of educated but unemployed city-dwellers. The bulk of the peasant population was hardly involved in any direct manner, although the Wafd manipulated them through a tightly organized control of village and town mayors.

The constitution was violated by the King in the very first year of its promulgation and adoption, 1923–24, and again in 1928; it was suspended altogether in 1930, and nullified to a

great extent by martial law during eleven out of the fifteen
years from 1937 to 1952. As a popular party the Wafd led the
struggle against the monarch's suspension of constitutional
government between 1924 and 1944. Between these two poles
of political power floated a number of lesser parties such as
the Constitutional Liberals, the Palace-inspired Union party,
Ismail Sidky's People's party, and Ahmad Maher's Saadists.
These parties provided the bulk of deputies in Parliament between 1924 and 1952. The Wafd's popularity among the
masses between 1919 and 1924 was neutralized by the autocratic behavior of the monarch, who was assisted in his attack
upon the Wafd by the pervasive influence of the British Embassy. Exercising to the maximum his constitutional prerogative to appoint and dismiss governments, King Fuad I, for
instance, managed to keep the Wafd out of power from 1930
to 1936, despite its undisputed success at the polls. Intervention by the Palace and the British Embassy rendered constitutional government and representative institutions mere for-
malities.

By 1936 the Wafd had developed into a mass movement
embracing all classes of the population. Nationalistic ferment
was aggravated by the privileged position and favored treatment which foreign communities still enjoyed in business,
legislation, and judicial procedures, although Egypt had been
formally independent since 1922. In 1936 the Wafd swept into
power ostensibly as the representative of popular discontent.
Its accession to power by popular mandate tended to keep out
the smaller groups of politicians represented by the Palace
party, the Liberal Constitutionals, the Saadists, Azhar Conservatives, and several small radical groups like the Young
Egypt (Misr al-Fatat) of Ahmad Husein. Up to this point the
Wafd was not just a party, it was synonymous with the nation
in contrast with the King on the one hand, and lesser political parties on the other.

The next ten years, 1936–46, were characterized by a struggle
for predominance between the Palace and the Wafd at the

expense of basic questions of policy. This conflict created a deep chasm between the Wafd and its constituents, as well as between the King and every one else. Although Parliament continued to function after 1936, its influence on the making of policy was slight, for it was either controlled by a Wafd cabinet, or, in the absence of a Wafd government, its members were overshadowed by the real government—the Royal Cabinet. The latter acted under the comfortable umbrella of martial law. In the fifteen years from 1937 to 1952 Parliament was unable to check or balance executive authority and the power of the King acting under martial law. Egypt was a police state with a Parliament.

A peculiar interpretation of constitutional provisions tended to weaken parliamentary government. The King—Fuad and his son Farouq after him—was prone to use his power to dissolve Parliament in such a way as to extend his own authority. He also interpreted the formal power of the monarch to appoint and dismiss ministers as giving him a veto over the formation of governments unacceptable to him. Executive power was thus extended, and basic constitutional rights were suspended through legislation by decree. The monarch's power to appoint one-fifth of the senators was an additional instrument of control, while financial conditions for parliamentary candidacy tended to confine the privilege to very few Egyptians. The throne's authoritarian tendencies created the anomalous situation of a predominantly Wafdist Parliament when elections were held, which would go into intransigent opposition when a non-Wafdist, King-appointed government was in office, and which would relegate itself into a rubber-stamp body when a Wafdist government was in office.

Meanwhile the period 1937–45 was one of great social and ideological ferment as well as economic development. It saw the rise of new groups in Egyptian society outside the triangular struggle between the King, Wafd, and the British. The 1930's witnessed perhaps the most rapid evolution of social and political ideas in the country's history, which was to undermine both the unpopular minority of Palace favorites and the allegedly popular Wafd.

The conclusion of the Anglo-Egyptian Treaty of Alliance in April 1936 and the abolition of capitulatory privileges at the Montreux Convention in 1937 were symbolic of complete Egyptian independence. It was expected that Egyptians would concentrate henceforward on the formulation of a national policy and the crystallization of national sentiment among the people. The task proved to be complicated, for there was no agreement among intellectual or political leaders on the basis for an Egyptian national platform.

Two sharply opposing trends dominated Egyptian national thought in the 1930's: modern secularism and fundamentalist Islam. Each claimed to provide a philosophy for Egyptian government and national development. Their antagonism was a symptom of the social tensions resulting from the establishment of a modern state superstructure in a strongly traditional society, permeated by religious precepts that were different from the basic ideas underlying the modern European concept of a nation-state, if not actually opposed to them.

Modern secularism began to appear as a liberal movement at the turn of the century, and reached the height of its activity in the 1920's and 1930's. It questioned the efficacy and the necessity of an Islamic base for the state. It also doubted political authority derived from other than human sources. Both Taha Husein in his *Pre-Islamic Poetry* and Ali Abd al-Raziq in his *Islam and Political Authority* outlined the attack upon the social and political tenets of Islam as a prelude to its exclusion from the ordering of mundane human affairs.

Unfortunately for Taha Husein (a garrulous writer and not always an honest thinker) and Ali Abd al-Raziq (who was more courageous), their secularist views were largely derived from Western liberal sources, and they tended to enunciate abstract concepts with insufficient attention to the practical difficulties of applying them. Their liberal position was not original or even indigenous. Indeed, most liberal-secular thought in inter-war Egypt suffered from the stamp of importation.

While the influence of modern secularism was visible both in theoretical writing and in the adoption of certain forms in government, administration, and financial and commercial practice, the pattern of power in the country was not affected. Nationalists enthusiastically urged the expulsion of the British, but were less interested in working for the limitation of executive authority and the diffusion of political power. These defects of secular nationalism tended to compromise its leadership, while the public questioned its efficacy. Consequently the people responded readily to the re-entry of Islam into politics (not that it had ever really left it), not merely with the traditional themes of Holy War, theocracy, and caliphal institutions, but with modern techniques of organization and propaganda, and with a highly effective leadership. The advantage of Islam in politics over the secular national formula was its indigenous character.

Until the early 1930's the small elite of landowners who made up the Wafd leadership as well as that of other political parties actively participating in the government was fairly secure in its monopoly of Egyptian politics. This leadership and that of Palace cliques were gradually being challenged, however, by small industrial, commercial, and professional classes whose ideological and political orientation in the early 1930's was as yet undetermined. Entering the political scheme of things as a large body of malcontents—from the ranks of white-collar workers, unemployed high school and university graduates, from small industries such as tobacco, transport, and textiles, from public services and British military installations —their demands were not confined to the evacuation of British forces from Egyptian soil. Concentrated as they were in urban centers, these new groups soon acquired political awareness and demanded social and economic reforms. They were not closely connected with the existing parties but were of a more

radical bent, representing the nucleus of a new urban prole-
tariat, a "younger" Egypt.

One would have expected the newly emerging groups which
sought to influence political life naturally to gravitate toward
the Wafd, as the representative of national aspirations against
British interests in Egypt, and for many years the champion of
the national struggle. But the Wafd and the other political
parties represented clubs of gentlemen whose access to political power and public positions was determined by their wealth
in land. The Wafd's hierarchy consisted of the same persons
year in and year out, creating a fairly rigid elite whose inner
confines no lesser member of the rising classes could invade.
Its popular character seemed to subside with the conclusion
of an unsatisfactory treaty of alliance with Britain in 1936, as
well as its return to power in February 1942 with the assistance of British armed strength. The Wafd's failure to deal successfully with the British question and to satisfy inflated popular expectations was compounded by its reluctance, hesitation,
and, in the final analysis, inability to face internal social and
economic problems. By the end of World War II the alienation
of the Wafd's inchoate mass constituency was a near-certainty.

When their demands did not find sympathy with the so-
called popular party, the people were not able to influence
political institutions such as Parliament through normal political expression. The frequent suspension of constitutional government, especially during the periods 1930–35 and 1939–49,
did not permit the expansion of public participation in the
political process. None of the new classes was really permitted
to organize within the constitutional framework established in
1923. The only organized political expression open to them
was extra-legal and extra-parliamentary. And this ushered new
groups of the mass movement variety into the arena of Egyptian politics, because more Egyptians had by now acquired
educational and some economic status, but not social or political recognition.

The rise of industry, the experience of a second World War,

and the unsuccessful struggle for Palestine gave rise to new political groups nibbling away at the Wafd's popularity and challenging traditional leadership. The period 1946–52 was perhaps the most momentous in modern Egyptian history, for it marked the end of an era. Its sharpest characteristics were these: (1) Terrorism by extremist political-religious groups increased, despite government efforts to stifle it. (2) By insisting on absolute rule, the King dragged existing political parties into a struggle for survival ending in catastrophe. (3) The political vicissitudes of this period impressed on the people the idea that only revolution could bring about change.

Among the new groups that achieved any measure of success in Egyptian politics one may single out the Muslim Brethren. As a mass movement it introduced into Egyptian politics a dynamism which the traditional old-style political parties lacked. To be sure, there was political opposition to the Wafd between 1923 and 1951, especially from Constitutional Liberals and Saadists. But neither group really offered the kind of participation and political integration demanded by the new elements in society, since both parties were already discredited because they cooperated with an absolute monarch in his efforts to rule, and their structure and composition were similar to the Wafd's. This situation was successfully exploited by the Muslim Brethren between 1936 and 1952.

The Ikhwan, or Muslim Brethren, of Hasan al-Banna began modestly in 1927 as a religious teaching and reform movement but soon acquired organizational skill for the eventual formation of a strong mass political movement with fanatic religious appeal. In contrast to previous attempts at religious reform, which were largely of a theological-ethical nature, the Ikhwan preached a total message of religious, social, economic, and political reform. For the social and economic betterment of the believers, it established solid programs and operated institutions—schools in various parts of the country, cooperatives, textile factories, and hospitals. By 1946 the Brethren had infiltrated the ranks of high-school and university students, oc-

cupational and business associations and guilds, and the
younger sector of the Army Officer Corps, and therefore
claimed a following which represented all classes of Egyptian
society. The movement spread swiftly, and branch organizations were formed in the neighboring Arab countries of Syria,
Jordan, and Palestine. Above all, the Brethren established a
well-armed, trained, and organized militia, placing weapons—
a strategic instrument for the seizure of power—at its disposal,
and a private army available to lead an insurrection. With a
membership of approximately one million in 1946, the Muslim
Brethren became a major contender for political power. It
was actually able to influence so large a portion of public
opinion that it forced a succession of governments from 1947
to 1951 to utilize most of their security resources to combat it.

The Ikhwan's success as a major political group in Egypt
after World War II may be partly explained by its ability to
channel national-religious emotion into serious and meticulous
planning. Although it operated on autocratic hierarchical principles, the organization found a task for every Brother in its
extensive activities. This gave the top as well as low man a
share in its apparatus. It afforded the politically and economically frustrated Egyptian, for the first time, experience in
organized, although often violent, political expression. It filled
the vacuum that had been created by the gulf existing between
the few leaders of traditional political parties who ruled and
the apathetic, yet volatile, masses who followed. Between this
new constellation of potential political leadership and the
traditional politicians stood a large proportion of the uncom-
mitted public and the army.

Beginning with the Ahmad Maher Government in early 1945
each successive cabinet, especially Ismail Sidky's in 1946 and
Nuqrashi's in 1947 and 1948, used terrorist methods to stamp
out agitation for social and economic reform. Meanwhile successive governments promised repeatedly to raise the living
standards of the *fellah*. The extent to which the government's
ability to maintain order had been weakened was indicated

not only by continued riots and demonstrations between February 1946 and January 1952, but also by labor unrest. There were strikes in 1946 at the largest textile factories of Mehalla al-Kubra and Shubra. The tram-workers went on strike in the same year. The strike by the male nurses in the Kasr al-Aini hospitals was soon followed by the general strike of the Egyptian police forces in April 1948. As Muhammad Husein Haikal remarked in the second volume of his *Political Memoirs,* "the political system had not settled upon definite principles accepted and respected by all. There was still much public difference of opinion as to the King's authority as Head of State, and the Nation as a source of all sovereign power."[1] This understatement describes adequately the state of Egyptian politics in this period.

A generation of younger writers who had grown up during the Second World War began to produce fiction characterized by a strong revolutionary message. Their short stories, plays, and novels offered something new to the readers: a true picture of the life of a common Egyptian. These writers were not professional men of letters. They were young medical doctors, lawyers, engineers, and journalists who had come from humble backgrounds and shared the privation and frustrations of millions like themselves.

Attacks by these writers on established authority were directed at all fronts. Khalid Muhammad Khalid embarked on a socialist-inspired radical criticism of the deleterious effect of petrified religious thinking and leadership on the Egyptian body politic. His *Min huna nabda'* (From Here We Start), published in 1949, rocked Egyptian intellectual circles and invited the wrath of his fellow Azhar *sheikhs* and the government. Followed in quick succession by his *Muwatinun la ra'aya* (Citizens Not Subjects, or Citizens Not Cattle), *al-Dimoqratiyya abadan* (Democracy Forever), *Hadha aw al-tawafan* (This or the Deluge), and *Lillah wa al-hurriyya* (For God and Freedom), it encouraged radical writers to intensify their attack upon all aspects of social, economic, and political injustice.

Taha Husein insisted on the completion of his *Al-mu'adha-buna fi'l-ard* (The Tormented on Earth), a biting and naked description of the abject poverty of the average Egyptian, despite the obvious disapproval of the authorities. The pens of Muhammad Farid Abu Hadid and Yusuf Idris appealed to popular pride, while Sharqawi with his novels (*Earth,* etc.) gave vent to leftist views dangerous to the regime's security. Most intensive was the campaign initiated by *Rose el-Youssef* magazine, edited by Ihsan Abdel Quddus together with a core of radical writers, such as Ahmad Baha al-Din, Anwar es-Sadat, and even President Nasser under various pseudonyms at the time.

Much of this criticism and reappraisal by Egyptians was prompted by the failure of collective Arab efforts in Palestine. The Palestine War, moreover, precipitated a crisis in Egyptian politics marked by assassinations, increased para-military activity by the Muslim Brethren, a tightening of security measures within the country, and the eventual return of the Wafd to power. The failure of the Egyptian army in the Palestine campaign forced the government to impose a state of siege in the country and inflate to fantastic proportions the number of concentration camp inmates. It was indeed ominous, as anyone who was in Egypt in the winter and spring of 1949 can testify, to hear such slogans as "Allah is our goal, the Prophet our leader, holy war our way, the Koran our Constitution, and death in the cause of Allah our sole desire" chanted by the mobs in the streets of Cairo.

Evidence is now available showing the extent to which the King enjoyed absolute rule. It is no Egyptian exaggeration that when the Nuqrashi Cabinet met in secret session with Parliament early in 1948 to consider military action in Palestine, its view was that no large-scale operations should be contemplated. This recommendation was based on the detailed reports of General Headquarters on the operational, logistical, and general state of preparedness of the Egyptian army. Suddenly, on May 13, 1948, Nuqrashi reversed his position at the insistence of the King and his Chief of Staff, Haidar Pasha, in favor of battle against the Israelis. Indeed, some Egyptians, including Rafii in his *Muqaddamat thawrat thalatha wa 'ishrin yulio 1952* (Prelude to the Revolution of July 23),[2] and Ahmad Baha al-Din in his *Farouq . . . malikan* (Farouq . . . King),[3] argue that the King had already ordered the advance of troops into Palestine without informing, or even consulting, his Prime Minister. Muhammad Husein Haikal in his *Political Memoirs* cites the deteriorating internal situation as a major factor in precipitating Egyptian armed intervention in Palestine. "The resort to war," he asserts, "to distract attention from internal difficulties is a common policy frequently used by dictatorial states in modern and ancient history."[4] On the other hand, the decision of the Egyptian Government to participate in the Palestine War was motivated to a great extent by its desire to contain potential gains by King Abdullah of Jordan in Palestine.

On many occasions the King interfered in matters of policy without the knowledge of his ministers. In 1945 and 1946 he met privately with various Arab leaders to promote for himself a position of leadership in the Arab-Islamic world, without the previous knowledge, consultation, or presence of any member of his cabinet. Similarly he acquired or transferred *Waqf* properties (religious trusts and bequests) to the *khassa* or Royal Domains administration at his pleasure. He interfered directly and obnoxiously in political as well as in cabinet and Senate appointments.

Public irritation with the King's unconstitutional interference in the executive functions of the government was apparent as early as February 1946, when in the famous Abbas Bridge demonstrations students shouted calls for his demise, while others tore his posted portraits from University walls. Furthermore, the Metro Theater (cinema) was dynamited on May 6, 1947, an obvious insult to the monarch on the day celebrating his assumption of the throne. The author, who survived that explosion, never got to see Wallace Beery in "Bad Bascomb," the feature of that evening.

At the close of World War II, King Farouq tightened his control over Egyptian politics. He was encouraged to do so by the inability of the various parties to agree on a united national policy, especially over the resumption of negotiations with the United Kingdom early in 1946. Farouq became convinced that parties which could not unite against a common foreign foe would not be able to unite in obstructing his political ambitions. His humiliation by the British ultimatum on February 4, 1942, without a public stir in his support, convinced him further that he could not depend on popular support. He proceeded therefore to appoint capable public relations men and lobbyists to his royal court as "advisors." Such were the duties of Karim Thabit, as Press Secretary to the King, and Elias Andrawus as economic advisor. Farouq's growing dependence on these courtiers for the making of decisions tended on the one hand to nullify the importance of the Royal Cabinet as liaison with the government, and to alienate the legally constituted Cabinet on the other.

From 1946 until the return of the Wafd to power in January 1950, Egyptian politics was plagued with violence. Those new groups—Socialists or Green Shirts of Ahmad Husein, Communists, and Muslim Brethren—which did not "belong," politically speaking, declared war on the politicians of the old school in February 1945 by murdering the Prime Minister, Dr. Ahmad Maher, leader of the Saadist party. Another prominent figure in Egyptian political life, Amin Osman Pasha, Minister of Finance during the war, met the same fate at the hands of an assassin in January 1946 for his alleged pro-British sympathies. By the spring of 1948 the Muslim Brethren had completely terrorized Egyptian society by a series of political assassinations. Among their victims were the President of the Cairo Court of Appeals, followed by the Cairo Chief of Police, General Salim Zaki, outside the gates of the Medical School, and later Prime Minister Mahmud Nuqrashi. Bombings of courthouses and residences of political leaders became common in the capital, until the government itself had to resort to the violent elimination of Sheikh Hasan al-Banna, Supreme Guide of the Brethren, in February 1949.

National security required an extension of martial law in May 1949 for still another year during the Ibrahim Abdel Hadi Saadist Government. This was the major accomplishment of the Abdel Hadi Government from December 1948 to July 1949, unless one considers its public stunt in the form of the March 1949 parade celebration honoring returning Faluja veterans.[5] Its strict application of martial law led to the persecution of many Egyptians on suspicion alone, especially since the Brethren had been outlawed in December 1948.

The horrifying breakdown of public order in the country impelled all political party leaders to seek some rapprochement among themselves to provide the country with a coalition cabinet which could claim a measure of public support. Dissatisfied with its five years out of power, the Wafd, which presumably could invoke greater popular support than any other party, undermined any plans of a coalition that included other political party leaders. The King, on the other hand, who still felt he could always call upon *his* army for the retention of his throne, was opposed to any formula devised by political leaders which might bring the Wafd back to power. Finally, the crisis was inadequately met by the formation of a coalition Cabinet under the chairmanship of Husein Sirry, an independent, which included four Wafdists, four Saadists, four Constitutional Liberals, two National party members, and four independents.

A primary task facing the new coalition Government was again that of security. Although it released most political prisoners and prepared to end martial law, this Government did not have the unqualified support of all the political parties. Planning for new elections was apt to create problems in any discussion of electoral laws. The King was therefore only too happy to accept the resignation of the coalition Cabinet, and immediately requested Husein Sirry to form an independent caretaker Government to prepare for general elections.

The Wafd surprised everyone in January 1950 by winning the election with a crushing majority. It is not inconceivable that the outlawed Brethren, leftist groups, and the Communist party threw their support to the Wafd primarily to avenge Saadists who had persecuted them so severely from 1946 to 1949. But since the Government under which elections were held was independent or politically neutral, it strengthened the Wafd's chances of success. The latter's electoral organization in the provinces as well as its vast financial resources worked successfully. It captured 228 of the 319 seats in Parliament. But one must note that less than two-thirds of the registered eligible voters went to the polls: 2,959,741 out of 4,105,182. The Wafd, moreover, did not receive a majority of the votes cast, for their 1,135,642 was less than the remaining 1,724,098 votes.

The public expected the Wafd, now that it was back in power, to respond to pressing demands. Restoration of civil liberties seemed paramount. The failure of Anglo-Egyptian negotiations since 1946 clearly required the evolution by the Wafd of a general anti-British policy acceptable to public opinion. Finally, the public considered the Wafd the only group capable of curbing the King's proclivity to absolute rule and expected it to do so.

Responding to public clamor and assessing its strong position as reflected in the elections, the Wafd partially restored civil liberties in May 1950—enough to invite a vehement press campaign against the King's excesses and the government's failure to fulfill certain promises regarding inflation, unemployment, and public works.

In June 1950 the press, and especially the *Rose el-Youssef* magazine, began to uncover many improprieties in the King's behavior as well as in that of persons influential with the Palace. For example, the issue of defective arms purchased by

Egypt in Europe to supply fighting forces in the Palestine War was publicly aired. Ahmad Husein, leader of Misr al-Fatat (now the Socialist party) concentrated his attacks in the newspaper *Al-ishtirakiyya* upon the King's brutal treatment of peasants working on his many estates.

The Egyptian historian Rafii—a member of the Liberal Constitutional party—nevertheless alleges that the return of the Wafd to power proved a restoration of absolute rule.[6] The allegation is supported not so much by direct Wafdist persecution of the opposition as by its complicity with the King's desire to impose his will upon the government. This is borne out by an examination of specific incidents for which evidence today is indisputable.

In May 1950 Senator Mustafa Marei questioned the resignation of Mahmud Muhammad Mahmud, Chief of the Government Accounting Office. Mahmud had reported certain discrepancies in the accounts for the purchase of arms during the Palestine campaign, expenditures for the King's yacht, and transfers of monies to Karim Thabit, Press Secretary to the King, from charity hospital funds. The Wafdist Government declined a debate on these issues but agreed instead to appoint a parliamentary committee to investigate Mahmud's resignation. In June the Cabinet issued three decrees which affected the composition of the Senate. One decree ousted all senators appointed during the Husein Sirry Cabinet. The second appointed new senators friendly to the Wafd. The third dismissed Muhammad Husein Haikal, head of the Liberal Constitutional party, as President of the Senate, and appointed Ali Zaki Orabi, a Wafdist, in his place.

Public reaction to this clearly dictatorial action by the Government was widely reflected in the press. More important was the reversal of political party alignments. Now, the Wafd appeared as the willing and obedient servant of the King in opposition to Constitutional Liberals, Saadists, and National party members, who in October 1950 sent an open complaint to the King, deploring his trespassing of the Constitution and drawing his attention to his bad reputation at home and abroad. The text of the letter was not permitted by the Wafd Government to appear in the papers of October 21, 1950.[7] The Wafd, on the other hand, claimed privately that its acquiescence in the King's improper activity was only a temporary measure until it could successfully settle the Anglo-Egyptian question. By the autumn of 1951, the latter had erupted into armed conflict between British troops stationed in the Canal Zone on the one hand, and Egyptian police and irregular guerilla forces on the other. According to Muhammad Husein Haikal, however, whereas Fuad Serag al-Din, Secretary General of the Wafd and Minister of the Interior at the time, used to criticize Palace policy in the past, he now "whined that after ten years in the street, the Wafd had come to the verge of collapse. It is justified therefore now in coming to terms with Palace policy." "Then," continues Haikal, "I realized that the kissing of the King's hand by Nahhas had become the accepted policy of the Wafd in retaining office for many years to come."[8]

Worse, though, was the Wafd's complicity in the King's attempt to tamper with the institutions of justice. In September 1951 the King, who had been used to sending verbal and written directives to the Cabinet via his courtiers, requested, while on a European honeymoon with his second wife, Narriman, to have the Council of State reconstituted or, preferably, abolished. As the supreme judicial body in the country, the Council of State was to be free of any pressures from other branches of the government. Unfortunately, the King was encouraged to proceed with such a request by previous attempts on the part of the Wafd to undermine the Council. As early as January 1950, that is upon assumption of power, the Wafd had asked Abd al-Razzaq al-Sanhuri to resign his post as President of the Council on the ground that he had once served as minister in a partisan cabinet. The King, on the other hand, was by May 1951 anxious to have Public Prosecutor Muhammad Mahmud Azmi removed from his post to prevent him from carrying out an investigation of the "defective arms" case, in which Palace employees were seriously implicated. The Wafd, meanwhile, had regretted the freedom it had given to the press and, by late 1951, it issued decrees curbing freedom of expression. But once they were challenged in the courts or the Council of State many of these decrees were thrown out.

Despite the unilateral abrogation of the Anglo-Egyptian Treaty by the Wafd Government in October 1951, and its encouragement of the national struggle against British troops in the Canal, the Wafd was by now thoroughly identified in the public mind as the King's "stooges." Governing practically by royal directives, Nahhas and his Cabinet strengthened the King's autocratic hand. The latter already held the view that there was no such thing as a "public will." It is reported, for instance, that when the parliamentary committee headed by Abdel Salam Fahmi Gumaa, responding to the speech from the throne in 1944, referred to the "will of the people," Farouq retorted, "My good Pasha, the will of the people emanates from my will!"

More irresponsible was the blatant intervention of the King in the appointment of ministers to the royal Cabinet—a matter clearly requiring Cabinet approval—when at the height of the Anglo-Egyptian dispute in December 1951, he appointed Hafiz Afifi to head it. This was considered by most Egyptians as a direct insult to their cause, as Hafiz Afifi was considered to be "more British than the British." At the same time the King placed Elias Andrawus, his economic advisor, on the governing board of Bank Misr, and appointed the just-recalled Ambassador to London, Abdel Fattah Amr, his "special advisor on foreign affairs." When Abd al-Majid, Sheikh of the Azhar, alluded to the laxity of royal conduct at home and abroad, the King summarily dismissed him. Similarly, the King usurped a clear-cut cabinet responsibility in the appointment of the Supreme Commander of the Armed Forces, when he rammed his own candidate, General Muhammad Haidar, down the throats of the Cabinet.

These highly improper actions of Farouq did not go un-
noticed by the general public. During December 1951 violent
demonstrations against the King spread in Cairo, Alexandria,
and all the provincial capitals, forcing the Government to
close by decree all universities including the Azhar, and secondary schools in the major cities as of December 29, 1951.
Fiercer outbreaks protesting the King's conduct occurred in
mid-January 1952, led once again by students. Some days later,
reacting to the Ismailia incident (the armed clash between
British forces and Egyptian auxiliary police), politically disaffected groups—the Communist party, Socialists, and the Muslim Brethren—led the mobs in the burning of downtown
Cairo.[9] The six months following the riots of January 26,
1952 saw the total collapse of political leadership in the country and the vacuum created by its utter defeat at the hands of
an absolute ruler, Farouq.

The four cabinets between the fall of the Wafd and the
army coup in July 1952, those of Ali Maher, Nagib Hilali,
Husein Sirry, and Nagib Hilali again, were desperate attempts
by highly qualified civil servants to salvage the situation. Being non-partisan and largely Palace-appointed, the cabinets
were not assured of the cooperation of the constituted political
parties.

Egyptian politics from 1923 to 1952 may be summarized
thus: the adoption of modern constitutional forms and parliamentary government; the emergence of political parties
which unfortunately were the instruments of a socially conservative upper class; the continuation of a national struggle
directed chiefly against the privileged position of Britain in
Egypt; the reopening of the question of secular nationalism
versus political Islam; the intensification of economic and
social unrest (the "haves" versus the "have-nots"); and the
search for a new formula for salvation in violent mass eruption.
Indeed, national frustration, compounded by the absence of a
satisfactory accommodation with Britain, and aggravated by
the humiliating fiasco in Palestine and by the subsequent eco-

nomic plight of the Egyptian masses, pushed the average Egyptian by January 1952 into a ferocious nihilistic explosion against organized authority. Any movement which satisfied, or at least sympathetically responded to, his frustrations was welcome.

The politically literate Egyptian was faced by a situation where a mere constitutional framework provided a cloak of legitimacy for unrepresentative governments, never fully accepted but largely imposed. A rigidly stratified social system prevailed, characterized by disparities and inequalities between rich and poor, male and female, peasant and town-dweller. The absolute authority at the top was helped in governing by blocs of families of landowners, businessmen, and bureaucrats, whose extreme sense of family loyalty extended into nepotism. Outside the chambers of constitutionalism there were highly influential and unrepresentative antechambers. Any semblance of democracy or of a representative political system ended with a few forms: a parliament, a formal separation of powers, and a bureaucratic administration. There were few if any extra-parliamentary institutions such as pressure groups which could influence policy or legislation and act as checks on established authority. Thus the public was denied practical experience in politics, public responsibility, and self-confidence—the safest evolutionary means perhaps to an integration of national life, and to unregimented political institutions. Exclusive control prevented controversy or organized dissent. The political discipline which comes with criticism thus remained unknown to the Egyptian political community. Moreover, the lack of genuine party conflict and compromise fostered blind obedience as the price of political achievement, and conspiracy as the only avenue of opposition and criticism.

The King, on the other hand, always felt that so long as he controlled Army Command, he held the trump card for predominance over the Wafd and other parties. No doubt until 1945 the King exerted a great measure of control over the

armed forces. He appointed senior officers to General Headquarters and insisted on approving every applicant to the Military Academy, placing a line of ministers of war in an embarrassing position. He also had commanded the allegiance
and loyalty of most army officers. The popular belief that he
was "manhandled" by British tanks in February 1942 seemed
to increase his popularity with the army. Moreover, so long as
the British supplied arms to the Egyptian forces his position
was fairly secure. But with the exposure of the defective arms
deals in 1950, the publication of the irresponsibility with
which the army was committed to battle in Palestine, and the
King's complicity in both cases, defection among army officers
was inevitable.

In all fairness to the civilian, albeit Palace-dominated,
period 1923–52 in Egyptian political history, one must remember that the 1923 Constitution was no Magna Carta. As a
written document, it was handed down rather than eagerly
sought or tediously won by any sizable portion of Egyptians.
It was furthermore not impressive to the average man, who
continued to adhere to the unwritten constitutions by which
his socio-political life had been managed for many centuries.
The customs and practices of the *fellahin*—the bulk of the
Egyptian population—continued to form the basis of the distribution and utilization of social power in their community
and to govern their existence independently of any central
ruling institution. The new Constitution was good for a central executive authority in Cairo which, in the average Egyptian's view, was no different from the many he had known
before. Authority, for him, emanated from the traditional
structure of his small society on the village level. The customs
and practices of his village, Bedouin clan, or religious brotherhood were the only sources of legislation he easily recognized.
And those were usually accepted unquestioningly.

The unresponsiveness of the people to a modern constitutional system, with its emphasis on the limitation of executive
power by a legislature drawing its authority from the people,

was in itself a rejection of limited government. Nor were the central government or the new institutions of the state viewed by the average Egyptian as instruments of social control. Indeed, in his view, they had no positive role or function. Inevitably, these new institutions were used by the sophisticated few for the promotion of their own ends. Unfortunately, the category of the "sophisticated" increased in number, and the ensuing struggle for admission into the political arena brought the whole structure down.

As recently as 1952 the conflict for political leadership involved a very small percentage of the Egyptian people. Did the events of 1952 fundamentally alter the old pattern of control and structure of political power? Has political conflict extended far into the countryside, upsetting traditional social and political processes? Is there greater concern today with the checks on legitimate authority—more bluntly, executive power? Are all of these concerns recognized by the new leadership as crucial aspects of meaningful nationalism to guide political development?

3. The Free Officers Group

FOR CENTURIES, at least since the Arab conquest, Egypt has lacked a military tradition. Britain, after occupying the country in 1882, merely extended the policy of permitting Egyptians a minimum of military experience. The decree that British authorities managed to extract from the Khedive Tewfiq in September 1882, only a month after the occupation, in effect disbanded the Egyptian army as a fighting force. Whatever troops remained were dispatched to the Sudan to help quell the Mahdi revolt. Most of this expeditionary force under General Hicks was annihilated by the Mahdist forces in the November 1883 battle of Shikan. The British authorities reorganized an Egyptian armed force under their direct control through the newly created institution of a British *Sirdar,* or General Commanding Officer. Although not altogether responsible for the institution of a payment (*badaliyya*) in lieu of military service in 1886, Britain was not uninterested in this arrangement as it would obviously result in a minimum of Egyptians receiving military training. Naturally, the poor and illiterate *fellahin* who could not afford the payment constituted the bulk of the British-controlled army between 1886 and 1914.

With the Declaration of February 28, 1922, making Egypt an independent monarchy, Britain retained the right to defend British communications. This permitted continued British supervision over the Egyptian military establishment. Although the murder of Sir Lee Stack Pasha, *Sirdar* of the Egyptian army, in November 1924 had serious repercussions on Anglo-Egyptian relations, a crisis did not really arise until June 1927, when the Budget Committee of the Egyptian Parliament recommended certain reforms in the army, among them the abolition of the *Sirdar*. The British objected, insisting that there be a British Inspector-General and that the Frontier Force remain under his supervision. Not until 1936 did the Egyptian army achieve some measure of independence from British control, although in the Anglo-Egyptian Treaty of that year it was stipulated that arms and military instruction be provided by the British.

Responding to nationalist revulsion against the Anglo-Egyptian Treaty in 1936, the Wafd Government liberalized the admissions policy of the Military Academy soon after it assumed power in May 1936. Until then, as noted before, an army career was open only to members of the aristocratic class, most of whom were of Turkish origin or background. The Wafd now opened the doors of the Academy to native Egyptian youth, regardless of family background, social class, or economic status.

Of the eleven men who composed the founding committee of the Free Officers group in late 1949, eight entered the Academy in 1936. These were Lieutenant Colonel Gamal Abdel Nasser, Major Abdel Hakim Amer, Wing Commander Abdel Latif al-Boghdadi, Lieutenant Colonel Anwar es-Sadat, Wing Commander Gamal Salem, Lieutenant Colonel Husein Shafei, Lieutenant Colonel Zakariyya Muhieddin, and Major Salah Salem. Major Kamal al-Din Husein and Squadron Leader Hasan Ibrahim, also members of this founding committee, were graduated from the Military Academy a year later, in 1939. Another member, Major Khaled Muhieddin, was graduated in 1940.

Table I on pages 48–49 shows the background and activities of these officers.

Five of them were born in 1918, two in 1917, and one each in 1920, 1921, and 1922. The average age of the members of the Revolutionary Council in 1952 was thirty-three years. Only three of them had higher education other than military training. With one exception all had seen active service in the Palestinian War. Excluding General Muhammad Naguib, all had been involved in some kind of political activity earlier in their careers.

Most of these officers were of humble origin, from all parts of Egypt. Their fathers and grandfathers were peasant farmers, small landowners, or minor officials in the Delta and Upper Egypt provinces. They were sent in the early thirties to the towns or cities—Alexandria, Cairo, Port Said, Tanta, Zaqaziq —for secondary education in preparation for the civil service or the university.

However, outside this core group, one finds other adherents to the Free Officers movement of aristocratic background and comfortable economic status. Such, for example, are Wing Commander Ali Sabri, Minister in Charge of Presidential Affairs, and his brother Hasan Dhu'l-Fiqar Sabri, Deputy Minister for Foreign Affairs, both of whom were flight officers in the Air Force. The same is true of Colonel Sarwat Ukasha, Minister of National Guidance and Culture for the Egyptian region of the U.A.R. It is difficult to classify all the officers who have been appointed to high administrative and diplomatic posts in the U.A.R. However, Table II below comprises a sample of some of those who have achieved cabinet rank under the present executive structure of the government.

Secondary schooling during the early thirties meant contact with the pre-1936 agitation directed against the British, and also over Palestine and the Suez Canal. Student political activities of those days were under the influence of the ultra-nationalist Wafd. Moreover, these young men attended the Military Academy during the period of an all-nationalist government. During World War II they witnessed the greatest concentration of British troops ever seen in the Middle East, and found their duties limited by the British, who were wary of them. Some of them even hoped for an Axis victory as an easy way to the fulfillment of national aspirations. Many of them viewed the Fascist military states of the day as models to be emulated.[1] Ironically, those who went to Staff College had the benefit of British instructors, who, as part of military training, introduced them for the first time to the systematic study of the political history of the Middle East. One of these British instructors has stated to the author that Gamal Abdel Nasser, Abdel Hakim Amer, Zakariyya Muhieddin, and Anwar es-Sadat were exceptionally good students, highly motivated, with a genuine interest in social reform.

The political education of this core of younger army officers was not uniform in its development or intensity. It was most intense in the cases of Gamal Abdel Nasser, Anwar es-Sadat, Kamal al-Din Husein, Abdel Latif al-Boghdadi, Abdel Hakim Amer, and Khaled Muhieddin. The cases of both Nasser and es-Sadat are interesting and illuminating.

Contrary to popular belief, President Gamal Abdel Nasser was not born in Beni Merr of Assiut province, but in the city of Alexandria. Although his father, Abdel Nasser Husein, in his capacity as assistant postmaster, was frequently transferred from one place to another, it was in Alexandria and Cairo— the two major cities of Egypt—that Nasser received his primary, secondary, and military education. He was exposed at an early age to both Egyptian environments: Upper Egypt in the Said, and Lower Egypt, or the Delta region, in al-Beheira, where he began his schooling in the Khatatiba primary school. The remainder of his elementary schooling was completed in Alexandria and Cairo. His secondary schooling began in Helwan, outside Cairo, continued in the Ras el-Tin Secondary School in Alexandria, and was completed in the Nahda Secondary School in Cairo in 1936. The location of the schools Nasser attended at an early age influenced his political orien-

TABLE I

Name	Rank	Birth Date	Birth Place	Military Academy	Staff College	Other Education or Training
Abdel Hakim Amer*	Major	1919	(Istal) Minia	1938	1948	
Abdel Latif al-Boghdadi*	Wing Cmdr.	1917	(Shawa) Daqhaliyya	1938	1948	Air Force Academy, 1939
Kamal al-Din Husein*	Major	1921	Benha	1939	1949	
Hasan Ibrahim*	Sqdn. Leader	1917	Alexandria	1939		
Khaled Muhieddin*	Major	1922	Kafr Shukr Mit Ghamr	1940	1950	B.S., Commerce, 1951
Zakariyya Muhieddin*	Lt. Col.	1918	Kafr Shukr Mit Ghamr	1938	1948	
Mohammed Naguib	Maj. Gen.	1901	Khartoum Sudan	1917	1939	LL.B., 1927
Gamal Abdel Nasser*	Lt. Col.	1918	Alexandria	1938	1948	5 mo. Law College, 1936-37
Anwar Sadat*	Lt. Col.	1918	Qaliubiyya	1938		
Gamal Salem*	Wing Cmdr.	1918	Sudan	1938		
Salah Salem*	Major	1920	Sudan	1938	1948	
Husein Shafer*	Lt. Col.	1918	Tanta	1938	1953	

* Founder member in Free Officers movement.

Revolution Command Council

Troop Command and/or Branch	Other Special Military Assignments	Political Activity	Other
Infantry Staff GHQ		Muslim Breth.	
Air Force Fighter Cmd.	Mission to Yemen, 1948	Anti-British Sabotage, 1940–42	Misr Air, 1946–48
Artillery	Instr., Staff College, 1951	Muslim Breth.	Supervised *fedayeen* training, 1947–48
Air Force		Misr el-Fatat, 1930's	Overseas missions after World War II
Cavalry Armor		Communist Party	
Infantry		Free Officers	
Infantry	Chief, Infantry, 1950–51	None known	Free Officers candidate for Pres., Officers' Club
Infantry	Instr. Infantry School; Instr. Admin. School; Instr. Staff College, 1951	Wafd Party; Muslim Breth.	
Infantry		Misr el-Fatat, 1930's Muslim Breth., early 1940's; Anti-British sabotage, 1941–42	
Air Force		Egyptian Socialist Party	
General Staff	Instr. Tactics, Staff College, 1951		
Cavalry Armor			

tation. It is well known among Egyptians that the Nahda School student body in Cairo was always in the forefront of political demonstrations.

Political demonstrations were commonplace among Egyptian secondary school students in the thirties. Nasser's experience in this regard began in Alexandria and continued through 1936 in Cairo. The period 1930–35 was one in which the Constitution was abolished, Parliament suspended, and rule was by royal decree. The Wafd, which was still the party of the masses, was able to rally most of the students in demonstrations against Ismail Sidky's government in 1930, and against succeeding governments, until the Wafd returned to power in 1936. It is almost certain that Nasser was at the time a Wafd sympathizer, if not a follower. His attachment to the cause of the party was perhaps strengthened a year later when the Wafd made it possible for him, as well as other secondary school graduates, to enter the Military Academy. His first application for admission to the Academy, immediately upon graduation from secondary school in June 1936, was turned down. He proceeded to enroll in the College of Law in Cairo, where he spent five months between October 1936 and February 1937.

Other events influenced the development of Nasser's political career. Graduating as a second lieutenant from the Military Academy in 1938, he was posted with a line infantry outfit in Manqabad, Assiut province, in Upper Egypt. His promotion was rather fast. He reached the rank of captain in September 1943, at the same time receiving an appointment as instructor in the Military Academy. All this occurred soon after an event that left an impression on many Egyptians: the Palace incident in February 1942, when a British ultimatum to the King supported by tanks led to a change of government.

Until this time Gamal Abdel Nasser probably did not have any definite political aims. No doubt, like many other young Egyptians, he felt humiliation over the easy compliance of his government with British dictation. He was aware, too, of the economic and social backwardness of his fellow Egyptians, for such is the testimony of his colleagues: Anwar es-Sadat in *Revolt on the Nile (Qissat al-thwara kamila)* and Abdel Latif al-Boghdadi in the Anniversary Volume, *Hadhihi al-thawra.*[2] Nasser's own *Philosophy of the Revolution* is to the same effect.

Nasser's sophistication in politics began with his attendance at Staff and Command College between 1945 and 1948, followed by his appointment as instructor in the Army Administration School in July 1949. Between these assignments, he had seen duty in the Palestine campaign, including a difficult siege at Faluja. By the time he was assigned to the Staff College as instructor in November 1951, his political ideas had taken definite shape, and plans for revolutionary action had already taken the form of the Free Officers movement.

Nowhere in Nasser's activity prior to the coup of July 23, 1952 is there any suggestion of rash behavior. With the exception of his own admission of complicity in the attempted assassination of a prominent political figure, which, according to *Philosophy of the Revolution,* he later regretted, there is no known instance in which Nasser engaged in premeditated acts of violence. Although intensely political, Nasser must, contrary to the common view, be considered cautious, deliberate, and calculating.

Contrasting sharply with Nasser's lack of an activist record is the case of Anwar es-Sadat, first Secretary-General of the National Union and Islamic Congress. Although it is extremely difficult today, as in the forties, to say with certainty who were members of the Muslim Brethren—they were outlawed in December 1948—it is fair to assume that es-Sadat had strong connections with that organization and access to Sheikh Hasan al-Banna, its Supreme Guide. His political career is difficult to follow as he moved from one adventure—mishap, perhaps—to another. In the 1930's he could conceivably have been attracted to the Green Shirts of Misr el-Fatat. We know definitely from *Revolt on the Nile* that he was implicated in the attempt of General Aziz al-Masri, Chief of Staff of the

Egyptian Army, to defect to the Nazi forces in the Western Desert in 1941. He was subsequently imprisoned, having collaborated with two German spies in Cairo. Accused also of complicity in a plot to assassinate Amin Osman Pasha, he was cashiered from the army. Confirming the tradition of British leniency, after eighteen months in prison at Minia and elsewhere in Egypt, he managed to escape in November 1944.

Es-Sadat was also active in a small and highly secret group of young officers which in 1941 concentrated on obstructing and undermining any possible mass withdrawal of British troops from the Libyan front via Egypt. Most members of this group were first lieutenants. Es-Sadat, incidentally, was well placed for such an eventuality as Communications Officer in Meadi, a suburb of Cairo. The group managed to collect maps of British installations, military roads, and other strategic points with a view to organizing raids on supply and communications lines. The arrest of es-Sadat and another of his companions in 1942 broke up this group. His is definitely a more reckless record than Nasser's.

Wing Commander Abdel Latif al-Boghdadi appears to have been a more sophisticated revolutionary. Although he was only a year older than es-Sadat, his attendance at the Air Force Academy in 1939, after graduating from the Military Academy the preceding year, afforded him more formal training. His brief experience in 1947–48 with a civilian airline, Misr Air, and his assumption of administrative responsibility as Chief of the West Cairo Airport in 1948, as well as his mission to Yemen the same year, gave him the chance to mature faster than the regular army officer performing routine duties. Yet together with es-Sadat he participated in the secret group mentioned above, which was bent on sabotaging British military installations during the war.

The resumption of political activity by Boghdadi in 1948 shows at least some planning before plunging into action. For example, he met in Damascus with Fawzi Qawuqji, leader of the armed irregulars in the Palestine conflict, to discuss ways by which the Egyptian Air Force could render assistance. He thought of smuggling Egyptian Air Force planes onto a secret Damascus airstrip. In fact, Boghdadi appointed Squadron Leader Hasan Ibrahim, another Free Officer, to select a suitable place for an airstrip. According to Boghdadi, Qawuqji never asked for the planes.

Major Kamal al-Din Husein, whom the author met in 1958, appeared diligent, devout, and devoted. He was a few years younger than any of the officers mentioned above, and his political sensitivity was intensified by his devoutness. The Muslim Brethren could have been his avenue of political expression. But his actions appeared more precipitous than anything Nasser did before 1952. At the outbreak of the Palestine conflict, early in 1948, he resigned his army commission to join volunteer irregular forces engaged against the Jews. For some time he trained and supervised *fedayyeen* (commando operations) in Palestine, and later, in 1951, he supervised them in the Canal Zone. His political views derived largely from his efforts in the Palestine conflict.

Of the same age as Kamal al-Din Husein but equipped with more formal education (B.Sc. in commerce and economics), Major Khaled Muhieddin could qualify as an "intellectual revolutionary." He was perhaps the most active contributor to the secret pamphlet publications of the Free Officers in 1950 and 1951. His political training was based more on theoretical speculation of a leftist character, less on involvement in revolutionary activity. He was a convinced Marxist-Communist by 1954, distressed by the "reactionary" proclivities of his colleagues on the Revolutionary Council.

Were one to analyze in detail the background of every officer active in the Free Officers movement he would find at least one common factor behind their involvement in politics: frustration with an autocratic regime which could not handle the question of Anglo-Egyptian relations and—worse still—betrayed the army in battle. A corollary force affecting their

TABLE II Sample Officers Who Have

Name	Age*	Rank	Ministry
Tawfiq Abdel Fattah†	38	Lt. Col.	Social Affairs & Labor, Egypt
Tu'ma al-'Awdat Allah	37	Lt. Col.	Municipal, Rural Affairs, Syria
Mohd. Mahmud Nassar	46	General	Health, Egypt
Abbas Radwan†	38	Lt. Col.	Interior, Egypt
Fathi Rizk†	48	General	Industry, Egypt
Husein Dhu'l-Fiqar Sabri†	48	Wing Cmdr.	Deputy Foreign Min.
Sarwat Ukasha†	37	Lt. Col.	Culture and National Guidance
Kamal Rifaat†	37	Lt. Col.	Min., State; Acting Min. of Waqfs

* Age at time of appointment, October, 1958   † Free Officer

Attained Cabinet Rank in Present Executive of UAR

Education	Political Activities	Positions Held
Military Academy, 1940 Staff College, 1952		Staff Officer Infantry Corps 1952: Dir. Bureau of C-in-C for Operations 1953; Sec. Gen. to Council of Ministers 1958; Chief Office of Com. Gen. Staff, Arab Pact Armies, 1955; Joint Chiefs of Staff
Military College, Syria; 1st Army Armd. Corps	Socialist	
College of Med., Cairo, 1936		Genl. Officer rank 1957; Pres., Egyptian Med. Assn.; 1st Lt. Army Med. Corps; Dir. al-Maza Hosp.; Dir. Military Hosp.; Chief Med. Officer Military Med. Commission; Dir. Gen. Med. Service
Military Academy, 1942; Staff College, 1951		Instr. Infantry School 1952; Dir. Public Affairs Bureau of C-in-C 1952–53; Dep. Dir. Military Intelligence 1958
Military Academy, 1932		Dir. Military Supply; Chrm. Committee on Transportation; Petroleum Commission; Chrm. UAR delegation for agreement on Naval Transport between UAR and West Germany; Dep. Min. of War
Military Academy, 1932; Air Force Academy, 1935	Flew Gen. Aziz al-Masri toward German lines in West. Desert 1941	Air Fleet Cmdr.; Mem. Sudan Governor's council; brother of Ali Sabri, Min. in charge of Pres. Affairs; Consultant to Pres., Egypt. Republic 1956–58
Military Academy, 1939; Staff College, 1948; Diploma, Journalism, 1944		Military Attaché Berne, Paris; UAR Ambass. to Rome, 1956–58
Military Academy	Subversive Activity vs. British in Egypt	Cmdr. Kantara Dist. 1956; elected member National Union from Kantara without opposition; appointed dep. to Ali Sabri, Min. in charge of Pres. Affairs

political behavior was identification of the ruling institution as an evil to be dispelled like a foreign occupying power.

Further reasons for the political concern of this army officer group emerge from an examination of how and when the Free Officers group was organized. Recruitment techniques for membership in the group are also revealing. We might readily accept one or more accounts of the formation of the Free Officers group as given by some of the so-called founding members themselves. Anwar es-Sadat, in his account referred to previously, intimates that the group existed as far back as 1941. He also implies that it rallied then around General Aziz al-Masri in his efforts to sabotage the British war effort in the Middle East. Es-Sadat also claims that the revolutionary officers met in Zamalek in 1942 to discuss the February Palace incident, and that by 1945 the group had outlined its plans for attaining power. Es-Sadat talks of two branches organized within the movement: one military under the command of Gamal Abdel Nasser, the other civilian or "popular" under his own command. There was a third, a small terrorist or suicide group headed by Captain Mustafa Kamel Sidki. Infiltration of army commands and secret recruitment of sympathetic officers had, according to es-Sadat, brought membership by 1947 to the thousand mark.

Tom Little in *Egypt* accepts the above account, but it is prudent to entertain the view that between 1941 and 1949 there was no organized group of Free Officers. Rather, many of the Free Officers operated independently of, yet sympathetically to, one another in infiltrating army personnel and spreading their message. The message was vague at this stage, for many of these officers continued to adhere or even belong to one or another of the organized political groups, such as Misr al-Fatat (by then the Socialist party), the Muslim Brethren, and the Communist party.

Any cohesion among these officers was based until 1949 entirely on their personal relations and contacts. There was, as suggested earlier in this chapter, a nucleus of officers who were contemporaries in the Military Academy and Staff College, many of whom had served together in various commands and capacities. One hears and reads about relations between Nasser, es-Sadat, and Zakariyya Muhieddin in Manqabad on their first army post assignment. Similar relationships and close friendships between Nasser and Abdel Hakim Amer developed while both were serving in the Sudan. Naturally, these were strengthened during the Palestine War. But it would be hasty to presume any ideological cohesion between these men in their early contacts, or any collective conspiracy based on neatly organized plans for revolutionary action. Not all of the Free Officers acquired political aspirations—even views—by way of revolutionary activity, adherence to, or affiliation with one or another of the existing political and religious groups. Many of them may well have been "converted" politically by their colleagues over a long period, during which they maintained friendship with one another.

Generally speaking, until 1949 the defense of the Suez Canal and, in effect, of Egypt was a British responsibility. Consequently the activities of the Egyptian army between 1939 and 1948 were limited. Chances for active comradeship among Egyptian officers resulting from extensive and strenuous battle duty were almost nil. Most of the Free Officers were by 1945 occupying desk or staff jobs in major cities. Freed from sustained attention to military strategy or continuous training, they could direct their thoughts and energy elsewhere. Occasionally, and more frequently between 1945 and 1949, they were called on by the government to restore public order in the major cities during serious political disturbances.

It seems likely that the Free Officers movement began in the early 1940's as an informal "fraternity" of friends among junior officers who had been posted together at one time or another. Even so, camaraderie was not enough to transform this fraternity into a Free Officers group with some organization by 1949. What factors, then, can one isolate as most instrumental in bringing about the Free Officers Executive?

Attendance at the Military Academy between the years 1936 and 1939 no doubt fostered the earliest contacts and friendships between members of this small group. Attendance at the Staff and Command College between the years 1945 and 1948 by Gamal Abdel Nasser, Abdel Hakim Amer, Salah Salem, Zakariyya Muhieddin, and Kamal al-Din Husein renewed these contacts at a politically critical period in Egypt's history, while it probably strengthened the political overtones of their personal relations. Those members of the Free Officers who did not attend Staff College at this time had attended later (Shafei, 1953). Most of them therefore shared this experience. Almost immediately upon graduation from Staff College several left to participate in the Palestine campaign, so that their contacts with one another continued. So far, however, these officers held no particular view on political action or the role of an army officer in the process. Despite their earlier indulgence in student political activity, or wartime sabotage against Britain's position in the country, the idea that they, as army officers, had a role to play in Egyptian politics had not yet crystallized in their minds.

It is also difficult to establish their motives in choosing a military career. To a large degree, as many of these officers would readily admit, an army career offered financial security as well as prestige. The patriotic view that they would be defending their country would have been fatuous at the time, when defense was for all practical purposes a British concern.

It has been suggested by students of Arab politics that a career in the army was an avenue to political office. Majid Khadduri, in his "The Army Officer: His Role in Middle Eastern Politics," argues this motive for officers in the Iraqi army, especially in connection with the Bakr Sidki coup in 1936.[3] The situation was different in Egypt, where in the thirties an army career was the least likely avenue to political power. The British exercised direct control over the Egyptian army for many years, while the monarch carefully maintained it as his loyal praetorian guard against predominantly civilian politicians.

A series of crucial experiences between 1948 and 1951 alienated the young officers' loyalty to the Crown and led to the organization of the Free Officers group, for which a nucleus, or inner circle, already existed. The Palestine War was for these officers their first serious combat experience. Failure to defeat the Jewish state in Palestine was humiliating for the army in general and its officers in particular. Subsequent exposure of the defective arms scandals, the levity with which the King and Cabinet committed the army to battle, together with the widespread publicity of both of these facts, provided a sympathetic though unofficial link between these younger officers and rising popular disaffection with the *status quo.* Their sympathy with radical and extremist organizations, such as the Muslim Brethren and the Socialist party, increased in direct proportion to their disappointment with the King and civilian politicians in power.

There is no indication at this stage, however, that the Free Officers contemplated an active part in the struggle for political power. They merely complained against the authorities and the monarchy for failure to manage properly the Palestine affair. The Free Officers group took no positive action until the King as well as his civilian ministers extended their control into the military hierarchy. When Palace politics began to affect seriously the position of the younger officers—who now possessed a more intense political awareness—organization in the form of a movement within the army became a tactical necessity.

Rashed al-Barawi claimed in *The Military Coup in Egypt*[4] that as early as 1945 a group of officers issued secret circulars under the general heading "The Army Gives a Warning," signed "The Free Officers." These circulars were allegedly concerned with evacuation of British troops from Egyptian soil and demanded vigorous action by the Egyptian Government to achieve this end. This may well be true. Still, Barawi may be

confusing these secret pamphlets with the circular "An Appeal
and a Warning" issued by the Free Officers early in 1950. The
latter is more probable, for it has been established that the
first Executive Committee of the Society of Free Officers was
constituted late in 1949.

Other circumstances support the view that the Free Officers
group was not formally organized until 1949. Upon returning
from the Palestine campaign in March 1949, Gamal Abdel
Nasser, Kamal al-Din Husein, Salah Salem, Abdel Hakim
Amer, and other Free Officers received assignments as instructors in both the Military Academy and the Staff College.
Favored by the prestige attached to heroism in the siege at
Faluja, they were in a position to infiltrate a large section of
the student body in both institutions. But the Chief of Staff
suspected their political activities. Many of them were known
members of the Muslim Brethren, an organization outlawed
since December 1948 for its terrorist acts. Nasser himself reported publicly on July 22, 1953 that in the summer of 1949
Premier Ibrahim Abdel Hadi accused him of unlawful political activities in the presence of General Osman Mahdi, Army
Chief of Staff.[5]

Undoubtedly officers who showed the slightest signs of discontent with the *status quo* after the Palestine War were suspect. Possibly Gamal Abdel Nasser and his associates realized
the importance of organization both as a safety measure and
a device for expanded operations. Their experience in Sinai
convinced them that the King and his government were not
interested in the nation's or army's welfare. They accepted
the proposition that so long as the King and the usual type
of civilian government continued to exercise political control
the country was doomed to national frustration and foreign
domination. Thus they were equating national liberation with
destruction of the regime. Up to this point, however, they
were not clear as to who or what group would lead a struggle
for liberation. Some of them, to be sure, placed their hopes
in the Muslim Brethren, others in a socialist revolution. With

the exception of Nasser perhaps none of them had seriously accepted the idea that the army should lead in bringing political change.

The assumption of a political role for themselves was nevertheless encouraged by the fact that in neighboring Arab states army officers were replacing traditional civilian leadership on the grounds of treason, incompetence, and unrepresentativeness. In Syria alone three consecutive coups led by army officers occurred within six months (March to August 1949).

Free Officers met informally at the end of 1949 to discuss plans for organizing a Free Officers group. This gathering consisting of Lieutenant Colonel Nasser, Major Amer, Major Kamal al-Din Husein, Major Salah Salem, Wing Commander Gamal Salem, Squadron Leader Hasan Ibrahim, Wing Commander Boghdadi, Major Khaled Muhieddin, and Lieutenant Colonel es-Sadat, constituted itself as a founding committee. Soon thereafter, in January 1950, it met again to elect an Executive Committee and a Chairman. Gamal Abdel Nasser was elected the first Chairman of the Executive, and elections for the Committee were to be held in January of every year. In January 1951, Nasser was re-elected Chairman.

The activities of the Free Officers Executive in 1950 and during most of 1951 were confined to (1) publication and circulation among members of the armed forces as well as student and other civilian groups of pamphlets attacking government policies and the King, and (2) efforts to infiltrate army commands for the recruitment of members. Non-member sympathizers were sought among civilian groups opposed to the *status quo*. The Committee also enlisted the support of opposition journalists who, in 1950 and 1951, were conducting a vigorous press campaign against the King. Through these journalists the Free Officers were able to air some of their views and grievances.

Within the army the Society of Free Officers used the cell system. A cell consisted of not more than five to ten members. An intelligence network was possible because members of the

Executive were placed in staff positions close to the Army
High Command. Major Salah Salem, for example, had access
to the office of the Chief of Staff, whereas Lieutenant Colonel
es-Sadat managed a "pipeline" to the Palace through contacts
with the King's private physician. Major Khaled Muhieddin
and Lieutenant Colonel Nasser were close to such influential
journalists as Ahmad Abul Fath of the daily *al-Misri* and
Ihsan Abdel Quddus of the weekly *Rose el-Youssef*.

When in 1949 the government of Ibrahim Abdel Hadi extended martial law after the termination of military operations in Palestine, some members of the Free Officers came
under surveillance of the political police. It was necessary,
therefore, for the Society of Free Officers to anticipate eventu-
alities by imposing tight security measures within the group
and maintaining at all costs its access to information from the
Palace, the government, and Army Headquarters.

Needless to say, the Abdel Hadi Government of 1949 as well
as that of Wafd in 1950 and 1951 knew of the existence of the
Society. Strangely, they did not take drastic action against it.
Nor did they seem capable of assessing its danger. The King
must be held largely responsible for such complacency, for he
continued to believe that his control of the top personnel in
Army Command was in itself a guarantee against any radical
political movement by army officers. What is more puzzling
is his continued optimism when his contention was proved
wrong late in 1951.

General elections for the Army Officers Club were scheduled
for December 1951. The King had always paid special attention to this club in his efforts to retain the loyalty of army
officers. In doing so he succeeded year in and year out in getting his chosen candidates elected to its governing board. As a
rule, the Chief of Staff was elected President. Now for the first
time in the history of the Club, there emerged opposition to
the King's routine control of the elections. The Free Officers
organization had thus already prepared its position for a

genuine electoral contest, and it conducted a vigorous campaign among fellow officers for its nominees.

The meeting of the Club's General Assembly was scheduled
for December 27 to elect a President and members of the governing board. Shortly before the meeting it became known
that a faction in the army would be nominating General
Muhammad Naguib, General Officer Commanding Infantry,
for President of the Club, along with a full slate of candidates
for the board. The King, on the other hand, was anxious to
have his own man, General Husein Sirry Amer, Chief of Staff,
elected to the presidency. He interpreted the existence of an
opposition ticket as a mutinous act on the part of the army.

While hundreds of officers were arriving at the Club for the
scheduled meeting, Army Headquarters suddenly ordered the
meeting adjourned and elections postponed indefinitely. But
some 350 officers from all branches of the service were already
at the Club, and the meeting proceeded as scheduled without,
however, an election. The members present, especially those
adhering to the Free Officers movement, took the opportunity
to circulate the names of their candidates. The assembly agreed
to hold elections at a meeting a few days later. More important,
however, was the fact that the officers present at the meeting
had disregarded the order of Army Headquarters not to meet,
and rebuffed the wishes of the King.

The meeting early in January 1952 to elect Club officers,
attended by some 500 officers, was prefaced by a resolution that
the army was in full sympathy with the Egyptian people in
their struggle against imperialism and that it was always at
the service of the nation. Proceeding to the elections, they
chose General Naguib as President and a governing board of
fifteen members which included at least five known members
of the Society of Free Officers. The remaining members elected
were known sympathizers of or adherents to the Free Officers
movement. The Free Officers had succeeded in getting their
slate elected—a clear victory over the King. Among those
elected were Lieutenant Colonel Zakariyya Muhieddin (Free

Officer), Lieutenant Colonel Rashad Mehanna (Free Officer), Lieutenant Colonel Anwar Abdel Latif (Free Officer), Squadron Leader Hasan Ibrahim (Free Officer), Lieutenant Colonel Abder Rahman Amin, Wing Commander Bahgat Mustafa, Lieutenant Colonel Galal Nada, Brigadier Hasan Hishmat, Lieutenant Colonel Ibrahim Fahmi Dabas, Lieutenant Colonel Abdel Aziz Gamal, Lieutenant Colonel Ahmad Obeid, Lieutenant Colonel Hafiz Atif, Captain Ahmad Ghani Mursi, Brigadier Ayad Ibrahim, and Major Gamal Hamad (Free Officer). For the first time members of the Club Board included junior officers, lieutenant colonels and majors, with only two brigadiers.

The Officers Club election crisis of December 1951–January 1952 constituted the second major event which, after the Palestine War, further alienated the army officers from the King. The success of the Free Officers in the elections marked the beginning of a campaign for membership in the Society and the establishment of a wide range of contacts with opposition groups in Egyptian politics. Such was the objective of the many pamphlets issued by the Society between January and July 1952, which circulated widely among the Armed Forces, university students, and the Muslim Brethren. In these pamphlets the Free Officers expressed their opposition to martial law in the country, the police methods of the Interior Minister Murtada al-Maraghi, and the policies of the Army Chief of Staff, General Husein Sirry Amer. In other pamphlets they demanded reforms in the army, and criticized the Commander-in-Chief, General Muhammad Haidar, for the debacle in Palestine. Moreover, having just won the Officers Club elections against the King, the Free Officers were now assured of a strategic position from which to infiltrate all ranks of the Armed Forces and to challenge seriously the authority of the government and the Palace.

Meanwhile the attitude of the Free Officers toward the Wafd had changed drastically. When the Wafd came to power in January 1950, the Free Officers, like most other groups, hoped for an improvement in the political situation, believing that the Wafd would be able to circumscribe the King. By the autumn of 1951 they were disappointed with the Wafd's performance and proceeded to include it on their list of political opponents.

The Free Officers' distrust of the Wafd became clear during the Suez Canal crisis between October 1951 and January 1952. There is some evidence that the Wafd Government indirectly encouraged the participation of army officers in the training and supervision of guerilla forces operating against the British in the Canal area. They hoped to divert attention from the political situation. But the Free Officers had already decided on a political role which they would some day play against the whole regime. They were not prepared to dissipate their strength and efforts in what then seemed a futile struggle. With shrewd political insight Gamal Abdel Nasser withstood all pressure from his more hot-headed colleagues to participate in the Canal battle. It is also to his credit that he disregarded attempts by the British government to dissociate the army from popular anti-British sentiment, when Sir Anthony Eden in December 1951 announced in the House of Commons that the Egyptian army was the most peaceful group among Egyptians, and the most friendly to Great Britain.

The crisis in the struggle between the army and the Palace arose at last on July 22, 1952, only a day before the Free Officers embarked on their successful coup d'état. Since January 26, 1952, the Free Officers had barely avoided the destruction of their movement by the Palace and a succession of so-called independent governments. Chagrined by the defeat inflicted on him by these younger officers in the Officers Club elections a few months earlier, the King now sought to tighten control over senior appointments and to punish those involved in the campaign against his candidates. He was actually losing confidence in the ability of General Muhammad Haidar to keep the army loyal to him, and wished to replace him as Commander-in-Chief by General Husein Sirry Amer. To accomplish this, the King put Haidar in an untenable position. Early in July he instructed the Royal Chamberlain, Hafez Afifi Pasha, to deliver a note to the Prime Minister in which the latter was directed to order General Haidar (1) to disband the Officers Club governing board, and (2) to transfer to distant posts its elected members. Failure to comply with both of these royal requests would mean Haidar's dismissal as Commander-in-Chief. To avoid serious trouble Premier Husein Sirry suggested to the King the appointment of General Muhammad Naguib, President of the Club, as Minister of War before dismissing the Club's board. This measure, Sirry felt, would placate the younger officers while it would satisfy the King by closing the Officers Club. The King's intransigence over this issue, however, forced Husein Sirry's Cabinet to resign on July 22, 1952.

When the King asked Naguib Hilali to form a new Government, he insisted on appointing his brother-in-law, Colonel Ismail Sherine, as Minister of War, a choice hardly acceptable to the army officers. Ismail Sherine's "honorary" rank had been bestowed on him when he married Fawzia, one of the King's sisters. He had never attended the Military Academy, and he had no known qualifications for the appointment other than his relation to the monarch. This open affront to the army spurred the Free Officers to action on July 23. Convinced now that no government, including that of the capable Ali Maher between January 26 and March 1, 1952, could curb the King's absolute power, they also felt that the existing hierarchy of Army Headquarters (Husein Sirry Amer, Muhammad Haidar) was nothing more than a tool in the hands of the King for control of the army. When viewed in conjunction with the virtual collapse of civilian political leadership between January and July 1952, the situation was propitious for the action the Free Officers took on July 23.

The July 23, 1952, coup d'état in Egypt represents the culmination of a struggle between two factions in the Egyptian army: the Palace-appointed and supported officers versus the Free Officers led by Gamal Abdel Nasser. One hypothesis as to the easy success of the Free Officers is that the Society had a double advantage. In the first place, it was able to identify its cause within the army with popular discontent over the King and his civilian government. Secondly, members of the Society were closer in social and economic status to the bulk of the army officers than were the high-ranking officers in Army Command.

If one were to accept the account of Anwar es-Sadat (repeated by Tom Little in *Egypt*) regarding the beginnings of the Society of Free Officers at Manqabad in 1938, one would also have to accept the proposition that the society was a "party" within the army, deliberately planning for some fifteen years the achievement of political power. This view is difficult to substantiate. Es-Sadat has published his story; so has Nasser. But we have not heard, so far, from Abdel Hakim Amer, the brothers Salem, Zakariyya Muhieddin, and others. Indeed, al-Boghdadi's recollection points more to conspiracy and sabotage against Britain as the primary activity of these like-minded officers during World War II, under the inspiration of the intransigently anti-British General Azi al-Masri. It is difficult, therefore, to show conclusively that the Society of Free Officers was a long-standing army organization with definite political objectives. It is even more difficult to establish whether its members chose an army career as a means to political power.

It is tempting to compare the Free Officers to the Committee of Union and Progress in the Ottoman Turkey of 1909. The leaders of this Committee, Enver, Talaat, and Jemal, deposed Abdel Hamid only to replace him with a weaker Sultan and proceed with the strengthening of Ottoman ruling institutions. Among the active members of the C.U.P. there were also many civilians. Neither of these elements is to be found in the Society of Free Officers. Once the coup was successful, the Free Officers proceeded to eliminate all vestiges of the old regime. Nor were civilians actively involved in their society.

One looks in vain for a clear view of the role these officers envisaged for themselves even as late as 1951, other than resisting the King's abuses of their profession. One also finds few indications of any political program or plan of action. The fact that the Free Officers decided on a serious play for power as late as March and July 1952 suggests that their chances for political success emerged only after civilian authority had collapsed.

This reasoning suggests that the Society of Free Officers did not become an active political group within the army, an organized contender for power, until (1) the safety of its leading members was in question; (2) grave doubt had been cast on the competence and loyalty of Army Command; and (3) conditions in the country had deteriorated to the point where revolution was not unlikely.

There were perhaps as many shades of political belief as there were members of the Free Officers Executive. Views ranged from extreme rightist, Islamic fundamentalist, and Fascist to left-wing radical socialist and Communist. Any contention therefore that the Society embraced a group of officers with a common ideological or political persuasion is erroneous.

There is a parallel between Gamal Abdel Nasser in 1952 and Ahmad Orabi Pasha in 1882. Nasser, like Orabi, rallied native Egyptian army officers against those persons identified with the ruling institution or monarch. Both men prefaced their movements with a demand for reforms in the military establishment. Orabi sought the Ministry of War for himself, whereas the Free Officers seventy years later sought appointment of a senior ranking officer, General Muhammad Naguib, acceptable to them. Both Nasser and Orabi were "underdogs," men derived from the "people." There is, however, a sharp difference, advantageous to Nasser, which Orabi could not have hoped for in his time: the Egyptian army after seventy years had achieved a greater degree of Egyptianization. The political experience of army officers in 1952 was derived from thirty years of intense Egyptian nationalism, culminating in their participation in an all-Arab national struggle for Palestine in 1948 and 1949. The conspiracy of Orabi, Fahmi, and Abdel Al in 1881 was not bound up with the aspirations of a sophisticated Egyptian nationalist class, as was Nasser's Free Officers' conspiracy.

Part II

The Transformation of the Military Group into a Ruling Elite

4. Early Consolidation of Power

As EARLY as February 1952 it was obvious that the army was the only national institution in Egypt that could provide law and order, and the only dynamic element in a disrupted Egyptian state that could assume the role of political arbiter.

The story of the July 23, 1952 coup d'état led by Gamal Abdel Nasser and his Free Officers has been told several times. Among foreign analysts of the Egyptian scene, Tom Little in *Egypt* and the Lacoutures in *Egypt in Transition* have given readers complete accounts of this momentous event in modern Egyptian history. Three persons directly involved in the coup have also published their accounts: General Muhammad Naguib in his apologia, *Egypt's Destiny,* Gamal Abdel Nasser in *Egypt's Liberation: The Philosophy of the Revolution,* and Colonel Anwar es-Sadat in *Revolt on the Nile.* A general discussion of the significance of the coup entitled *The Military Coup in Egypt,* by Rashed al-Barawi, appeared very soon after the event in 1952. Another account here would be repetitious.

What concerns us is the further evolution of the Free Officers group once they achieved political power. Between July 1952 and October 1954 the Free Officers Executive succeeded in transforming itself from a conspiratorial group to the most effective ruling elite in the Arab Middle East. Beginning merely as the organizers of a military coup d'état against a

71

discredited civilian regime, the Free Officers Executive emerged as the spearhead of revolution. Constituting, with their adherents within the Egyptian army, a political group approaching the proportions of a party, the Executive evolved techniques of political control as well as a distinguishable political ideology and program. How it has exercised political control, formulated and executed public policy, recruited followers, and responded to public demands are the essential queries in any assessment of the present regime in the U.A.R.

Students of the Middle East, absorbed in the Big Power politics of the area, have neglected to look seriously at the emerging political system of the U.A.R. Such a task is difficult, involving grave risks of misinterpretation and plain errors of fact. But this need not preclude the formulation of certain hypotheses regarding the highly interesting developments in Egypt and the U.A.R. which are paralleled by the emergence of military regimes elsewhere in the Middle East and Asia. In drawing these hypotheses we shall endeavor to avoid, on the one hand, moral condemnation of governments headed by ex-army officers, and on the other, the enthusiastic approval of such governments evident in some quarters.

Those impatient with the chronic instability of the Arab countries recite the common refrain *"plus ça change, plus c'est la même chose."* Of course it would be impossible for any ruler to create an ordered, prosperous, and responsible Arab political community overnight. Nasser's ability to survive and thrive politically for more than eight years has been in itself a notable achievement. To ascribe his political longevity to chance, or mere force, would be fatuous.

Some observers initially felt that the coming of the army to power in 1952 was nothing more than a simple military mutiny. They argued that a true revolution produces fundamental changes in the socio-economic structure of a society, and transforms its major institutions. They hardly considered the possibility that the army coup might be the harbinger of revolution. On the surface, of course, there were few signs of any upheaval of the Egyptian masses; there was a marked absence of people's barricades in the streets. A superficial assessment of the situation in 1952, however, utterly fails to explain the nature of the army movement, its relation to other groups in Egyptian society, or its role in the political reorientation which followed its accession to power. Admittedly, there was at the time scant indication of the aims of the Free Officers group or its plans of action. Today we possess sufficient perspective to permit a detached and discerning study of the character and consequences of the army movement.

How the army group has consolidated its power and legitimized its authority should be our first concern. An analysis of the elements on which the new political power elite has tried to base its power and the manner in which it has, so far, sought to broaden the base of its support is helpful in understanding its political behavior.

The secrecy surrounding the Free Officers movement within the Egyptian army confused public speculation over its immediate plans once the coup occurred. If Muhammad Husein Haikal's reaction reported in his political memoirs—"I rushed back to Cairo, cutting short my summer vacation in the Lebanon"—is any indication of the reaction of all political party leaders, they must have considered the army coup a military action directed primarily against the King and the existing government and not against the existing political system. They obviously hoped the coup leaders would return to their military duties once a civilian government acceptable to them was constituted. The group most guilty of such gross miscalculation was the Muslim Brethren, which believed that its extensive organization would force the military junta to request its assistance in governing the country.

The first public announcement of the coup broadcast on the morning of July 23, 1952, contained no precise announcement of goals and plans. It merely informed the citizens that the army had acted on their behalf to "cleanse the nation of its tyrants, and to reform the constitutional life of the country."

As it turned out, neither the public nor the junta knew at the time exactly what this meant. But the expectations of civilian political leaders were heightened when the junta asked Ali Maher to form a government. They were not apprehensive over the deposition of the King so long as Ali Maher headed a cabinet of civilians. But the speed with which the army leaders then proceeded to neutralize all civilian political groups was a reflection of the latter's weakness, unrealistic optimism, and unpopularity, as well as of the army's evolving inclination to assume total power.

The civilians gathered by Ali Maher to serve as a government in the first days of the coup derived their appointment as well as their authority from the revolutionary officers. Their appointment was a matter of convenience enabling the junta to gain time for its next move. It did not reflect any desire of the army to encourage a civilian government to rule the country. Actual authority rested with the Free Officers Executive, now reconstituted as the Revolution Command Council.

As much as one may like to think of the July 23 coup as a popular revolution, and irrespective of its causes, the Revolution Command Council (RCC, or *qiadat al-thawra*) was notable for the absence of any substantial popular participation. The RCC consisted of the original members of the Free Officers Executive in addition to one or two others. Its membership was as follows: General Muhammad Naguib, Lieutenant Colonel Gamal Abdel Nasser, Major Abdel Hakim Amer, Major Salah Salem, Major Kamal al-Din Husein, Squadron Leader Hasan Ibrahim, Wing Commander Abdel Latif al-Boghdadi, Wing Commander Gamal Salem, Lieutenant Colonel Anwar es-Sadat, Major Zakariyya Muhieddin, Lieutenant Colonel Husein Shafei, and Major Khaled Muhieddin. Colonels Ahmad Shawqi, Abdel Moneim Abdel Rauf, Kamal Rifaat, and Lutfi Wahid, and Captains Ahmad Anwar and Yusuf Sadiq were associated with the RCC but not voting members in its inner circles.

The RCC was the forum in whose secret and prolonged

deliberations the conspiring Free Officers matured into a ruling elite. It was a Command Council, and it could not be a popular council. Command decisions were necessary to see the coup through its danger period, to marshal army units behind it, to obstruct countermoves by other army officers, and ultimately to win public confidence.

One thing quickly became clear: the Free Officers did not overthrow the monarchy in alliance with friendly political groups seeking power. Farouq was deposed so confidently and firmly that any groups inclined to obstruct his removal never had time to devise the means for it. Thus the swift abolition of the monarchy, the order to political parties to purge and reorganize their ranks, and the promulgation of the Agrarian Reform Law were all frank indications of the Free Officers' aspirations to political leadership and control.

The Agrarian Reform Law promulgated in September 1952 was one of the first in a series of political measures aimed at consolidation of power by the Free Officers. Generally speaking, it limited land ownership in Egypt to a maximum of 200 *feddans* (approximately 200 acres). Foreign observers have been piqued by the economic nonsense of this measure. But sound economics was not the only rationale for agrarian reform. It was rather a means by which to strike a sensational political note with the Egyptian masses. Considering the premium placed on land by rich and poor Egyptians alike, agrarian reform with its redistribution of large estates to the *fellahin* was a potent psychological measure. It gave the Free Officers their first political link with the peasant masses. Regardless of the economic and agricultural problems pertaining to the profitable utilization of a five-acre farm by an Egyptian *fellah,* the uplift to his morale was impressive. Having tilled but not owned the land for most of his life, he now viewed the young army officer who deeded it to him as a benefactor and liberator.

Although it limited land ownership to 200 acres, the Agrarian Reform Law did not amount to economic hardship by any standards for the small percentage of big landowners in Egypt. Nevertheless, the landowners affected objected to its implementation and questioned its economic wisdom. Both Premier Ali Maher and Regent Bahieddin Barakat were opposed to it. It was, of course, difficult for Ali Maher and his civilian Cabinet to accept wholeheartedly the drastic measures imposed by the RCC, whom they considered totally inexperienced in politics. Naturally, Maher was reluctant to encourage agrarian reform, reduction in land rents, and changes in *Waqf* (religious trusts and bequests) legislation. Thus, early in September it became apparent that his Cabinet could not withstand the radicalism of the RCC. Ali Maher resigned and on September 7 General Naguib formed a new Government, which was still a cabinet of civilians. It included mainly technicians and administrators, who, it was hoped, would heed and implement the "revolutionary changes" decreed by the RCC.

Meanwhile, as early as July 31, 1952, the RCC, through General Naguib, issued a call to all political parties and associations to purge themselves of undesirable elements and declare publicly their reconstituted hierarchies and platforms. RCC members argued that "if the primary objective of the army coup was the destruction of undesirable elements in the country, the government and civilian groups should proceed to purge such elements from among their ranks." By August 2 the RCC asserted that it would never use its influence to interfere in this purging process within the government. But by August 10, it was obvious that the RCC was not satisfied with the "fake" reorganization of such parties as the Wafd, and Naguib went so far as to announce that "after the warning period" the army might use force. But throughout this period, and until the resignation of the Maher Government on September 7, there was no clear indication of the RCC's intention to dissolve political parties. Nevertheless the reluctance of political parties to respond to the RCC demand—indeed, many of them did not take it seriously—on the one hand, and the army's growing resolution to carry out sweeping changes in the political life of Egypt on the other, sharpened the conflict between the RCC and traditional politicians. The RCC was now convinced that there could be no compromise with professional politicians. Their outright neutralization became necessary if the army regime were to carry on.

Among the political groups in Egypt the Free Officers had to contend seriously with two: the Wafd and the Muslim Brethren. The leadership of both groups believed in their ability to command the support of many Egyptians. Mustafa Nahhas, head of the Wafd, for instance, continued to claim that his party represented the nation, while the Supreme Guidance Council of the Brethren, headed by Hudeibi, contended for pre-eminence in any remaking of the Egyptian political system. It cannot be denied that both groups had many adherents among students, working and merchant classes. More serious was the active connection of some Free Officers (Abdel Moneim Abdel Rauf, for example) with the Brethren. The latter group was thus a more dangerous rival of the Free Officers than the Wafd, as they presumably had direct access to active sympathizers among the Free Officers.

The Brethren emerged from the January–July 1952 chaos as the strongest political organization in Egypt. There is no clearer proof of this than the fact that the junta initially considered possible cooperation with them. It is difficult to say whether the Free Officers offered the Brethren a share in government because of fear or genuine desire to cooperate. But the Brethren did enjoy at that time great popularity among militant radicals who were disillusioned with the Wafd. And this was exactly the type of following the Free Officers hoped to attract.

The invitation to participate in the government extended to the Supreme Council of the Brethren was misinterpreted by Hodeibi, Supreme Guide, and Ashmawi, his second-in-command, as a desire on the part of the Free Officers to embrace the Brethren's cause of an Islamic state. The three members nominated by the Brethren in August 1952 to serve in the

Cabinet came with the proposal that their Supreme Council should also have the right to pass on legislation by the new regime to assure its Islamic orientation. This presumption was unacceptable to the RCC, and the proposal was flatly refused. One of the Brethren nominees, Sheikh Hasan al-Baquri, was accepted by the RCC to serve in the government as Minister of *Waqfs*. Baquri's acceptance, however, terminated his association with the Brethren.

Faced with the reluctance of political parties and the Brethren to take them seriously, the RCC realized that a campaign to legitimize their authority and leadership with the people was urgent. Three themes were essential for legitimacy. First, the army had to dissociate itself from previous nationalist agitation and political development led by discredited civilian politicians. Second, the army had to connect its movement somehow with the Islamic ethos but distinguish it from the Muslim Brethren. Finally, it had to seek acceptance by the economically less privileged classes—workers, peasant farmers, and students—by preaching a vision of an equitable society with higher standards of living for all. In short, the RCC had the difficult task of asserting effectively that the army represented the nation.

Between September 1952 and June 1953 the RCC concentrated its efforts on a campaign to secure public acceptance of its undisputed leadership. While it paid attention to the behavior of the Wafd, Muslim Brethren, and other political groups, the RCC went directly to the people. On September 29, 1952, it sent its leader, General Muhammad Naguib, on a tour of the Delta region, where Wafd influence had been strongest. Naguib's public appearances evoked enthusiastic response from the masses. This in itself was some evidence of the waning influence of the Wafd in the Delta.

The RCC campaign among the people was extended during February, March, and April 1953 to all parts of the country. Leading RCC members, Gamal Abdel Nasser, Kamal al-Din Husein, Abdel Hakim Amer, and Abdel Latif al-Boghdadi, embarked on a systematic rallying of popular support. In fact, the RCC called this program "the conscription, or mobilization, of national sentiment" (*ta'bi'at al-shu' ur al-watani*). The RCC used the ingenious device of sending its members to campaign in their respective home districts. Thus Kamal al-Din Husein worked in Qaliubiya and Beheira, al-Boghdadi in Daqhaliyya province and its capital Mansura, and Abdel Hakim Amer in Minia. Throughout their tour, RCC members stressed that the army is the army of the people, that its aims are popular. So far, however, the RCC insisted that the army did not aspire to political power, but only planned to purge the country of undesirable elements and to re-establish genuine constitutional government. At the same time a new theme was injected into the officers' campaign: the era of outcry and demonstration was over. What was needed now was unity, order, and work. The economic plight of the country inherited from the previous regime was also emphasized to justify not only stringent RCC measures in that direction but also the time required to meet the economic crisis.

But Wafdist and Muslim Brethren strength was not confined to the farming population, or to village *sheikhs* and mayors of the provinces. The RCC recognized from the beginning the importance of winning the support of students in the urban centers, for it was among this group that the Wafd and Muslim Brethren had their best organized followings. Both Naguib and Nasser frequently addressed university students in Cairo and Alexandria during November 1952. Their appeal to the students also carried with it a warning against the usual political agitation for which this group was so well known.

Although industrial labor in Egypt is a very small fraction of the working force, the RCC was forced to pay special attention to its ranks. The earliest incidence of violence after the coup was labor unrest in Kafr-al-Dawar on August 13, 1952, which led to armed clashes between workers and government security forces. It ended with the government taking strong measures against labor by summarily executing two of the ringleaders. The RCC was in no mood to permit labor unrest or any type of revolutionary activity so soon after its own coup, but neither did it wish to appear unresponsive to labor demands. From September to November 1952 both Naguib and Nasser, in addressing labor groups in Cairo, stressed the army's serious concern with labor conditions and emphasized the importance of sound labor legislation. An apology for the Kafr al-Dawar hangings is detected in Naguib's plea with the workers at Embaba on November 20 for more time to devise progressive labor laws.

Difficulty with the Muslim Brethren strengthened the RCC's belief that an accommodation of their movement with public religious sentiment was imperative. One must still accept the proposition that although Arabs generally, and in this case Egyptian Arabs, are not overconcerned with an Islamic political system or state, their traditional and emotional adherence to an Islamic heritage weighs heavily in their assessment of political authority. It can actually make a difference in whether they accept a ruler as legitimate or reject him. For this reason alone the RCC wisely sought to associate the movement it led with the purported Islamic ideal of justice and equality. Thus in May and June 1953 Husein Shafei, Anwar es-Sadat, and Kamal al-Din Husein took to the pulpit to preach Friday sermons at various mosques, and to plead the basically Islamic character of their planned reforms. They reminded the believers, moreover, that fanaticism was not the only variety of devoutness.

This RCC campaign on all fronts must be viewed only as a general appeal for mass acceptance of the coup. It was by no means the prime method by which the Free Officers secured consolidation of their power. The RCC was not really seeking votes of confidence or popularity. Rather it was gradually preparing the people for full submission to the new regime. In order to assert their undisputed authority, the Free Officers had to destroy the existing organized political activity, on the one hand, and to achieve absolute control over the military establishment on the other. Regimentation of the Egyptian population could follow only after these two objectives had been accomplished.

Alongside its country-wide appeal for support the RCC made changes in all aspects of government which eventually led to total political control on a new basis. This institutionalization of control was as thorough as the measures for obtaining it were drastic. It involved the displacement of all vestiges of civilian authority and influence by the appointment of military personnel to the Cabinet and other posts. The RCC as the policy-making group for the Revolution necessarily extended its authority over the execution of policy as well.

The first Naguib Cabinet, announced on September 8, 1952, featured one army officer—himself. Although predominantly civilian, it presented a new departure from pre-coup policy in that the RCC consciously tried to cooperate with known progressive citizens. Fuad Galal, who became Minister of National Guidance, and Abbas Ammar, who took the portfolio for Social Affairs and Labor, were both prominent leaders in the *Ruwwad,* or Pioneers, movement of the thirties. The Pioneers had brought together a group of sociologists and economists to work for the social betterment of Egyptians. They came equipped with the pragmatic training of Anglo-American social science in contrast to the predominantly French legal background of professional politicians. The army now sought the cooperation of those civilian elements who appreciated the importance of social and collective welfare, in preference to the highly individualistic values of those steeped in French-conceived liberty.

Although the purge within the army was still in its first stages, the RCC instituted a general purge of organized political parties in January 1953. The parties were formally dissolved, their properties and funds confiscated, and a military dictatorship announced for the next three years. Military tribunals established in January to try defecting officers were supplemented later in the year by the Court of the Revolution to try leading politicians of the previous regime. Extreme right as well as extreme left publications were suppressed when press censorship, lifted on August 12, 1952, was reimposed on October 21 of that year.

In order to thwart any attempts by the Wafd to challenge legally the Parties Reorganization Law in the Council of State, the RCC on November 13 made General Naguib "Chief of the Revolution" by decree. By January 23, 1953, when the Liberation Rally was inaugurated and mass oaths of loyalty to the regime were taken by civilians and members of the Armed Forces alike,[1] the RCC showed unmistakably its intention to rule without accommodating existing civilian political groups. Gamal Abdel Nasser became Secretary-General of the Rally on February 6, 1953, and a fifty-member commission was appointed to draft a new constitution. All the members of the RCC automatically became members of this committee in addition to a select number of former senators, premiers, and ministers.

With the inauguration of the Liberation Rally, a three-year transition period was formally announced by General Naguib. Eleven Rules of Government for the transition period were proclaimed on February 10, 1953. The last four are significant. By Rule 8, the Leader of the Revolution and President of the RCC assumed full sovereign powers to protect the aims of the Revolution. He was empowered to appoint and dismiss ministers. Rule 11 described the RCC and Council of Ministers as jointly composing an Executive Council to consider general policy of the state. Every minister was formally responsible to this Council.

The Manifesto of the Liberation Rally published on January 16 outlined the national aims of the Revolution, among them the determination of the regime to "drive out occupiers from the Nile Valley unconditionally." Other aims were to "establish a sound community, to rid the country of all elements of retrogression and weakness, to set up an economic system based on social justice, to create industry on a large

scale, to protect citizens against unemployment, and to en-
lighten all citizens in their duties through unity and cooperation in productive work."

Defense of the Revolution was now linked with a complete
change of regime. "The Liberation Rally is not a political
party," declared Gamal Abdel Nasser at Mansura on April 9,
1953. "It is a means to organize popular strength for the reconstruction of a society on a sound new basis." At the same
time Nasser made it clear that those who thought the army
coup merely aimed at overthrowing King Farouq were mis-
taken. "This aim," he declared on February 23, 1953, "is a
minor objective compared to the over-all idea of our Revolution. The latter seeks to change the political system for the
benefit of the people. It is therefore necessary to defend the
Revolution against those who try to deter it from its course
and prevent it from attaining its ultimate goals."

In launching the Liberation Rally the RCC was not necessarily seeking to broaden the base of the support for its movement. It was more interested in creating a vehicle through
which it could forestall political agitation by the Wafd, the
Ikhwan, and other elements.[2] As the Free Officers contemplated
the final dissolution of all political associations, they established the Liberation Rally as a measure against disruption
resulting from the chasm existing between them and the people.
Thus, though it did not become the Party of the State, the
Liberation Rally served the RCC in helping clear labor unions,
trade federations, and student organizations of antagonistic
elements. This pattern became evident when Nasser formed
his first Cabinet in April 1954. The key ministry of Social
Affairs and Labor, for instance, went to a member of the Free
Officers inner circle, Kamal al-Din Husein. The latter system-
atically purged trade unions and labor organizations of possible
opposition. He performed the same operation successfully
among student organizations after he became Minister of
Education in June 1956. That the purpose of the Liberation
Rally was one of regimentation was asserted by Major Salah

Salem—the bluntest member of the RCC—when on April 11, 1953 he informed an audience at Mit Ghamr, "We did not come to you for votes, because we do not aspire to rule, or to become members of parliament. We came to seek your co-operation and unity."[3]

The determination of Gamal Abdel Nasser to make a clean break with the past was apparent long before he achieved total control. Throughout 1953 Nasser was the undisputed mouthpiece of the RCC on matters of basic policy. This fact has eluded those who have insisted that Nasser maintained his leadership in the background at this time. Major pronouncements on domestic and foreign policy consistently came from him, and the first indication of a republican regime is found in one of Nasser's press interviews on June 17, 1953.

When the Republic was announced on June 19, 1953, Major Salah Salem, in a prepared statement to the press, emphasized the security of the regime as a major reason for the abolition of the monarchy. For the same reason, he explained, it was necessary that members of the RCC join the Cabinet. Gamal Abdel Nasser was appointed Deputy Prime Minister and Minister of Interior, Wing Commander Abdel Latif al-Boghdadi Minister of War, Major Salah Salem Minister of National Guidance and Sudanese Affairs, and General Abdel Hakim Amer Commander-in-Chief of the Armed Forces.

The appointment of leading RCC members to key ministries implied three things. First, it reflected tighter control by the RCC over the army as well as the civilian population. Second, it indicated the pre-eminence of Gamal Abdel Nasser in making policy for the regime. Third, it was a preventive measure against the possible political accommodation of General Naguib with civilian personnel in government. The army officers who became cabinet members for the first time retained their army commissions but received ministers' salaries. This misled many people to believe that the assumption of cabinet posts by these army officers was a temporary arrangement, despite the implausible public explanation that they were re-

taining their army commissions to permit liaison with the
RCC. As the Council of Ministers—which also acted as a
Sovereignty Council—was really controlled in matters of policy
by the RCC, the inclusion of the above-mentioned four officers
clearly meant greater consolidation of army power.

Major Salah Salem, in further public explanations for these
drastic changes, attacked the previous civilian Cabinet for its
shortcomings. He claimed in June 1953 that RCC members
originally intended to return to their barracks six months after
the coup. The adverse machinations of some "seventeen political parties"[4] and the reluctance of civilian ministers to implement revolutionary policies recommended by the Free Officers,
Major Salem contended, necessitated the assumption of executive positions by RCC members. In a public statement regarding the establishment of a republican system on June 20,
Nasser reiterated the same reasons. Both Salah Salem and
Nasser made it clear, however, that the army was until then
the only major source of positive power for the regime. General
Naguib emphasized this fact during a ceremony in which a mass
oath of allegiance to the new Republic was taken by army
officers. "The Army officers," exclaimed Naguib on that occasion, "are the pillar of the revolution. The whole movement
was initiated by you; the nation looks to you for leadership.
. . . Do not ever forget that the army is the vertebral column
of this movement in the country, even though all citizens have
blessed it."[5]

The abolition of the monarchy was not, however, a gesture
in favor of less absolute rule. If few Egyptians showed any
regret over the passing of the monarchy, it was because the
institution was largely an imported one, the dynasty was foreign, and experience with the behavior of its members in the
country unpleasant, if not bitter. Moreover, it was difficult even
for those who might have regretted it to express their feelings
under military government. The average Egyptian still thought
in terms of a *ruler*. One ruler had been replaced by another,
the new republican system to the contrary notwithstanding. In

the establishment of neither institution did the average Egyptian have a choice, or a voice.

There were, however, grounds for public acceptance—even enthusiastic acceptance—of the army officers that must not be overlooked. The Free Officers, even as *rulers,* represented a cross-section of native Egyptian society. The previous dynasty, of course, did not. Among politically conscious and sophisticated Egyptians the active leadership of the army was also in many respects acceptable. Aspiring to a number of economic, social, and political goals, and despairing of the inadequate civilian leadership which had just collapsed, these intensely political Egyptians saw in the army a highly organized and disciplined force to advance national aims. "The people," as Marei and Afifi put it in *thawrat sha'b* (A People's Revolution), "had found someone to defend the rights so long denied them."[6] The people now claimed—or imagined—that in recent Egyptian history army officers had been willing to use force to obtain national rights. Even a writer as critical of the Egyptian military junta as George E. Kirk conceded that "it was at least something that the army was associated with reform rather than reaction."[7] The RCC nevertheless was, until the end of 1953, still distinguishing between a "government" and the Army Officers Corps. At the same time it was threatening to take over full control in view of the situation. This, however, did not occur until the RCC had eliminated its major rival, the Muslim Brethren, and purged its ranks within the RCC and the army.

When the Free Officers acceded to power most groups, including the Muslim Brethren, seemed, on the surface at least, to favor the coup. The Muslim Brethren especially, counting on the association of certain Free Officers (Anwar es-Sadat, Rashad Mehanna, Kamal al-Din Husein, and especially Abdel Moneim Abdel Rauf) with their movement between 1940 and 1950, hoped for the best. They were further encouraged in their competition for power with the Free Officers when the dissolution of political parties in January 1953 did not initially affect them. Officially considered a religious association, the Muslim Brethren survived the January 16 decree. But they could not very well have viewed favorably the simultaneous inauguration of a Liberation Rally mass organization, which meant a possible invasion of their ranks. Hodeibi, the Supreme Guide of the Brethren, insisted that his association was adequate to provide the popular base needed for the Revolution. What disturbed the Brethren more was the establishment of a republican regime so soon after the coup. This RCC measure was too secular to suit the Brethren's designs. Indeed, the RCC had rather hastily decided on a republican regime to counteract mounting religious opposition to their movement, and to disarm such conservative elements as the Azhar and the Brethren.

As early as December 1953 disagreement among the members of the Brethren's Supreme Council leaked out. The *Ahram* of December 10, 11, and 12 published obscure news items indicating that Hudeibi, who was inclined to cooperate to some extent with the RCC, was being opposed by Ashmawi, Muhammad Ghazali, and Ahmad Abdel Aziz Galal. The latter three were temporarily expelled from the Supreme Council. Their exclusion from the hierarchy weakened the Brethren's top leadership while the struggle with the ruling army officers was in progress. Nevertheless, the Brethren shrewdly foresaw the growing rift between General Naguib and his younger colleagues on the RCC, and they sought his cooperation in any future showdown with the army. In the meantime, Naguib, as President of the Republic and Prime Minister, had succeeded in amassing tremendous popularity and good will in the streets. His moderation immediately attracted the sympathy of the outgoing civilian political groups, who saw in him now their hope for a return to power.

In January 1954 the Brethren's highly organized cadre precipitated disorders of some magnitude in Cairo University and among workers. They interpreted the "moderation" of the RCC in concluding an agreement with Britain over the Sudan

in February 1953, and the initiation of negotiations over the
Canal Base, as a betrayal of national aspirations. They agitated
for a Holy War against British troops still stationed in the
Canal Zone. A rally of university students on January 12 was
addressed by Brethren representative Hasan Duh, who, in
turn, introduced to the crowd Nawab Safavi, leader of the
Fedayan-i-Islam, a similar extremist Muslim organization in
Iran. A violent clash between pro-Brethren and pro-Liberation
Rally students erupted after the harangue.

These disturbances caused by the agitation of the Muslim
Brethren afforded the RCC sufficient cause to seek the dissolution of that group on January 14. Lieutenant Colonel Husein
Shafei, a member of the RCC, in a speech at Minia on January
13, accused the Brethren of being a subversive political party.
"Islam," said Shafei, "is not an industrial enterprise or monopoly for the Ikhwan (Brethren); neither is it idolatry."
Lieutenant Colonel Zakariyya Muhieddin, Chief of Military
Intelligence at the time, announced the arrest of 400 Brethren,
including Hudeibi, the Supreme Guide, and other leading
members of the Supreme Council, among them Sheikh Muhammad al-Farghali. Enough members of the Council, Abdel Sattar,
al-Khouli, Kamal Khalifa, and Mahmoud Seif en-Nasr, were
left free, however, to arrange a "United Front" with Wafdist,
Communist, and Socialist elements and precipitate a crisis in
February–March 1954.

Encouraged by General Naguib's apparent receptivity to
the idea of a return to parliamentary government, opposition
groups hoped to drive a wedge between this senior officer and
his younger colleagues in the RCC. Although the Communists
were active in this drive, the Brethren's leadership cannot be
disputed. Thus, while Nasser paid tribute to the "fallen
martyr" Hasan al-Banna, founder and first Supreme Guide of
the Brethren until his assassination in February 1949, by at-
tending a memorial service at his tomb on February 12, 1954,
he did not hesitate to describe the organization as "a state
within the state." Arms caches were in the meantime discovered

in the home of Hasan Ashmawi, a high-ranking member of the Supreme Council, further intensifying the Army's campaign against the organization.

The opposition United Front that was active from June 1953 until March 1954 cannot be assessed, however, separately from the opposition to the RCC within the Army Officer Corps and the internal power plays which occurred among RCC members. The attraction of dispossessed political groups to General Naguib encouraged him to seek greater authority in the RCC. Unfortunately Naguib was not in a position to claim total identification with the Revolutionary Free Officers. His sympathy with the grievances of younger officers prior to the 1952 coup notwithstanding, he never belonged to the Free Officers movement. Inevitably, therefore, his bid for power was obstructed by his inability to command the loyalty of leading Free Officers. They were already committed to the leader of the army movement, Gamal Abdel Nasser. Naguib was thus left with two alternatives: to accept the role of figurehead assigned to him by the RCC and hope for a better future, or to make a serious bid for power with the aid of existing opposition groups within the army and the civilian population. His choice of the latter course eventually cost him his position and his freedom.

Involved in the internal crisis of February–March 1954, which was caused mainly by a struggle for power within the army officer corps between the Nasser-led forces and those in favor of Naguib, were two considerations: (1) What was the aim of the army movement? (2) When should the role of the army be publicly announced? Naguib, for one, felt that a return to constitutional and parliamentary institutions was the logical next step. It is possible also that favorable reaction to his view by interested political groups heightened his personal expectations for a brighter political future. What General Naguib apparently failed to realize was that his hopes would be frustrated without the unequivocal support of the army. He evidently failed to appreciate the cohesiveness of the Free Officers group in their determination to destroy all political opposition to their evolving objectives, just as he failed to assess the fundamental direction in which the group's sense of purpose was moving. The leader, in short, failed to discern the route being taken by his followers, as other leaders have been known to do at momentous but fluid periods of national history. The popularity of General Naguib with his countrymen was not a practical source of strength sufficient to permit him to bypass the wishes of the new power elite: the inner core of the Free Officers movement.

In practical terms the time had come by February 1954 for the junta to declare its political intentions. An agreement over the Sudan had been successfully concluded with Britain in February 1953, and negotiations for the settlement of another national problem, the British evacuation of the Canal Zone, had begun late in 1953. The prognosticated solution of the latter "imperialist" issue left the junta face to face with internal considerations of political, social, and economic reforms. But the RCC was not in a position to assess its real strength within the Army until a crisis situation tested it.

General Naguib's resignation on February 25, following his disagreement with RCC members over matters of policy and the allocation of authority, had serious repercussions among the public, disconcerting to the junta. But the public aspect reaction to Naguib's resignation was not the decisive element. The junta was alarmed, rather, at the division among officer ranks over this issue. Muslim Brethren sympathizers, upper-class and Communist-following army officers rallied to restore Naguib to office. The story was circulated at the time that Cavalry Corps officers, commanded by Major Khaled Muhieddin, a member of the RCC, led an armed demonstration in favor of Naguib, and that Nasser had to "talk himself" out of this difficulty in Abbasieh Barracks. Naguib was brought back to the premiership three days later, on February 28.

This incident was the first serious indication that the ranks of the junta were divided. It also underlined the necessity of a more complete and systematic purge of these ranks. This does not mean that the RCC or its effective leader, Gamal Abdel Nasser, had not realized this necessity earlier.[8]

At the same time, the incident encouraged disaffected political groups to intensify their courting of General Naguib. Before making him Prime Minister again the junta appointed Nasser Military Governor of Egypt, a measure intended to obstruct the possible alignment of Naguib with the civilian political forces. It also permitted the RCC to institute sweeping purges of the Armed Forces. Publicly, though, Nasser employed ingenious tactics to disarm his enemies. By March 5, 1954 he feigned a rapprochement with political groups, announcing a decision to restore parliamentary forms beginning with a constituent assembly to be elected in June of that year. Under this scheme the RCC was supposed to disband, permitting political parties to contest the elections in the absence of martial law. To confuse its enemies further, the junta ordered the release of certain political prisoners, especially members of the Muslim Brethren who had been arrested earlier in the year. The question which remained unresolved and which eluded the rejoicing political parties was whether the adherents of the Free Officers in the army and the junta would permit the voluntary self-liquidation of their movement.

Wafdists, Socialists, Communists, Muslim Brethren, and left-wing journalists were now lured by the junta's relaxation of repressive measures to align themselves with Naguib. Meanwhile, the originally secret organization of the Free Officers set to work independently to counteract a possible return to power of old political groups. The Liberation Rally, controlled by its Secretary-General Nasser and loyal Free Officers, was able to organize students and trade union members into mass demonstrations against the proposed return of constitutional life. The demonstrations of March 25–27 in Cairo and Alexandria and the ensuing general strike in public transport were manifestations of the total control and regimentation achieved by the Liberation Rally as an arm of the RCC elite. More important was the protest of Free Officers against the proposed relinquishing of authority by the junta in July 1954 and their virtual threat to assassinate those junta members in favor of this change. This, in effect, was an expression of loyalty to Nasser's leadership of the army movement and implied a mandate to the RCC to eradicate all opposition to the army. On March 28 the junta announced the indefinite cancellation of the proposed June elections for a constituent assembly, and ousted General Naguib from the premiership and the RCC.

The removal of Naguib and the victory of the Nasser faction in the army placed all political groups, and especially the Muslim Brethren, in a difficult position. While the junta now retained Naguib in office as President of the Republic to placate public sentiment as well as Sudanese feelings—Naguib was half Sudanese—it simultaneously set out to consolidate its absolute control in the country. Before announcing his new Cabinet, Nasser on April 15 issued a decree in the name of the RCC depriving all those Wafdists, Liberal Constitutionalists, and Saadists who held cabinet posts between 1942 and 1952 of their political rights for ten years. His Cabinet of April 18 featured most of the RCC members: Lieutenant Colonel Nasser, Prime Minister; Squadron Leader Hasan Ibrahim, Minister for the Presidency of the Republic; Major Salah Salem, Minister of National Guidance and Sudanese Affairs; Lieutenant Colonel Zakariyya Muhieddin, Interior: Lieutenant Colonel Husein Shafei, War; Wing Commander Abdel Latif al-Boghdadi, Municipal and Rural Affairs; Wing Commander Gamal Salem, Communications; Major Kamal al-Din Husein, Social Affairs and Labor. Thus eight out of the eleven members of the original Free Officers Executive at the time of the coup assumed ministerial posts. Significantly, Major Khaled Muhieddin was excluded for his Communist leanings, but more so for his having supported General Naguib in February against Nasser.

The final battle between the junta and the Muslim Brethren was fought later in the year under circumstances definitely favoring the success of the army. In July the RCC succeeded in initialing a Heads of Agreement with Britain for the complete evacuation of the Canal Zone within twenty months; the final agreement was signed in October. Meanwhile, in April, the junta was able to silence major opposition journalists critical of their rule by closing down the largest formerly pro-Wafd daily, *al-Misri,* and subsequently trying its editors, Mahmud and Hasan Abul-Fath, in a military tribunal. Ihsan Abdel Quddus, editor and publisher of the weekly *Rose el-Youssef,* who enthusiastically supported the army movement in its first stages, now criticized it bitterly for its unwillingness to re-establish constitutional life. Consequently, he was imprisoned in the spring of 1954. Misr al-Fatat or Ahmad Husein's Socialists, Wafd students, and National Democrats of Mustafa Kamel Sidky were successfully combated from April, especially when control over the Liberation Rally was tightened by the appointment of a Supreme Supervisory Council consisting of Nasser, Kamal al-Din Husein, and two rising young Free Officers, Ibrahim Tawfiq al-Tahawi and Ahmad Abdallah Tu'aimah. The Court of the Revolution delivered its judgments on leading politicians of the old regime between December 1953 and January 1954, thus striking another blow at their organized resistance.

When a Muslim Brother tried to assassinate Gamal Abdel Nasser in Alexandria on October 26, 1954, the junta moved easily to crush the organization and knock it out of the political running indefinitely. The trial of the conspirators in November implicated President Naguib. He was quietly removed from his office and placed under house arrest on November 14.[9] The execution of seven conspirators, among them such leading members of the Brethren Supreme Council as Abdel Qader Oudeh and Sheikh Muhammad al-Farghali, made the official dissolution of the organization the following day the subject of an edict. With the destruction of the Brethren organization, the elimination of General Naguib, and the virtual suppression of all organized party opposition, the junta emerged by the end of 1954 as the undisputed ruling elite of Egypt.[10]

The pattern followed in consolidating the Free Officers' hold over the political and administrative structure of the state is revealing. Besides key ministries controlled by RCC members, the army had to ensure the loyalty, or at least guard against the defection, of the civilian administrative cadre. By December 1954 Nasser was able to appoint trusted army officers in key bureaucratic offices to supervise the work of civilian departments. Despite the use of civilian economic and other experts in cabinet posts (Finance, Economy, Commerce, Industry, Justice, Foreign Affairs, and Agriculture), Nasser was able, through the device of committees and commissions directly responsible to him for coordination of policy, to impose effective army control over all activities of the State.[11]

Within the RCC and the Free Officers group, personal loyalty to Nasser soon became the criterion for political longevity. Those who initially harbored independent political views were either relegated to unimportant positions or ousted. Colonels Ahmad Shawqi and Lutfi Wahid of the Infantry, for example, were ejected early for their leftist tendencies. Khaled Muhieddin paid the price for his defection during the Naguib-Nasser rift with exile to Europe. Although Anwar es-Sadat and Kamal al-Din Husein may have been just as far right in the political spectrum as Muslim Brother Colonel Abdel Moneim Abdel Rauf, only the latter was expelled from the Officers Executive. Colonel Rashad Mehanna, who tried to use his position on the Regency Council to bid for power in alliance with Muslim Brethren leaders and with the aid of artillery and cavalry officers, was dismissed from the Regency on October 14, 1952. When a rival group of army officers sought to elect him President of the Officers Club in December 1952, Colonel Rashad Mehanna was cashiered from the army, placed under house arrest, and his fellow conspirators were tried by a military tribunal.

Some observers of Egyptian developments during this period

have decried the illegal methods used by the junta to consolidate its power. They felt that the behavior of its members after the coup robbed the army movement of any legitimacy it might have secured through a rapprochement with existing political groups. The issue, however, was not one of legitimacy through any "representative" institutional device. Granted that by December 1954, legitimation of the junta's rule depended on the army's unequivocal support and loyalty, organized political groups had ceased to exist, and a political void between the military rulers and the population resulted. But Nasser and his new political elite of army officers could now proceed to legitimize their authority through devices of their own choice, as will be argued later in this discussion.

When the coup occurred all groups rushed to influence its political direction and orientation. The Brethren hoped to control the junta in favor of a traditional fundamentalist orientation. The Wafd, on the other hand, expected that by forcing a return to constitutional forms they could find their way back to power. The Communists, Socialists, and other radical leftist groups within and outside the army viewed the coup only as the first phase of a more radical revolution. But Nasser apparently was not prepared to commit himself or his movement to any one group, at the end rejecting their terms by suppressing every one of them. Thus the questions facing the RCC in March 1954 were answered—by actions rather than words—in the only way capable of producing hard, tangible responses to the issues facing that group at the time of Thermidor.

To the credit of Nasser and his junta were already such popular measures—regardless of their practical effectiveness—as agrarian reform, labor and social legislation, and the evacuation of the Canal Zone by the British. The attempt on Nasser's life in October 1954 further enhanced his popularity and rendered all opposition groups by definition "enemies of the Revolution" and, therefore, of desirable change. In Egypt at the time, as well as in most other Arab countries, such mass popularity frequently replaces the need for more formalized institutional legitimacy. The lack of organized political expression and experience among the masses helps them to overlook the institutional aspect of legitimate authority.

In the first two years of its rule, the junta was not prepared to accept dictation from any political doctrine represented by prevailing political groups, or even by some of its own members. Although radically nationalist in the eyes of the public, it affected to portray an abhorrence for partisan politics. Its determination to become the ruling elite in the country precluded any long-range alliances with rival groups. Its political interest—the desire to rule in order to carry out the Revolution—could not have been accommodated with other group interests. As such, therefore, the junta consisting of members of the Free Officers Executive became the nucleus of a new ruling class whose membership, as we shall see below, continued to be recruited largely from the army officer corps, but which was slowly invaded by certain professional groups in Egyptian society, whose services the military power elite could not dispense with or easily replace. At the same time, the increasingly secure position of the junta in authority permitted it, as will be argued in the following pages, to venture into schemes of social and economic reform as well as to experiments with limited popular participation in politics—two possible sources of potential opposition.

5. The Search for a New National Myth: The National Union Scheme

By the end of 1954 the consolidation of the junta's position as the ruling elite in Egypt was in an advanced stage. All serious opposition from the landowning old guard politicians, the mass organization of the Muslim Brethren, the extremist Misr al-Fatat, lesser leftist radical groups, and Communists had been crushed. The partly armed confrontation between Communist and Brethren-inspired army officers on the one hand, and Nasser loyalists on the other, in February–March 1954, had ended in a clear victory for the latter. The assumption of the functions of government in addition to those of policy-making by the members of the RCC in the spring of 1954 had completed the coup d'état by imposing the rule of Nasser-led Free Officers over the entire political community. So far, however, no revolutionary change in the structure of government (as distinguished from policy) had occurred. The appointment of army officers to executive positions in the bureaucracy was more of a control device by the junta than a means of introducing structural change. Nasser was not only anxious to extend his army-based control but also to compensate Free Officers for their part in the Revolution. As a leading young Egyptian intellectual put it, "there was not much of a revolution until 1956; after the Suez affair the Free Officers sensed the urgent need to marshal popular forces at home instead of merely concentrating power in their own hands."

External events helped permit this incomplete consolidation and extension of army power to persist for another two years. The Baghdad Pact of February 1955, the Israeli attack on Gaza in the same month, and the arms purchase agreement with the Soviet bloc in September 1955 increased the popularity of the army rulers and gave them greater freedom of action in the Egyptian political scene as well as in the wider Arab arena. In the face of obviously grave threats and problems in intra-Middle East and international politics there was no pressing need to buttress military rule with revolutionary domestic policy changes or to de-emphasize it by recourse to ostensibly popular institutional devices. Indeed, the Egyptian sense of inimical isolation from the North engendered by the conclusion of the Baghdad Pact and the Israeli attack in the same month seemed to justify, if not further legitimate, the "transitional" rule imposed by the junta.

The "representative committee" appointed in 1952 to draft a constitution never completed its work, and the RCC continued to rule by decree on the basis of a brief stopgap document adopted in February 1953. To prepare a replacement for this transitory document Nasser selected a smaller committee dominated by his RCC colleagues and himself. This group drafted a Constitution that was presented to the nation on January 16, 1956, and adopted by plebiscite on June 23. Its preamble reaffirmed the six major objectives of the Revolution: the abolition of imperialism (presumably achieved by the Anglo-Egyptian agreement in October 1954); the destruction of feudalism (presumably ended by the Agrarian Reform Law in 1952); the combating of monopolies and capitalist control of government (presumably struck down by the establishment of the Permanent Council for National Production in January 1953); the establishment of a strong army (to have begun with the arms purchase agreement with the Soviet bloc in 1955, and the promulgation of a new uniform military service law in the same year); the achievement of social justice in a "democratic socialist cooperative" society. The latter two objectives are yet to be achieved.

The new Constitution inaugurated a system featuring a strong executive with ministerial responsibility directly to the President. Political parties were temporarily replaced by a National Union through which "the people would realize the aims of the Revolution." Attempts at mass organization of a popular political following were not intensive during the "transition" period.[1]

However, regimentation and security were not the only concerns of the army regime. Much more important was the maintenance of the Egyptian state. Indeed, this is the major concern of all Arab Middle Eastern governments today. Maintaining a state in an environment which does not encourage the emergence of viable nations has been a basic task of all government in Middle Eastern countries which attained independence after World War I. Considerations of the type of political system—representative, democratic, or otherwise—appear secondary, while questions of social and economic reform take still lower priorities.

Democratic institutions and representative systems of government developed in the West long after the existence of the state was secure. In countries like Egypt and Syria the establishment of democratic institutions must draw from other than Middle Eastern sources, while the maintenance of a state, let alone a particular kind of state, is not a fundamental value commonly shared among their inhabitants. Premature adoption of representative or democratic institutions could therefore prove disruptive to the fabric and existence of the state, if indeed it were feasible at all.

It is incorrect to argue that the old regimes in Egypt and Syria were overthrown because the people ceased to accept their legitimacy. Legitimacy was not yet an issue in nations in which few classes and groups of the population had entered politics at all. In spite of the constitutional formula for male suffrage in both countries, the predominantly poor and illiterate masses did not achieve a high voting rate, and to expect from them active and discerning participation in political affairs would be absurd.

Incipient labor groups have yet to achieve sufficient economic emancipation (acceptance of trade union activity by the government, recognition of the right to strike, and collective bargaining) to exert any influence on political decisionmaking. Industrialization on a large scale has hardly begun in these countries. Agricultural workers—some 40 per cent of the rural population in Egypt—have only recently been officially recognized as part of the country's labor force. There was thus neither a sizable and expanding emancipated citizenry interested in preserving the status quo nor an articulate, organized opposition to it. As was suggested in Chapter 3, the challenge to and ultimate attack upon the old regime came from the army, the most powerful organized group in the state, which was primarily dissatisfied with the effectiveness and political performance of that regime.

There exists in the Middle East today, contrary to the European pattern, a paradoxical situation: radical nationalist ideology promising unlimited social and economic benefits to the underprivileged classes, without the necessary conditions of an industrial state which alone can make these benefits possible. The formula devised to fulfill this promise is one of rapid industrialization for massive economic development, which in turn, is expected to lead to a "socialist democratic" society. It is not at all certain, however, that economic development will lead to a socialist *democracy,* but the theory is presently accepted by most of the so-called underdeveloped countries of Asia and Africa.

Sociologists and political scientists since de Tocqueville have argued that the more numerous the cleavages and levels of conflict in a society, the greater the chances for the evolution of a free political community.[2] Their argument derives from the Western assumption that groups within a society or political community are a good thing, and that they should be permitted to express their differences. It further assumes that, within limits, non-violent dissent and conflict are political values universally accepted by members of the community, regardless of their religious background, or their economic and intellectual tradition.

Although we may accept the proposition that the free expression of cleavages and the existence of conflict in a particular society lead to more democratic institutions and practices, we cannot easily apply it universally. In Egypt, for instance, until July 1952, this principle was formally recognized by constitutional provision. It did not, however, lead to a properly functioning democratic system, because certain underlying requisites were lacking: a high degree of literacy, social and economic mobility, a high rate of industrialization, an equitable agrarian system, an emancipated middle class of professionals and workers, and in general a reasonably stable political climate. The tendency of the masses under stress to join extremist political movements, moreover, presented fertile ground for revolution against the status quo rather than loyalty to it. Those in power did not recognize any basic rights of majorities or minorities out of power, and those out of power had no choice but to remain passive or to reject the authority of the rulers and seek to replace them by force. An acceptable formula for the orderly transference of power from one group to another never really existed. Violence was therefore an acceptable—unavoidable—instrument of change.

The tendency in the U.A.R. until this writing has been to prevent the proliferation of political groups, open cleavages in society, and thus to suppress the areas and sources of conflict. Instead, integrative movements or state parties were devised for the "political and economic enfranchisement" of the people. Trade unions, for example, have not so far been permitted autonomous organization outside the integrative superstructure. Vehicles of national endeavor such as the National Union were devised to stimulate populist expression of support for a leader and his supporting power elite. But it cannot be too frequently stressed that the Nasser regime did not depend for its essential power or position in the 1950's on positive popular support. Such support was essentially supplemental and stabilizing, and to a large degree intended as a deterrent to opposition. At the same time, unilateral promises of new standards in political and economic performance became the chief criteria for popular acceptance of a strong revolutionary regime. Of course, there is a vast gap between popular acceptance of this sort and democratic society in the traditional Western sense.

Past experience in Egyptian politics at least favored the organization of the masses by the ruling elite. The Wafd founded its Blue Shirts in 1935 as an athletic organization for its younger followers, possibly with a view to making mass violence available as an additional prop to its political position. The fanatical Green Shirts of Ahmad Husein, also organized in the thirties, reflected, as did the more numerous Muslim Brethren, the ease with which the masses could be rallied to extremist political activity. The lack of differentiated political associations expressing articulated interests made this possible. A well-defined but small party elite was able to use the device of mass organization as a useful adjunct to its apparatus.

The National Union Scheme

It is often difficult to say why a military regime decides on certain measures. Why should a leader like Nasser, backed by the armed forces as he was, feel compelled to provide the people with a national mass organization, especially after he had crushed all sources of organized opposition to his authority? Was he concerned with the expansion of the political franchise for the citizens? It is difficult to conceive of the right to vote as an effective index of political emancipation without the right of free and voluntary association, free expression and press, and other basic freedoms. These freedoms, in turn, would inevitably lead to groupings and parties. These freedoms were not commonplace in the U.A.R. in the 1950's. Nasser repeatedly condemned partisan politics, "fake" parliamentarianism, and "paper" constitutionalism. Indeed, he emphasized the absolute need for a period of political, economic, and social regimentation in order to achieve the necessary conditions for a "true" democracy: social and economic equality, higher production, and higher standards of living. This, in the view of President Nasser's regime, would be best assured through some mass organization device.

Article 192 of the 1956 Constitution provided for the establishment of a National Union to replace all political parties. It has not been clear so far whether the National Union is a state party, or merely a state agency for political control of the masses. Nor is it developed enough at this stage to compare or contrast it to Ataturk's early organization of the People's Republican party in Turkey. But according to its army officer designers, the National Union was to represent a revolutionary concept in the political development of the U.A.R. In explaining its rationale, Anwar es-Sadat, first Secretary-General of the National Union, as well as President Nasser in his speeches on many occasions, has referred to it as a device to organize the masses so that they may acquire the means for achieving the goals of the Revolution. The army, which led the Revolution, argued the elite, was not a political organization, nor was leading revolutions its proper function. It was only a means ultimately resorted to by the people because all other means and organizations available in Egyptian society had failed. The army's involvement in politics was therefore temporary and exceptional.

A revolution, according to National Union theorists (Nasser and es-Sadat), requires a revolutionary elite or cadre (*jihaz thawri,* literally, revolutionary apparatus) to undertake its organization, planning, and leadership. This is the tool of revolution. It is not enough to have a revolutionary apparatus in the army—the junta. A mass apparatus is needed also.

These theorists have argued further that Egypt had been a country of masses without organized leadership. Consequently, imperialism, corrupt political parties, and fake parliaments were able to exploit them and render abortive their rebellions for political freedom and independence in 1936, 1948, and 1951. In 1952 the search for revolutionary leadership found no response among the unorganized masses or the organized political groups. The army, therefore, acted through the RCC as executive leader of the Revolution. But the RCC was not a government; it was merely an *ad hoc* executive. It is nevertheless inaccurate to argue, as Colonel es-Sadat of the Free Officers often has done, that the RCC led and governed a completely unorganized public, for he has overlooked the presence of the Muslim Brethren until 1954.

The purpose of the National Union and the motives for its establishment by the military ruling elite cannot be explained in the same terms for both regions of the U.A.R. In Egypt, at least, one can identify specific reasons and justifications for it. Officially the regime rationalized the National Union as the means to achieve the final goal of the Revolution: "a socialist, democratic, cooperative society." "As for the existence of a new generation, fit to assume political control and the functions of government according to the new mentality," declared Anwar es-Sadat in an interview with *Rose el-Youssef* on June 1, 1959, "it already possesses many qualifications. It still needs, however, a school to develop soundly these qualifications." This "school" is presumed to be the National Union. Another member of the junta, Lieutenant Colonel Zakariyya Muhieddin, Central Minister of the Interior, described the National Union as "a historical, economic, and social necessity before it can be thought of as a political necessity."

While the power elite through its leaders, President Nasser and the Secretary-General of the National Union, Colonel Anwar es-Sadat, hailed the new organization for the masses as necessary for the achievement of the social revolution, it never stated clearly the relation between the National Union and political emancipation, or more specifically the entry into politics of the Egyptian public. The regime was undoubtedly concerned with the question of loyalty to its rule, if not to the abstract concept of the state. It was also concerned with the transition from a provisional arrangement to a more permanent relationship between the military rulers and the people. Having committed itself to major economic planning and rapid industrialization, it found that "guidance" of a mass population became essential. The new Egyptian leaders, moreover, recognized the facility with which Arab as well as Egyptian masses were usually drawn into extremist movements in the absence of institutional frameworks for their political satisfaction. They were also impressed by the lack in the past of a homogeneous citizenry. The National Union, according to spokesmen of the military regime, controlling all aspects of public activity—students, labor, agricultural effort, economic and occupational associations—was expected to become the appropriate instrument for the development of a homogeneous political culture.

The National Union was formally created in May 1957, and played its part in the elections of July 1957 for the first Egyptian Assembly. The Electoral Law promulgated on March 1957 provided for a National Assembly of 350 seats, an allocation legalized by the April 18 districting law (65,000 inhabitants per district). Candidates had to be approved by the National Union Executive Committee, consisting of Wing Commander Abdel Latif al-Boghdadi, Lieutenant Colonel Zakariyya Muhieddin, and Field Marshal Abdel Hakim Amer. These three leading members of the junta were at the time Minister in Charge of Economic Planning, Minister of Interior, and Commander-in-Chief, Armed Forces, respectively. They screened 2,500 registered candidates for the 350 single-seat districts from sixteen provinces and three governorates and rejected 1,182 of them, leaving 1,318 actual contestants from which the six million registered voters aged over eighteen might choose. The £E50 (£E is approximately equal to £1) deposit required by law for filing candidacy naturally confined the contestants to prosperous lawyers and businessmen (about 33 per cent of those elected); town and village mayors already in office (about 10 per cent of those elected); high ranking civil servants, ex-ministers, and army officers who resigned their commissions in order to qualify for election (about 30 per cent of those elected); and landowners (about 12 per cent of those elected). Labor accounted for a mere 3 per cent of the total 350 seats, and peasant farmers, *fellahin*, won practically none. In contrast to many countries with established parliamentary traditions, voting was compulsory. Defectors were liable to fine or imprisonment, or both. Women were granted suffrage for the first time but only two were elected to the Assembly.

Besides the limitation on candidacy imposed by the required £E50 deposit (roughly twice the annual per capita income of Egypt), the screening of candidates by the junta virtually meant the disqualification of anyone suspected of opposition to the regime. Moreover, once elected, the candidates had no clear understanding of the functions of the Assembly when it met on July 22, 1957. The Assembly met between July 1957 and March 1958 mainly to hear lengthy statements by the President and members of his Cabinet on government programs undertaken and policy decisions made. These were hardly debated but merely approved.[3]

Union with Syria rendered academic the function of the Egyptian National Assembly. During its short life it merely lent an aura of legitimacy to the undisputed authority of the army Free Officers. The formation of the U.A.R., an organic union of Egypt and Syria, called for the dissolution of legislative assemblies in both countries and the projected formation of a single Assembly for both regions of the new Republic. Article 72 of the provisional U.A.R. Constitution, promulgated on March 5, 1959, on the basis of which the plebiscite legalizing union and accepting Nasser as the first President of the U.A.R. was held, provided for the reorganization of the National Union to include both regions, as a first step toward the elections for a U.A.R. legislature.

Before discussing the development and organization of the National Union after the formation of the U.A.R. and the elections of July 1959, certain propositions about its purpose are in order. These propositions are meaningless unless they are viewed in direct relation to the new problem of political and economic integration of Egypt and Syria. In Syria, it will be recalled, agitation for union with Egypt was led by a political party, the Baath, in alliance with a clique of army officers. Normal party life was functioning until January 1958, with representation and active debate in a parliament. It is now clear that the anticipated replacement of Syrian political parties by the National Union was intended to (1) impose firmer control by the Egyptian army over Syria, by diminishing the role of political parties and their clientele, (2) achieve a measure of political and economic integration between Egypt and Syria by reorganizing the political and administrative structure in the North, and (3) further cement union by the imposition of an emerging U.A.R. ideology upon both provinces of the Republic.

The structure and organization of the National Union, continuously revised from September 1958 onward, is confusing and difficult to fathom. Reports in the press, official interviews with junta leaders, and proclamations to the public have been often inconsistent. One reason for this confusion is that responsibility for the final organization of the National Union in both regions of the Republic has been shared by certain key members of the government. Colonel Anwar es-Sadat, Secretary-General of the National Union, was responsible, along with the President's National Union Executive Committee, for the initial preparations. Later, in 1959, Major Kamal al-Din Husein, Central Minister of Education, was appointed by the President to supervise the final stages of National Union organization in Egypt. Similarly, Lieutenant Colonel Zakariyya Muhieddin, Central Minister of Interior, was given direct control over lists of candidates as well as future members of committees on the many local levels.[4] Field Marshal Abdel Hakim Amer, Commander-in-Chief, Armed Forces, as Governor of Syria from October 21, 1959, was finally given unlimited powers over the formation of the National Union and the conduct of elections in Syria, coordinating his efforts with those of Kamal al-Din Husein in Egypt and Colonel Abdel Hamid Serraj in Damascus.

Another source of confusion has been the intention of the government to link the National Union with its new plans for local government organization, which at this writing are not yet finalized. It has never been made clear whether the older local institutions such as the *sheikh, umda,* and others would be modified, abolished, or continued. Nor has the government stated precisely the relationship of these older institutions of local government to the new reorganization plan under the National Union. The continued operation in 1960 of provincial government on the principle of control by the central authority (appointment of provincial governors by the President) leaves the whole question of local government plans uncertain.

Roughly, the National Union structure as explained publicly by those responsible for its organization presented a system of committees beginning on the village level in the country, or the *quartier* level in the major cities, working upward through district and provincial committees to a General Congress from which would be chosen half the members of the new National Assembly. The latter, scheduled to meet in February 1960,[5] would not be exactly a legislative house, but would serve as a Constituent Assembly for the drafting of a new constitution for the U.A.R.

Parallel to this basic structure of the National Union were the various local government councils devised under a separate plan of the Ministry of Social Affairs in conjunction with the

Ministry of Municipal and Rural Affairs. The relation between the two structures has been unclear except for the statement in 1959 by the Minister of Interior that the local government council members must be chosen from the National Union membership or approved by it. Another statement at the end of December 1959 by Lieutenant Colonel Husein Shafei, Central Minister of Social Affairs and Labor, and the person directly responsible for local government planning (in 1960 Kamal al-Din Husein, Central Minister of Education, was appointed Minister in charge of Local Government Administration), implied that members of rural, municipal, district, and provincial local councils would have to be chosen from those elected to the National Union at these various levels. They would also have to be permanent residents of these localities. Some members of these councils would be appointed by the Central Government from among its officials operating on these levels.[6] Those town mayors, *quartier sheikhs,* and village *umdas* not approved by the National Union or unable to succeed in the National Union elections would lose their offices. Local National Union committees were also to (1) recommend candidates for the local government councils, (2) guide their societies to cooperative production, and (3) study local problems and make policy recommendations to local government.

Under this scheme, the National Union and its various committees were linked to the Central Government through local government councils. The provincial governor was to rule through provincial councils, representing various government agencies and services, but also including two of the National Union executive committee members of the district or province. Thus, for the first time, the office of provincial governor would presumably become a political one, as he was to become automatically chairman of the National Union Provincial Committee.

When one looks at the upper levels of the National Union hierarchy the structures become somewhat clearer. Election for the various committees was by degrees: village-elected district committee, district-elected provincial committee, which elected representatives of the province in the General Congress. Each higher committee presumably supervised the work of the lower ones. At the top, however, there was a Higher Executive Committee for all National Union organizations which acted as the highest supervisory and executive body for all aspects of the National Union. This Committee was not elected but appointed by the President of the Republic. It was the immediate link between the National Union and the government. Before discussing the implications and importance of this Higher Executive Committee for the National Union, it must be noted that the organization also had a Secretariat. The latter, headed by Colonel Anwar es-Sadat, did not seem to be a politically important office but mainly an organizational, publicity, and planning agency.

The Secretariat was the creation of the President's Office. It featured four committees: (1) Political, with subcommittees on research and foreign affairs; (2) Organization, with regional offices, a department for youth guidance, a section for feminist organizations, labor, trade unions, professional associations and guilds, cooperative affairs; (3) Publicity; and (4) Finance. The members of these committees were chosen from those elected to provincial committees of the National Union. Originally the two assistant secretaries appointed by President Nasser were army officers: Ibrahim Tahawi and Ahmad Tuaimah. The latter is at this writing Minister of *Waqfs*. The Secretary-General was a member of the Free Officers Executive and the Revolutionary Command Council. Among its many organizational functions the Secretariat concentrated on publicity, propaganda, and the preparation of social and economic educational materials for the enlightenment of the public. Significantly, the Secretary-General held the same office in the Islamic Congress, which permitted him to combine the Islamic ethos with the attempted evolution of the new secular ideology for the Revolution. An important aspect of the Secretariat's activities was the establishment of National Union operations within the professional and business associations and guilds: bar association, societies of accountants and auditors, the medical association, and others.

In October 1959 the President suddenly appointed Kamal al-Din Husein, Central Minister of Education, to supervise the final stages of the formation of the National Union in Egypt after the general elections of July 8, 1959. A few years earlier Kamal al-Din Husein had been not only a member of the Liberation Rally screening committee but also briefly Minister of Social Affairs and Labor. In the latter capacity he purged labor ranks in consonance with the regime's requirements. Subsequently, as Minister of Education, he carried out the policy of organizing students within the National Union to the exclusion of all other student organizations. Moreover, as Commander of the National Guard, Kamal al-Din Husein, along with Abdel Hakim Amer, Zakariyya Muhieddin, and Abdel Latif al-Boghdadi, was one of the small circle of original Free Officers who remained personally loyal to, as well as influential with, the President. He participated in major decisions of policy regardless of the formal cabinet structure.

To assist Kamal al-Din Husein in his task the President created the Central Office for Operations, which became the first Higher Executive Committee for the National Union. The three main assistants to Husein were Salah Dasuqi, Secretary-General to the Central Cabinet and an ex-army officer; General Amin Anwar Sherif, Director-General of Mobilization; and Yusuf Sibai, Secretary-General of the Higher Council on Arts, Letters, and Social Sciences, and an ex-colonel in the cavalry. There were actually twelve staff members in the Central Office, each heading various activities such as the Youth Committee, Labor, Professional Associations and Guilds, Feminist Organizations, and so forth. Ahmad Baltaji, Secretary-General to the Office of the Presidency, was the Administrative Officer of the Central Office. Later evidence indicated that the Central Office was more directly responsible for the final formation of the National Union than the Secretariat established earlier under Colonel es-Sadat.

All U.A.R. citizens over the age of sixteen (*sinn al-rushd*) were automatically considered potential members of the National Union. They were, however, to apply in writing and their qualifications were to be "in agreement with the goals of the National Union." Annual membership dues amounted to 12 piasters (approximately 35 cents; there are 100 piasters to £E1). This constituted inactive membership. Active members were to be those elected to any of the National Union committees on the village level or above. Their annual membership dues amounted to 60 piasters. To become active a member was expected to work in one of the Union's organizations. He was to be seconded or recommended by at least two active members and approved by both the local and provincial committees of his region.

Although general elections were held in July 1959 for some 16,000 local council members and thirty-three provincial councils in both regions of the Republic, the final election of members of the various committees did not take place until November 2, and in Syria had not at that time yet been completed. The President was to choose half the members of the National Assembly from the General Congress of the National Union and the other half was to be made up from members of the 1957–58 National Assembly in Egypt and the Syrian Parliament prior to union, respectively. Most of those elected in Egypt to head local, district, and other committees were members of the old National Assembly. Eighty per cent of the election returns were available a few hours after the opening of the polls. All members of the Central and Regional Cabinets were elected either by unanimous vote or by a majority. Generally, in Egypt, the elections did not reflect signs of older party cleavages and conflict. It was in Syria that the experiment revealed some interesting phenomena and precipitated serious political repercussions, many of which were already apparent before the National Union scheme and general elections of July–November 1959. The special case of Syria, however, which is inextricably linked with more complicated political forces, will be discussed after a few words about the functions of the total organization as recently expressed by its leaders.

In answer to queries in the press, especially the weekly *Rose el-Youssef,* Anwar es-Sadat, Kamal al-Din Husein, and Zakariyya Muhieddin have all claimed that the National Union in its final form would set general policy for the nation. It would make known to the government the demands and desires of the public as they came up from local levels through the Higher Executive and the National Assembly. It would also check the execution of policy by the government. This projected picture is at present vague, because it does not state clearly in terms of legislative functions what the National Union is empowered to do or will be able to do. Nor does it present a clear formula of checks by the National Union upon the Executive. What is clearer is the statement by these leaders that the National Union committees will have the right to accept or reject candidates to membership in various occupational and professional guilds, trade unions, local offices, and so forth. This in effect meant that no person not approved by the National Union would be able to participate in the governing or steering bodies of any groups in U.A.R. society.

The National Union in the Syrian Region

Work for the final organization of the National Union in the Syrian Region is at this writing still in progress. It has been under the direct supervision of Field Marshal Abdel Hakim Amer, personal representative of President Nasser in Damascus, and Governor of the Northern Region.

The establishment of the National Union in Egypt was not particularly difficult, for it was meant to fill a vacuum created by the dissolution of the old political parties. In Syria, however, despite the formal dissolution of parties upon Union, political party groupings continued to function informally. No one could seriously question the fact of continued political activity of the Baath, especially when during the first year of Union it was the major source of administrative and political leadership in the Syrian Region of the new Republic. One can actually claim that the official dissolution of political parties in Syria decreed by Nasser in March 1958 implicitly excluded the Baath. Freedom to become the predominant political group in Syria was the price the Baath thought it extracted from the arrangement since it was the most instrumental force in bringing about union. Moreover, without Baath support within and outside the Syrian army, Union in Syria could conceivably have collapsed during the first year. Similarly, President Nasser compensated the party when he appointed Baathists to both the Central and Regional cabinets of the U.A.R., as well as to key administrative positions in Syria.

The first year of Union between Egypt and Syria was beset by three specific difficulties. There was, first, the problem of integrating two economies diametrically opposed to one another: a guided, largely state-controlled economy in Egypt and a free, almost unregimented one in Syria. The second problem was the legislative, administrative, and financial integration of the two regions. Finally, there was the task of asserting Cairo control over the politics of Syria both in the army and among civilians. The latter situation created the greatest source of friction between the South and the North in the U.A.R. It presented the Cairo authorities with a rather delicate situation, for streamlining the Syrian armed forces under Cairo leadership meant the inevitable alienation of certain members of the officer corps.

Furthermore, economic and political integration also meant the invasion of prerogatives claimed by pre-Union political groups. It is doubtful whether the Syrians expected an earnest effort at political integration dominated by Cairo in the sense of total political control. They rather expected to continue running their own local political show. Indeed, during the first fifteen months of Union, power in Syria was in the hands of the Baath, which emerged as the "government party," and certain Baath-sympathizing army officers—Serraj, Hamdoun, Qannut, Nafuri. In Egypt, however, power was entirely in army hands. The organization of a National Union for Syria meant inevitable disruption of the Baath–army alliance and the end of Baath supremacy. Reaction and opposition were therefore inevitable.

Syrians felt perhaps that they did not lack a vehicle for the evolution of a new ideology. The Baath especially felt that it filled this role. Perhaps, too, the Syrians did not recognize the necessity of a National Union to achieve the goals of a revolution begun in Egypt. Indeed, many Syrians would object to the establishment of a socialist cooperative society, an avowed purpose of the National Union program. In practical terms, the success of the National Union meant the weakening of the Baath's position as a political group with an ideology and a program of its own. It also meant, initially at least, the loss of political power by Baath leaders and their inability to continue to make decisions even for Syria.

Objections to the National Union scheme in Syria appeared as early as the summer of 1958. In December of that year President Nasser appointed an Emergency High Commission, consisting of Vice-President Abdel Latif al-Boghdadi, Vice-President Akram Haurani, and Minister of Interior Zakariyya Muhieddin, with broad power to investigate the economic and political problems of Syria and to recommend plans for closer integration of that region with Egypt in accordance with the new over-all U.A.R. policy. Throughout 1959 the government announced from time to time its repeated efforts for the organization of the National Union structure in Syria. Evidence of difficulty in evoking the wholehearted support of the Syrians for the scheme cropped up early in the summer of 1959. Syrian opposition to the scheme and Baath alienation from Cairo increased in direct proportion to the growing rift between Cairo and Baghdad, Cairo's apparent rapprochement with Jordan and Tunisia at the time, and Cairo's accelerated efforts to impose army rule in Damascus.

Leading Baathists who were instrumental in the realization of Union, Hourani, Bitar, and others, were in October 1958 appointed to the U.A.R. Central Cabinet, in which the original members of the Egyptian army junta predominated. In a sense, therefore, they were politically neutralized when they were brought to Cairo—seat of the Central Cabinet—away from their old constituents in Syria. This left the field at home clear for Colonel Serraj, the Syrian proconsul. Dependent on the good graces of President Nasser and the supervision of Colonel Muhieddin's apparatus in the Ministry of Interior, Serraj could not very well have acted to the satisfaction of all Syrian politicians. Moreover, Baathist political leaders who expected to dominate the Syrian Executive Cabinet were frustrated when Nasser appointed Dr. Nureddin Kahhale, a politically unknown former public servant, to head it.

By May 1959 the estrangement between Cairo and Baghdad was serious enough to endanger the stability of the U.A.R. in Syria. President Nasser, at the recommendation of Boghdadi and Muhieddin, implemented the only policy available for securing his northern flank: a speeded-up program of total political integration, preferably to be based upon direct army rule over Syria, at the risk of alienating Baathist forces. It is reported, for instance, that Cairo wished to strengthen its control over Radio Damascus in order to better direct its propaganda activities against Baghdad. Riyad al-Malki, the young Baathist Minister of National Guidance and Culture for the Syrian Region, whose office had direct control over Syrian broadcasting stations, objected to this encroachment from Cairo on his executive domain. As a member of the Baath, he naturally turned for advice to older leaders of the party such as Bitar and Hourani in Cairo. For a while Malki considered resigning his cabinet post. He later resigned from the Syrian cabinet in September 1959, without any public explanation in the press.

The resignation of Malki touched off a series of disagreements between the leading Baathists, Hourani and Bitar, in the Central Cabinet in Cairo, and President Nasser. These disagreements centered on the future position of the Baath in Syrian politics. Cairo was loath to leave radio stations in Syria under control of Baathists who would use them for political advantage in elections. The Baath, on the other hand, was not prepared to lose its constituency in Syria by default, especially in the impending National Union elections, for the party had always considered itself the standard-bearer of unity in the Arab world. Feigning acceptance of the dissolution of political parties in March 1958, it nevertheless hoped to become the guiding force in the Syrian sector of the Nasserite National Union. But the Baath misunderstood Nasser's temporary and expediential acceptance of its pre-eminence in Syria as an admission of party control over executive power.[7] Hourani and Bitar argued with Nasser in the early summer of 1959 that they should be permitted to campaign in Syria on behalf of their group before the July National Union elections. They were, moreover, apprehensive of their loss of prestige within the Baath General Congress of the Arab countries. The latter, meeting in Beirut in August 1959, elected a new executive and leadership which excluded Syrian Baathist leaders.

President Nasser was thus faced with serious risks in Syria. His decision to cement a stronger economic and political union between Syria and Egypt was largely dictated by events in Iraq. The National Union scheme presented the best means for attaining this goal. At the same time, such a scheme obviously invited defection by the very architects of Union in Syria, the Baath. To protect himself, President Nasser had no apparent choice but to impose the National Union scheme by the establishment of total army control over Syria, too. As it turned out, in the July–November 1959 elections in Syria the Baath came out second best, while such conservative—and presumably discredited—elements as the tribal chiefs, old deputies among the Shaab party, Shishakli partisans, religious leaders (*ulema*), and even Muslim Brethren re-entered Syrian politics. It was now apparent that in order to end the pre-eminence of the Baath in Syria, Nasser could not at first rely on military control but had to enter into a rapprochement with the old populist, nationalist, and conservative elements.

Under these circumstances President Nasser designated his right-hand man, Abdel Hakim Amer, as Governor of Syria in October 1959. The powers delegated to Amer were broad and all-pervasive. His mission was to extract Syria's political obedience by accelerating economic and political integration, and to ensure the success of the National Union at all costs. This task required Amer's immediate attention to the Syrian First Army of the U.A.R. on the one hand, and to the speedy amelioration of the economic situation in the region on the other. His appointment with sweeping powers over Syria, however, reflected the obsolescence of the Syrian Executive Cabinet and implied the limitation of the power of proconsul Colonel Serraj.

Vice-President Hourani in his capacity as leader of the Baath protested to President Nasser, for in the July elections his party had received less than 5 per cent of the 9,500 seats contested in the National Union. Moreover, Hourani was unhappy over the incorporation of old rightist and conservative party elements in the new state party. He had already been made uneasy by the widely publicized statement on May 10, 1959, of General Bizri—leftist ex-Chief of Staff, Syrian Army, at the time of Union, and discredited after Nasser's attack on the Syrian Communist party—to the effect that Cairo dominated Syria. These and other irritating factors led to the resignation (probably ouster) of Hourani and Bitar from the Central Cabinet on December 25, 1959, as well as the resignation of Colonels Hamdoun and Qannut from the Syrian Executive

Cabinet.[8] This meant the absence of effective Baathist leadership from the government. Soon thereafter, on December 30, 1959, Abdel Hakim Amer announced in Damascus the formation of a special Advisory Committee to assist him in the formation of the National Union, consisting of Colonel Serraj, Ahmad al-Haj Yunes (Minister of Agriculture), Tu'ma al-Awdat Allah (Minister of Municipal and Rural Affairs), and Amjad Tarabulsi (Minister of Education). With exception of Colonel Serraj, none of these ministers was considered to have been associated with Baath leadership.

Direction of U.A.R. policy in Syria by Abdel Hakim Amer was a significant reflection of President Nasser's determination to strengthen his position in the Northern Region. A Vice-President of the Republic, Amer was also Commander-in-Chief of the Armed Forces as well as chairman of the all-powerful Central Economic Committee of the U.A.R. His very first measures upon arrival at Latakia on board the destroyer *Nasser* emphasized the seriousness of his mission.[9]

While he admitted the economic plight of Syria, Marshal Amer denied any connection between his assignment and the Iraqi situation. The October 21, 1959, decree by President Nasser clearly granted broad powers to the Commander-in-Chief, covering the reorganization of the Syrian regional government, the control and integration of economic planning, and the speedier execution of general policy. It made all Syrian Executive Cabinet members directly responsible to Marshal Amer.

By December the Egyptian press had begun to admit the difficulties faced in Syria and the real reason for Marshal Amer's mission. Among the problems recognized was that of separatist propaganda against the U.A.R. centered in Syria.

This danger to the Union made it necessary to place Syria under higher authority and supervision from Cairo. A personal representative of President Nasser was, furthermore, considered more capable of rallying Syrian support for the Union. To establish the principles of a general policy in Syria oriented toward the maintenance and support of the Union required central Cairo control over all propaganda media, including Radio Damascus. Moreover, immediate economic measures were called for to remedy a deteriorating situation. These, it was finally realized by Marshal Amer, did not have to be similar to economic measures taken for the Southern Region, but could be separately developed to meet Syrian conditions. Economic unification of the two regions could follow later. Cairo recognized that economic union must be evolutionary even though political union was consolidated by the forceful imposition of its authority on Syria.

The outcome of Cairo's difficulties in organizing a National Union in Syria is at this writing not yet clear. Much will depend on the ability of Cairo to impose a measure of army rule sufficient to compensate for the loss of Baath support. President Nasser may also have to continue to make concessions to the older political elements in Syria for the adoption of his program. As an instrument of control the National Union scheme under the supervision of Marshal Amer was at least a functioning entity. But it is difficult to assess its usefulness as an instrument of policy, since much of the latter has been so far formed in both regions of the Republic by decree of the Executive-in-Council.

Political Potential of the National Union

So far, in this study, the ambiguity of the National Union scheme has been stressed. Yet, in all fairness to the rulers of the U.A.R., it is necessary to consider the possible evolution and development of this attempt at populistic mass organization. At the beginning of their rule in 1952 the junta repeatedly deplored the lack of a social philosophy, ideology, or sense of collective and public responsibility among Egyptians. In devising a long-range program of national regeneration they promised to remedy this ill. They were, in a sense, admitting that while there was much nationalism in Egypt effective against an outside enemy, there was very little nationalism useful as a basis for a rational or viable nation-state. Significantly, the junta—which many have erroneously accused of inexperience in politics—refused to subscribe to any economic and social package doctrine or political dogma. They preferred to remain, as President Nasser put it, "empirically pragmatic."

Establishment of a homogeneous political community and a viable state in the U.A.R. clearly must involve gigantic efforts. In Egypt, Syria, and many other Middle Eastern countries the nation-state concept is a relatively alien superstructure, imposed upon an existing society that functioned on the basis of Islamic and local traditions, which were not congenial to the nation-state idea. A highly stratified agricultural society, with sharp divisions between a minority of rich landowners and a majority of poor peasant farmers, further complicated matters. The rise of populous and rather shapeless urban centers neither changed the basically agricultural character of the social masses nor produced anything like a sizable middle class. The proliferation of students in secondary schools and universities (75,000 in the latter in 1959–60) actually helped to aggravate endemic problems of urban unemployment, since economic development did not keep pace with educational advancement.

Another significant consideration in any basic assessment of the National Union scheme is its possible effect on the formation of an elite. Politics in the Arab countries so far have consisted largely of the struggle of emerging groups, such as teachers, lawyers, journalists, intellectuals, professionals, and students—commonly regarded as elements of a new "middle class"—to invade the ranks of the ruling elite, which until recently had consisted mainly of an alliance between landowners, rich bourgeois merchants and entrepreneurs, tribal chiefs, and religious hierarchs. The inability of the new classes to crack the elite edifice made it possible for the army group to attain political power. Many of these professional classes now came to identify themselves socially and intellectually with the Army Officer Corps and presumably to expect admission to the ruling elite. In Egypt, at least, their services have been utilized by the military regime. It is not certain, however, that they were or will be permitted to share in policy-making. The question must therefore be raised: Will the National Union scheme catapult these groups into political eminence, or will it merely regiment them under army control? If the latter turns out to be the case, is the National Union the reflection and the instrument of a totalitarian political system?

In *The Permanent Purge: Politics in Soviet Totalitarianism*, Brezinski refers to a totalitarian situation as occurring when "the complete mobilization of all human and material resources, and the dogmatic insistence on the pulverization of all opposition for the sake of ideologically proclaimed goals of social reconstruction have produced a total social impact. . . ."[10] Although President Nasser and his Free Officers may have pulverized all opposition, they have not proclaimed an arbitrary ideology, or new faith, in the sense of an all-embracing doctrine determining the whole of national life. In the case of the U.A.R. one cannot easily equate an authoritarian political regime with a totalitarian system—at least not yet. Even though President Nasser and his regime have initially rejected democratic institutions and processes, including the concept of constitutional limitations on executive power (the populistic limitation does not really qualify), they have never overtly rejected the traditional social order of Islam, which is independent of Nasser and his army-based power elite. Society at the lower levels is fairly stable—something a totalitarian dictatorship cannot tolerate at least in the long run. The lack of a developed ideological orientation in the U.A.R. has also restrained totalitarian tendencies.

The problem of elite formation in the U.A.R. is closely connected with the search for a new national culture, a national myth if you will. For a long time two social groups have been active in Arab political communities: the traditional ruling class allied with rich landowners and merchants versus a rising intelligentsia, small entrepreneurs, incipient labor groups, and masses of peasant farmers. Frustrated in their efforts to achieve social and political recognition, the latter groups became politically extremist in orientation, providing a following for such groups as the Muslim Brethren in Egypt and the Communist and Baath parties in Syria. A third force, the army, entered this struggle. Its prime positive link with the extremist groups was that of nationalism.

As competition between these groups intensified, the state became weaker. Generally, the Arab state has not been able to share the strong allegiance of the people to institutions like the family, the religious community and its leadership, and the tribe. The people, accustomed to an autonomous communal and tribal existence, have traditionally viewed central authority with suspicion. For many centuries under Ottoman rule, central authority was identified with tyranny. The introduction of a wider concept of nationalism embracing all the Arabic-speaking communities in the Middle East further injected a supra-national or regional element demanding allegiance to a larger Arab nation, which also has had a weakening effect on the bonds of the state.

U.A.R. rulers have thus been faced with a formidable task: to provide the basis for a viable nation which will sustain a state whose final character is yet to be determined. It is a dangerous task, too, because it is being attempted in an Islamic environment. Islam never succeeded in formulating a realistic theory of the state. It is only in the last fifty years that the ideas of a "nation" and a "sovereign people" have invaded Arab thinking and vocabulary. The traditional chasm between rulers, always viewed as aristocrats of some kind, and people is not easily overcome. The majority of the people still tend to treat as aristocrats even the army rulers of today. Instead, for example, of the old Pashas swarming in the exclusive Gezira Sporting Club in Cairo one now sees army officers and their families. The chasm must be bridged, however, because of the increasing unrest among a people that is acquiring education and some economic status, but not a satisfactory degree of political recognition.

There is also a different understanding of the term "the people." Radical revolutionary groups in the U.A.R., led by the revolutionary Army Officers, have purported to identify "the people" with the masses of peasants and workers. The term thus has acquired intrinsic economic as well as political significance. Meanwhile, national sovereignty continues to lack a developed ideology for a new society—an ideology which must be fully as much economic as political. Is the National Union to provide this ideology? If so, shall it provide the ideology of an Egyptian, a Syrian, a U.A.R., or an Arab society?

A hypothesis can be formulated that the establishment of the National Union does not resolve for the military rulers such problems as the nature of the ideology they must evolve for U.A.R. society. Should it be Egyptian *wataniyya* (patriotism) or Arab *qawmiyya* (nationalism)? Will the new citizen be a good Egyptian citizen, Syrian citizen, or Arab citizen? Will national training for good citizenship through the National Union be Egyptian, Syrian, U.A.R., or Arab?

For a long time in Egypt and Syria, as well as in other Arab countries, conflicting educational systems, including foreign missions and schools, weakened the opportunities for the development of a homogeneous national ideology. There were no thoroughly national public school systems. The result was a kaleidoscope of Francophiles, Anglophiles, German or Italian-oriented, and pro-American "citizens," who not only idolized the nation-states represented by each of these educational institutions, but tragically felt remote from their national governments when these finally came into being. Moreover, changing political conditions, revolutionary currents, and upheavals in neighboring Arab countries tended to produce a variety of often subversive reactions.

Another obstacle to the emergence of a uniform citizenry and a common allegiance has been the variety of concepts of citizenship prevalent among the Arabs: tribal, Islamic, and

modern secular. The object of loyalty may be a religious community, a communal group, or a tribal society rather than the
nation-state. The task of any contemporary Arab ruler is to
break down these barriers by asserting the supremacy of public
loyalty to the state. Will President Nasser and his National
Union, or their successors, be able to do this?

There are strong indications that the military power elite led
by President Nasser has tried to devise means by which to
achieve social solidarity as the basis for national life and a
national culture (Egyptian, U.A.R., or other). Besides the National Union, there are other national establishments which
the regime has sought to strengthen in its effort to create some
form of corporate life. Education, labor and social legislation,
national economic planning, national cooperatives, Islamic
ethical traditions, and compulsory uniform military service are
some of the fields of endeavor through which the present power
elite has sought to strengthen the fiber of national life. President Nasser's attempt to divorce the political elements from the
Army Officer Corps to the contrary notwithstanding, the army
has been a major source and instrument of power in his hands
as well as a political force in itself. Nasser has depended on it
as the most thoroughly organized national institution, and the
standard-bearer of a "middle-class" revolution. The army which
led the political revolt against oppressive oligarchs would also
lead the social and economic revolution against social injustices.

The question really is whether the army has been the instrument of the military power elite or of the people. This
question is not easy to answer. The current search for a
formula of national salvation in the U.A.R. also begs the
serious question of leadership. Will it be Egyptian, U.A.R.
(Egyptian and Syrian), or Arab in its composition? Whatever
it is, such leadership must contend with the problems of breaking down a hard cake of rural custom in Egypt and some tribal
communalism in Syria, and of giving shape to an amorphous
urban community in Cairo, possibly Damascus, and other major
cities, if the present regime or its successors are to create a

civilian political instrument and source of power to replace or complement the army.

Control of Intellectual Endeavor

There is evidence that the regime has sought to evolve an Arab-nationalist body of thought among its leading intellectuals. In the past, many Egyptian and Syrian writers represented French or English schools of letters. The present regime wants a school of "revolutionary letters" to meet the requirements of Arab nationalism. For this purpose, a Higher Council of Arts, Letters, and Social Sciences was decreed by the government in 1956 to direct, supervise, and channel literary, artistic, and research activities within the prescribed goals of the Revolution. Its exact title is "Council for the Guidance of Arts and Letters" (al-majlis al-a'la li-ri'ayat al-adab wa'l-funun, literally the patronage of arts and letters). In a moment of acute humor, one Egyptian writer cynically remarked, "I did not realize art required guidance."

Article 2 of the 1956 law decreed for the establishment of the Council states: "The Council shall coordinate the efforts of all government and non-governmental agencies in the fields of arts and letters . . . , and devise means leading to the upbringing of a generation of writers and artists who sense the need to assert the national tenor (al-tabi' al-watani) in Egyptian intellectual production." Articles 3 and 5 provide for the presentation of Council decisions relating to general policy of the state to the cabinet.

The Council, according to Article 6 of the 1956 law, is officially headed by the Central Minister of Education, a representative from each of the state universities (four representatives in all, selected by university faculties), representatives from the Ministries of Education, National Guidance, Finance, Economy, and Social Affairs, and no more than eight members appointed by the cabinet from among active artists, writers, and social scientists. The Council has a special budget provided by the state.

The Higher Council of Arts and Letters was actually administered by a Secretary-General, Colonel Yusuf Sibai (Cavalry Corps), a leading young novelist and eminent screen writer.[11] At the same time, Sibai was editor of the leading Egyptian literary monthly magazine, *Al-risala al-gadida* (The New Message), a government-subsidized publication issued under the auspices of Dar al-tahrir, the government publishing agency. As President since 1956 of the Short Story Club with its monthly writing contests, Sibai was in a position to aid and influence budding young writers in Egypt and Syria. In 1956, for instance, he recognized a short story by a young Egyptian, about labor conditions in the country, as a first-rate piece of literary creation but refused to give it top rating in the short-story competition "because the writer's ideology was confused."

Attached to the Office of the Presidency of the Republic, the Higher Council of Arts and Letters came under the direct supervision of Wing Commander Ali Sabri, Minister in Charge of Presidential Affairs, and therefore of President Nasser. Taha Husein, Tawfiq al-Hakim, Sami Dahhan, and other illustrious literary figures were on the Council's Advisory Committee in 1959 and 1960. The executive offices of the Council were heavily staffed with ex-army officers. The Council has worked closely with the Ministries of Education and National Guidance and Culture, headed by Major Kamal al-Din Husein and Colonel Sarwat Ukasha, respectively. Within the Council, however, there were in 1960 some fifteen technical subcommittees, formed in January 1959 under the supervision of the Minister of Education. These subcommittees, each headed jointly by an Egyptian and a Syrian, cover poetry, prose, folk art, translation, the theater, the cinema, music, representative arts (painting, etc.), architecture, philosophy and sociology, law and political science, geography, history and archeology, education and psychology, and economics. The Council has not as a rule subsidized promising writers or artists.[12] Most Egyptian writers today cannot support themselves on their literary earnings. Many of them are civil servants, doctors, and journalists.[13]

The Department of Fine Arts, a section of the Ministry of National Guidance and Culture, headed by Yahia Haqqi, has been a small operation. Popular as the theater is in Egypt today, stage facilities and the maintenance of a National Company are still wanting.[14]

Even the generation of new writers who grew up during World War II, and who enthusiastically prepared their readers for revolution and the acceptance of an army-led movement against the old regime, later became unhappy under an arrangement which still did not offer them economic security, social prestige, or political recognition. If, moreover, they must toe the line of decreed "nationalism" or "social realism" in their work, any creative ability they may have must necessarily suffer. When Muhammad Farid Abu Hadid, in *Ana al-sha'b* (I am the People), attacked the authoritarian methods of the old regime, and indirectly urged the masses to rebellion, he did not expect the prohibition of rebellion by a military junta later. Similarly Yusuf Idris, in *Hadithat sharaf* (a collection of short stories entitled "An Incident of Honor"), describes how things were in the country "under the old regime," implying with tongue in cheek that not much has changed really. Most good writers are torn between accepting the role of intepreting a regime-sponsored "culture" to the masses, and continuing to develop their creative powers to the maximum as independent artists. Some of them are even bold enough to doubt whether literature can be nationalized.

Education and the National Union

In the field of education the U.A.R. government is faced with three major problems: nationalization of schools to provide a uniform public and higher school system; achievement of a healthy balance between mass higher education on the one hand and vocational and technical training on the other; and development of a school system that will meet the needs of a rural population. The program outlined in 1958 by the Minister of Education to ruralize schools *"taryeef al-madaris"* is based on the need (1) to provide vocational-primary education to enable the *fellah,* or peasant, to achieve a self-sufficient society in the countryside; (2) to ease the pressure on urban centers (thousands of elementary school graduates come from the country to the cities each year for secondary training); and (3) to protect the universities from overcrowded enrollments.

Both the Minister of Education and the Director-General of the Ministry in 1958 argued the importance of "directed" and "directive" education. They both stressed the responsibility of all educators, writers, and intellectuals in Egypt today in building a new ideology for society. In this respect one can see the significant responsibility of Major Kamal al-Din Husein in supervising in 1959–60 the organization of the National Union. Together with the school, the National Union was to create a new ideology and especially one directed against extremist movements and Communism. The ideology was needed for the preservation of the *status quo* imposed by the military power elite, which from a revolutionary group was by 1959 turning into a conservative force against further radical movements in Egypt, Syria, or even the neighboring Arab countries.

Creating a nucleus of future leadership and a "new elite" loyal to the regime and to its projected revolutionary goals from a mass of university students many of whom cannot find jobs after graduation is a difficult proposition. In October 1959 the Ministry of Education, in conjunction with the National Union, launched the General Federation of U.A.R. Students. The main purposes of the Federation were to foster the growth of Arab nationalist consciousness among students and to encourage a nationalist, social, athletic, cultural, and military life; to strengthen the bonds of brotherhood and cooperation among students of the Republic, and between them and students in other countries; and to participate with all other youth organizations in the National Union for the development of a "new" Arab society under the general direction of the state's Higher Council for Youth Guidance. Tied in with this General Federation for students have been the activities of the various Youth Guidance Centers organized on all levels in Egypt and Syria under the supervision of the Higher Council for Youth Guidance.

The U.A.R. is faced, especially in Egypt, with serious problems of broad educational policy above and beyond the nurturing of an appropriately oriented intellectual elite. For a long time education did not particularly strengthen the rural society. In the villages, the *kuttab* (schools attached to the village mosques) taught children how to read to some extent but primarily made them memorize the Holy Koran. It did not do much else. Those who went on to the Azhar University became either religious teachers or religious judges (*qadis*) and, until a generation ago, were exposed to strictly medieval disciplines of study. The secular primary and secondary school system administered by the central government emphasized a highly theoretical curriculum along nineteenth-century continental lines, with very little attention to vocational training. As a result, graduates of these schools converged upon a limited number of white-collar jobs, primarily in the state bureaucracy. For those who secured a secondary school certificate, a civil service post in a city or town meant a relatively more comfortable existence than life in the Egyptian countryside. Theoretical curricula also produced a vast number of university students in law and the arts at the expense of applied programs in science and engineering. Trade and vocational schools were of course at a minimum.

Much of the military regime's preoccupation with technical and rural education in the past eight years was prompted by the need to provide technical services, to raise the general level of technical training as a prerequisite for industrialization, and to deter mass immigration of rural populations to the cities.

The development of needed skills to fit the economy and to balance the proliferation of intellectually trained but unemployable individuals is still at the heart of the educational problems.

The so-called rural program of education was also relevant to the projected schemes of local government development and the National Union. Although education was still centrally planned and administered, the military regime proposed to decentralize its operation through the National Union in order to instigate more rapid community development and greater local responsibility.

Closely connected with the regime's rural education program were the Combined Centers (*al-wahdat al-mugamma'a*). These were established to offer social, medical, health, agricultural, recreational, and educational facilities and services for clusters of villages. Begun in 1954, there were in 1960 about 250 of these Centers in Egypt. In January 1960 they came under the supervision of the National Union. But there were not enough doctors, agricultural experts, midwives, nurses, and teachers available to serve all of the Centers. One reason for the shortage was that university graduates, preferring to work in the city, did not apply for positions at the Centers. To remedy this, the government in January 1960 decreed legislation forbidding medical doctors and pharmacists, for example, to work in cities upon graduation unless they had already spent two years in the country. As incentive for rural employment, the government would pay an additional 100 per cent of base pay, plus 15 per cent of base pay for living quarters in areas where medical doctors cannot have any private practice after hours. It would pay only 25 per cent across the board when living conditions were better and free practice after hours was possible. Moreover, those physicians and pharmacists already in government employment could not resign their posts before completing five years of service. A fine of £E50 to £E100 could be imposed on violators of this law.

The National Union in Social and Economic Development

As an all-pervasive movement affecting every aspect of national life, the National Union was expected to invade the fields of social, economic, and industrial endeavor. Until recently, social legislation concerning insurance and other protective schemes for the working classes, especially agricultural workers, was minimal if it existed at all. Although the junta made clear as soon as they assumed power that their movement was not in any way a prelude to a proletarian revolution, they nevertheless recognized the importance of controlling as well as propitiating the working classes. Workers' unrest in various parts of the country was crushed in 1952, but the junta speeded up the promulgation of legislation on minimum wages, labor contracts, workmen's compensation, trade union organization, health and accident insurance.[15]

With the exception of agricultural workers, the industrial and commercial workers and the civil servants are the two single largest working forces in the U.A.R. today. In the absence of accurate statistics one might place the industrial labor force of the U.A.R. in 1960 at 2.5 to 3 million workers or about 11 per cent of the population. A small fraction of this number is employed in a very few large enterprises, such as textiles, oil refining, and transport. The majority is scattered over many small enterprises.

Although one may speak of labor agitation in these countries in the past twenty years, one cannot presume an active labor movement. Whatever labor organization exists in Egypt, for instance, is the result of direct legislation by the central government, specifically since World War II.[16] The U.A.R., moreover, lacks a tradition of industrial labor organization simply because industrialization is a new development. Until 1900 workers engaged in the small industries, craftsmen and artisans, were organized in guilds, or *asnaf,* following the medieval pattern. More recently industrial enterprises in Egypt were owned and operated by foreigners or individual Egyptian "tycoons."

These did not particularly encourage labor organization. The military regime's plans for rapid and wide industrialization were based on state-owned and state-controlled enterprises.[17] Consequently, the state has been interested in government-supervised labor organizations.

Trade unions attained legal status only in 1942, although tobacco workers, printers, and tramway workers were organized as far back as 1910. They were not permitted to form a national federation or confederation until 1956. They have yet to acquire the right to strike. The December 1952 law extended certain benefits, such as indemnities, holidays with pay, free medical care, and arbitration procedures over wage and hour disputes, but still permitted the government to exercise rigid control over the political activities of trade unions. A Supreme Advisory Council for Labor Affairs, established in September 1953, under the chairmanship of the Minister of Social Affairs and Labor, ensured governmental supervision. The exclusion of persons who are not actually workers in industrial or other enterprises has prevented lawyers, journalists, and other intellectuals from assuming positions of leadership in the trade union movement. Instead, the government instituted in 1954 a Trade Union Leadership Course to train workers in problems of trade union management. Offered and directed by Social and Educational Centers, these courses have come presumably under the supervision of the National Union organization.

Social legislation since 1955, however, has brought certain benefits to labor as well as to agricultural and other workers in the U.A.R. Insurance and provident fund laws, workmen's compensation, and minimum wage legislation have been enacted. It will be some time, however, before the implementation of these laws becomes uniformly effective. For example, the legislation setting a minimum daily wage for agricultural workers of 18 piasters is still a goal rather than a reality. Agricultural workers rarely receive more than 12 piasters, and they are still at the mercy of the labor contractor. The Nasser government hoped to avoid such "middle men" as the labor contractor through expanded cooperative unions and agricultural workers' unions. Accident and health insurance schemes were announced in November and December 1958, which will presumably extend to the total working force in the U.A.R.[18]

There are also numerous professional associations of lawyers, medical doctors, musicians, artists, writers, and others, which in 1957 numbered about 200. These should be distinguished from the labor trade unions. But both types of unions have been since 1958 in the process of reorganization under the general supervision of the National Union. One must bear in mind that the National Union can approve or reject candidates for the various offices in these organizations.

The whole question of labor and social legislation must be viewed in connection with the total economic and social planning of the regime. As President Nasser has often emphasized in his public speeches, especially since November 1958, "a revolution needs planning to achieve its goals." Lacking capital as well as the resources of a highly developed entrepreneurial class, the government is confronted with the limitations of a national economy based on a single exportable industrial crop: cotton. The junta, furthermore, has committed itself to raising the living standards of all Egyptians by increasing national production through improved agricultural methods, land redistribution, expanded cultivable areas, irrigation schemes, industrialization and various related services. This it has promised to accomplish within the next ten to twenty years while fully aware of the predicted 2.5 per cent annual increase in population.

The kind of society and political community the military power elite in the U.A.R. has sought to establish through the National Union will depend on its ability to mobilize human and material resources within the country for the achievement of a more advanced economy. Despite the numerous accusations one may justifiably make against the Egyptian President for his forays into Big Power politics, one cannot deny his efforts since 1952 at facing up to internal problems with greater determination (and fanfare) than any previous government. As early as December 1952, for example, the junta passed a law establishing a Permanent Council for the Development of National Production. This was an independent agency attached to the Presidency with the task of accelerating the building of priority industrial projects, such as electric power, communications, mining, basic industries, and the channeling of capital investments into industry including governmental participation. Briefly, it was assigned the task of spurring industrial output, which in 1952 amounted to £E92 million.

Industrialization aims cannot be assessed, however, apart from the regime's concept of planning.[19] It is the mark of a developing economy today to indulge in five-year plans. But planning in U.A.R. terminology extended to practically all fields of endeavor. One of its basic principles, for example, has been the synchronization of agricultural with industrial policy. Another was the premise that in countries like Egypt and Syria free private enterprise would not be adequate by itself to increase national production and income, or to assure their equitable distribution. State-wide participation and control of industry and agriculture was therefore regarded as necessary. The regime argued that in the past private entrepreneurs as well as foreign commercial institutions were not interested in large-scale industrial operations but preferred investments that produced quick profit. Native capitalists concentrated on enterprises which secured large net profits without the prospect of reinvestment. It also argued the lack of an industrial tradition among native capitalists, labor, and the rural population. And since Egypt and Syria could not depend on agriculture alone for a more prosperous community, planning with an emphasis on industry became necessary, according to the leaders of the regime.

However we define the political revolution in Egypt and Syria or any other Middle Eastern country, it is inescapably related to a social and economic revolution which has not yet occurred. Social unrest exists, to be sure, but it is not necessarily spread widely throughout the various elements of the U.A.R. population. An industrial worker's economic expectations in an urban center are obviously greater than those of the rural peasant of the Nile Valley. Similarly, the expectations of the professional class in terms of living standards and political desires far exceed those of the ordinary worker or peasant. Planning, or *takhtit,* in President Nasser's understanding was both a device to fulfill some of these expectations and a mechanism by which to preclude the possible advantage of one group over the other. This does not mean that planning aimed at some leveling process; it does, however, theoretically aspire to marshal human and material resources for a more equitable economic and social system.

The regime's initial heavy emphasis on planning indicated a desire to avoid the haphazard functioning of governmental departments and ministries allegedly characteristic before 1952. Apart from the Central Planning Committee headed by Vice-President Boghdadi, planning committees were established in every ministry, to coordinate efforts and avoid duplication. Vice-President Boghdadi and his Planning Committee were made responsible for economic and social planning for the next twenty years, divided into four five-year plans beginning in January 1960. The major objective of the Committee was to double the U.A.R.'s per capita income in twenty years. If, for example, gross national income in Egypt was £E900 million in 1956, of which £E100 million or 11 per cent was in industry, it must be raised to £E2,470 million in 1976, since population is expected to rise to 32 million in Egypt or 40 million in the U.A.R. by that time. The first two five-year plans must therefore raise industrial income to an estimated £E300 million or 19 per cent of the estimated total to permit a £E90 per capita income for U.A.R. citizens.

The Planning Committee has recently agitated for legislation in the field of taxation and government-guaranteed loans to encourage industrial investment.[20] It has also sought ways and means of narrowing hard currency expenditures by approaching self-sufficiency in all that can be produced locally, although Egypt is still an importer of most of its consumer needs. But economic and social planning in all its aspects (industry, agriculture, communications, etc.) is still faced with serious problems of labor, capital, and other facilities. Technical training of personnel is still primarily a responsibility of the Ministry of Education, and it must keep pace with industrialization programs. The Aswan Dam may well be completed by 1970, but its efficacy in the final analysis will depend largely on the availability of technical and skilled personnel to operate the industrial complex it is expected to produce.

Increasing the industrial working force is another objective of the Planning Committee within the next ten years. Proper distribution of the labor force is a still more serious problem. So far, with the exception of the sugar industry and mining, industrial enterprises are concentrated in Cairo, Alexandria, and Suez areas, with textiles in some medium-sized towns such as Kafr al-Dawar, Kafr ez-Zayyat, and Mahalla al-Kubra. The wider distribution of industrial centers both in Egypt and Syria must be faced by the Planning Committee of the U.A.R. For example, some raw materials are found in the southeastern desert of Egypt, the Sinai, and some oases in the Western Desert. The settlement of labor as well as the extension of public services and utilities become a major concern of wider industrialization efforts. In January 1960 the government announced a program to extend communications and public services to more geographical areas to permit thirty-seven industrial centers to develop in Egypt alone.[21]

Developing a market for industrial products is also a major concern. Without the required cash to sustain an industrial economy the whole planning program may come to naught. With a per capita income in Egypt estimated today at £E30 per year, the average Egyptian has practically no cash left over to become a consumer of manufactured goods. Similarly, the U.A.R. can hardly aspire to a strong military establishment without the necessary strength in industrial production.

Until 1956 efforts in economic planning, industrialization, social legislation, and agriculture were not as intensive as they have since become. To read President Nasser's speeches of 1958 and 1959 is to recognize the apparent shift in emphasis (temporary as it may have been) from the foreign to the domestic. How deliberate or earnest the regime's preoccupation with economic and other domestic advancement has been cannot be easily gauged. The present leadership insists on the efficacy of an authoritarian political style to achieve certain ends. Past experience, it has argued, does not justify the unfettered activity of a few citizens in any field of endeavor, especially in a society where capital is limited, economic differences sharp, and technical skill at a bare minimum. One can agree with Professor Edward Shils that the Egyptian, like many other people in poorer countries, is impressed by the "concentration of charisma" in authority or the ruler, and that he expects this charisma to lead and perform in all fields, including the economic.[22]

The choice of authoritarianism by the military regime of the U.A.R. may not be completely unjustified in this respect. President Nasser, we are told, at one time entrusted a young, able, and enthusiastic economist with the direction of the new Industrial Bank. Unfortunately, the young economist ended in prison on the charge that he had embezzled Bank funds. This incident may illustrate some of the reasons behind the continued traditional distrust of the state by the average citizen, his fear to invest, and his desire to make quick returns from temporary adventures. Under these circumstances, the state has no alternative but to become the major investor, industrialist, and economic planner. A feeling for community development is not yet common among Egyptians or Syrians, especially on the lower levels of society. Economic planning through the National Union organization is thus to be expected, but without any guarantee that it will instill community feeling among the citizens.

Closely connected with the government's planning program after 1955 for industrial development was the National Cooperatives program of the Ministry of Social Affairs, in agriculture, commerce, and other activities. It is not intended to discuss here the cooperative movement in Egypt, which has a respectable history, but merely to underline the significance of the new program. Besides the usual purpose of cooperative societies for marketing agricultural produce, or assisting consumer members, the National Cooperatives in the U.A.R. were tied in by the military regime with the general effort to elevate rural life through the Combined Centers and the National Union. Judging from the expenditure and special care the government has given to Cooperative Unions (£E8 million for 1,000 coops in 1959, with an additional 1,500 scheduled for 1960), the regime appears anxious to establish controlled communication between the power elite or government and the rural population to the exclusion of other groups. That the Cooperative Unions may become the vehicles for the political orientation of the peasant is a definite possibility. The great political importance attached to the cooperative program by the government has been evidenced each year when President Nasser has delivered a major policy speech to the annual Congress of Cooperative Unions.[23]

President Nasser's government seems fully aware of the difficulties ahead. The claims made by the leaders for the National Union have been sweeping, and the public expects some measure of performance. President Nasser, for instance, has argued that the National Union "is the whole nation," "an opportunity for all the people to participate in the revolution," and "a means to recruit new cadres of leadership." It remains to be seen how all these "directive" institutions such as National Cooperative Unions, trade and labor unions, student federations, youth guidance centers, and National Union committees will produce economically and politically more advanced *and* participant peasants, literate and skilled industrial workers, loyal, orderly, and employable university graduates, and responsible local and national politicians. The military power elite, in short, has practically decimated the old associational bases of Egyptian, though not necessarily of Syrian, society. Will it be able to provide new bases for this society in accordance with its professed revolutionary goals and national commitments?

6. Formation of the United Arab Republic and Its Executive Structure

ON FEBRUARY 1, 1958, a joint communiqué signed by Presidents Nasser of Egypt and Shukri Kuwwatli of Syria formally announced the formation of the United Arab Republic. Although one could find traditional, historical, or economic reasons for a political union between the two countries, it is now clear that the decision was taken abruptly and without sustained examination of the problems involved or the consequences. The political repercussions of this event in the Arab countries and elsewhere were many and far-reaching.

Egypt and Syria

The United Arab Republic represents a union between Syria, a part of the traditional Fertile Crescent in Asia Minor, and Egypt, a country in Africa. Although both countries may claim similar spans of historical importance and experience, they could not differ more widely in temperament, climate, economy, and, in many ways, social structure. The similarities are their Islamic faith and the language they speak. Historically, also, both have had to struggle for independence from foreign rule.

Egypt is insular by temperament, and the Nile Valley *fellah*,

140

or peasant farmer, has always been very much attached to that narrow strip of fertile land. He rarely leaves Egypt to settle anywhere else regardless of prevailing political, economic, or other conditions at home. One would imagine that the inhabitants of a country as overpopulated as Egypt would be eager to emigrate. Yet emigration from Egypt has been almost nil from time immemorial. It is true, on the other hand, that Egyptian skilled and unskilled labor (especially the latter)—navvies, minor civil servants, and teachers—have ventured out to such neighboring countries in the Middle East as the Sudan, Northwest Africa, and the Arabian peninsula. During the First World War, many of these followed the advancing British troops northward into Palestine.

The formation of the Arab League in 1945, and the Arabization of Egyptian policy toward the whole Middle Eastern region, spurred an exodus of qualified teachers and technicians from Egypt for employment in the various services of sister Arab states such as Iraq, Saudi Arabia, Kuwait, Libya, and at one time Jordan. These groups, however, represented a very small number in terms of Egypt's total population. The Egyptian military regime might conceivably have hoped that union with Syria would at last provide some arrangement for the gradual settlement of an Egyptian community in the North. When the author visited the two regions of the United Arab Republic in 1959, however, he not only found proof of the frustration of this hope but soon realized that a slight movement of population in the opposite direction had occurred. It was not uncommon to see at that time in downtown Cairo, Shubra, and Heliopolis an increasing number of Syrian shopkeepers running successful establishments. This phenomenon indicated the contrast between the enterprising, business-minded Syrian from the North and the conservative, land-conscious Egyptian in the South. The Syrians, in turn, found in their midst for the first time many Egyptian officials assigned to the Northern Region of the Republic by the Central Government in Cairo.

One may also profitably contrast Egyptian and Syrian attitudes to politics. The history of the national struggle for independence in Syria between 1920 and 1945 was marked by
intense emotionalism and recurring violence. A Syrian mass
demonstration was frequently a prelude to violent eruption.
The same may be said of Iraq. On the other hand, in Egypt,
with the exception of a few political assassinations and the
organized terrorism of the Muslim Brotherhood, political
demonstrations on a national scale between, say 1945 and 1951,
were not famous for their violence. The Egyptian appeared to
view participation in a political demonstration both as a political duty and as a sporting activity. It was not uncommon for
Egyptian students to combine a movie show with two hours of
political demonstrating. In this respect they display an incomparable sense of humor, which is utterly lacking among
their Syrian counterparts.

The Egyptian, moreover, conditioned as he is by geography
and an economic existence directly deriving from the Nile, is
more modest, relatively resigned, yet pagan in his love of life.
He has viewed rulers from time immemorial with sophisticated
reserve, and has never accepted any of them wholeheartedly.
This reserve is reflected in the native folk tales (*nuktas*) that he
builds around the central government and other institutional
manifestations of authority. The Ptolemies failed to Hellenize
the Egyptian, the Romans failed to Romanize him, the Byzan-
tines showed similar shortcomings, and the Arabs who Islam-
ized him and gave him a new common language failed, in turn,
to Arabize him completely; there was no clean break with his
Egyptian past.

The Syrian, on the other hand, is intensely aware of his
Arab national mission: he has a vague yet emotionally inflam-
mable recollection of the Arab Caliphate in Damascus. Consciously or unconsciously, he tends to identify himself with an
Arab "aristocracy" claiming definite prerogatives, among them
leadership of the Arab national cause. He is not primarily an
agriculturalist attached to the land, but shares in urban and

semi-urban attitudes regardless of whether he lives in a city or town or not. He is more prone to rebellion against central authority than the riverine Egyptian. In contrast to the Egyptian, who until very recently has been ruled by a royal oligarchy of foreign extraction, the Syrian affects a republican political preference.

Syrian Pan-Arabism: the Baath

We are told that Syria asked for union with Egypt to prevent a Communist coup in Damascus. Assuming this is so, one must still account for certain forces which made it possible for the rulers of Syria to carry out such a step, especially when men like Kuwwatli, President of the Syrian Republic at the time of Union, were identified with an old regime just as conservative and "corrupt" as that of Farouq-Nahhas in Egypt. It is now certain that the Arab Socialist Renaissance party—Baath—of Hourani and Aflaq had infiltrated, first, the middle and lower urban classes in Syria, such as the civil service, schools, and market place, and second, the ranks of younger army officers. The old-time politicians of the National Bloc headed by Kuwwatli therefore found a ready and receptive political force in Syria for the move toward union with Egypt.[1]

There is no accurate way of empirically assessing the public's active participation in and support of the project for Union. The plebiscite held on February 21, 1958, in answer to the questions, "Do you favor Union between Syria and Egypt?" and virtually, "Do you favor Nasser as the first President of the United Arab Republic?" recorded 99 per cent approval. At the time, however, no Arab doubted Nasser's popularity as the accepted leader of Arab "liberating movements" (*al-harakat at-taharruriyya*).

In analyzing the Egyptian-Syrian Union most foreign students have nevertheless emphasized the negative forces pressing the Syrians toward the merger, including the threat of a Communist take-over in Damascus. Others, such as Walter Z.

Laqueur in *The Soviet Union and the Middle East,* have consciously or subconsciously underplayed the genuine public desire for some form of Arab unity, regardless of the views of respective Arab governments.[2] It would be unfair to the Syrians to overlook the very active work of groups like the Baath for some form of union between Syria and Egypt dating as far back as 1949.

The Baath, or Arab Renaissance party, had its beginnings in the 1940's. Largely under the inspiration and intellectual guidance of Michel Aflaq, a young Christian, French-educated Arab historian, the party evolved over the years a systematic body of doctrine regarding the Arab problem. Starting with the major premise that greater Arab unity is the only basis for the solution of all other problems in the Arab world, it subordinated all other considerations to this view. After its merger with the Arab Socialist party of Akram al-Hourani, in 1953, the new Arab Socialist Renaissance party drafted a constitution which described the movement as "national, popular, revolutionary," "struggling for Arab unity, freedom, and socialism." In the section on Basic Principles, the party constitution lists the following: (1) The Arab nation is one, and must exist in one state. (2) The Arab fatherland is a political and economic unit which cannot be fragmented, and no one region within it can fulfill its national and communal aspirations separately from another. (3) The Arab nation is a cultural unit. All divergences and differences are unreal and incidental under the pressure of the renaissance in Arab existence. (4) The fatherland is for the Arabs: they alone can dispose of its affairs and wealth, and direct its destinies.

The radical tone of this new group extends to the general principles enunciated for the party. It is a universal Arab party, which views specific or regional political problems only in the purview of the interests of a united Arab world. It is a nationalist party; socialist, in the sense that socialism is a necessity for Arab economic development. It is a popular party, believing that sovereign power derives from the people; and it is revolutionary, because it contends that the renaissance of the Arab nation, as well as the building of a socialist Arab society, can come about only through revolution. Furthermore, the Arab nation is geographically defined as bounded by the Taurus Mountains in the north, the Persian Gulf and Arab Sea in the east and southeast, the Ethiopian mountain range and the Greater Desert in the south, the Mediterranean Sea and Atlantic Ocean in the north and northwest.[3]

Bearing in mind this brief general description of the Baath movement and party, one must consider its epochal significance. To be sure, many Arab political leaders before World War II and after paid lip service at least to Arab unity and the "unified" nature of Arab problems. Their preoccupation with strictly state-national problems and parochial jostlings for positions of power, however, rarely permitted the idea of Arab unity to develop into anything more than a politician's slogan. Here for the first time in 1949, a radical idea was presented as a basis for a mass movement that would transcend individual governments or states, and geographical-political boundaries.[4]

Two major factors—the failure of the Arabs in Palestine, and the retreat of Anglo-French influence from the Middle East generally—helped the Baath idea to develop from a movement confined to Syria into a pan-Arab aspiration, or better still, from an Arab politician's slogan to an Arab public cry. The monarchs in Egypt, Jordan, Iraq, and Saudi Arabia were gradually dissociated from the emerging popular revolutionary forces and separated from the national struggle.

The idea that unity could not be distinguished or separated from other national aims—such as those in Palestine—advocated by the Baath found wide public acceptance after the Palestine catastrophe of 1948–49. For the Baath, as well as the disillusioned Arab public everywhere, all national aims were now considered unattainable without unity. From a mere ideal, unity was now proposed as the only possible basis of successful national struggle.

The ideological and intellectual influence of the Baath, however, far exceeded its direct influence on any government, its policy, or institutions. Its break-through to the masses, especially between 1949 and 1957, on the other hand, only intensified the unrepresentative character of established governments and political leaders in the eyes of the public. But it met at the outset with the determined opposition and, at times, harsh repressive measures of the established regimes in Syria, Jordan, and Iraq. The Baath's growing influence and challenge to established authority became serious enough, however, for older parties and politicians to utilize some of its new ideas to placate the restless public. Both Colonel Zaim's cooperation with the Baath in 1949 and Shukri Kuwwatli's tactics later in 1956–57 are good examples of this.

It is certain that during this period, 1949–57, the Baath as the new radical national force infiltrated, as was suggested earlier, the middle and lower classes in Syria, including the army. This incidentally happened when the Baath had no extensive representation in the Syrian Chamber of Deputies under the Shishakli regime (1950–54). With the fall of Shishakli in February 1954 and the general elections of September 1954, however, the Baath won twenty-two seats in Parliament, and one of its leaders, Akram Hourani, was elected Speaker of the Chamber in 1957.

This ability of a party to create a large mass following without necessarily having representation in the formal or legal institutions of the state is an interesting phenomenon of the more dynamic nationalist and mass parties in the Arab countries, especially during and after World War II. It was true, for instance, of the Baath in Jordan with the exception of a brief interlude in 1956–57, when the party managed to form a government under the leadership of Nabulsi. It was also true in Iraq from 1949 until the July 1958 coup. And it was certainly applicable to the Muslim Brotherhood in Egypt from 1944 until 1952.

Reference was made earlier to the ideological preference of the Egyptian Free Officers for a link between their conspiratorial plans and popular sentiment in Egypt and elsewhere in the Arab world. Looking ahead for a stronger political platform that would appeal to Egyptians and other Arabs as well, the Free Officers privately adopted the Arab view expounded and widely propagandized by the Baath in Syria. Thus the beginnings of favorable sentiment on the part of the Egyptian junta toward the Baathist platform were already there, regardless of the practical problems of Union confronted in 1958.

Party principles and ideological mass preaching were not enough, however, to bring about the Union of Syria with Egypt. More decisive was the maturation of the Baath under the combined leadership of Aflaq and Hourani from an essentially intellectual party to a highly active political pressure group influencing the total apparatus of the state in Syria, while indirectly affecting neighboring Arab governments through its followers in other Arab countries. Although there is some truth in the allegation made by some at that time that the Baath program was as vague as it was radical, the party's political success must be measured in relation to its shrewd outmaneuvering of the only other well-organized and active political group in Syria between 1954 and 1957, the Communist party.

Munif al-Razzaz, one of the leading Baathist thinkers, has recently tried to emphasize the political affinity between the Baath and other radical groups on the one hand, and the revolutionary corps of army officers on the other. In *Maalem al-hayat al-arabiyya al-jadida* Razzaz has argued that as a result of the Palestine War in 1948–49, most traditional governors in the Arab countries were, within ten years, replaced by a new class of rulers closer to the aspirations of the people. Although Razzaz did not specifically refer to the Army Officer Corps in Egypt, Syria, or Iraq, he alluded to it together with the small but radical "middle class" which constituted the bulk of Baath following. He suggested furthermore that the 1950's witnessed the emergence of a new ruling class, at once revolutionary and socialist, radical and nationalist, but one which by force of events was identified with broader popular demands. This development, according to Razzaz, indeed marked a break with traditional politics in the Arab Middle East.

It should be noted, on the other hand, that historically, in the Middle East, the armed forces were allied to conservative ruling groups, dynasties, and monarchies. The 1950's marked a reversal of this phenomenon in the alliance between the emerging articulate political leadership of middle-class and professional groups and the dispensers of physical force, the army. It is against this background that politics in Syria prior to the formation of the United Arab Republic in February 1958 must be viewed.

The Syrian Army and Politics

September 1954 marks a turning-point in Syrian politics, and one might well describe the years 1954–57 as the period of pre-Union politics in Syria. In order to place in perspective the total Syrian political scene, and especially the political role of the army in modern Syrian politics, it is necessary to examine the situation after the spring of 1949.

The area constituting the modern Republic of Syria—the Syrian Region of the U.A.R. today—is not best known for its military tradition. For centuries Syria had been a province of larger empires, such as the Byzantine and the Ottoman. Even though under Ottoman rule Syrians had served as officers in the Ottoman armies, especially during the latter part of the nineteenth century and the first two decades of the twentieth, the French mandatory government between 1920 and 1945 did not encourage the further development of a modern military establishment in which many Syrians could participate. Most officer ranks in the Syrian militia during the Mandate were held by French, while the enmity of Syrian nationalists to the Mandate limited their enlistment or recruitment into the army. Independence in 1946 thus found Syria without a national army and with the gigantic task of forming one. It is not difficult to understand, therefore, the shortcomings of the Syrian army when three years later in 1948 it was called on to face armed enemies in Palestine. But since that time the Syrian army has received one of the largest single appropriations in the budget. By 1953 it could count some 25,000 men.

The Palestine affair was significant not merely in showing the army's professional shortcomings. It simultaneously brought a poor fighting force into the greener pastures of politics. Thus in March 1949 the army, under the leadership of Colonel Husni Zaim, overthrew traditional civilian leadership, represented by the famous National Bloc, on the grounds of treason, incompetence, and unrepresentativeness; for the debacle in Palestine had caused widespread public disillusionment with the existing political leadership. The army was now challenging for the first time the monopoly of political activity in Syria by the traditional power elite. But if disaffection with traditional political leadership were popular in character why should the army effect its overthrow?

A possible explanation is that not only did the army have ready access to organized physical force, but it was the only group that could act as an arbiter in a crisis. None of the existing or emerging political groups in Syria in 1949 commanded enough popular support to be able to succeed to power and, if successful, to legitimize its power—not even the Baath. The latter, and other groups such as the Nationalists of Sabri Assali, or the Communist party of Khaled Bakdash, had not been able thus far to break the "monopoly of politics" enjoyed by traditional politicians in the formal or legal institutions of the state. The military, however, smarting from humiliation and defeat in the Palestine campaign, accepted to advantage the courting of the various political groups which sought to gain power by infiltrating the Armed Forces. In following a pattern of competing for the allegiance of army officers, Syrian political parties—without exception—enhanced the political orientation of the Officer Corps, without any guarantee, however, of who would benefit from this love affair. As established civilian authority continued to wane in the wake of radical public sentiment, the military ultimately seized power for itself.

Simultaneously, the small professional urban "middle class" and masses of lower-class adherents to the emerging radical groups, like the Baath and the Nationalists, interpreted the Palestine defeat as a reflection of internal social and economic ills. They demanded internal reforms unacceptable to traditional politicians because of threats to their political influence. Thousands of high school and university graduates, as well as technicians, appeared to press on with their economic and social ambitions upon a system ill prepared to accommodate them without a fundamental change in its political-economic structure. The existing system simply could not absorb them because education had outdistanced economic development, and worse still, political enfranchisement. The end result was a latent revolutionary situation; for it was implicit that the rising yet politically disfranchised classes should seek to share in power and, if necessary, to wrest it from the traditional hereditary oligarchies. What these new groups among the educated class lacked was the physical means and organizational skills required to effect this take-over. Both of these were ultimately provided by the Army Officer Corps, which now hoped to assuage its humiliation in war by a political victory at home. Hence the series of coups between March and August 1949.

Momentarily, the coup d'état led by Colonel Zaim on March 30, 1949 against the existing government implied an expression of the public's frustrations—an identification perhaps of its interests with those of the army. Zaim was able to attract to his support at the outset both the People's party led by Rushdi Kikhia and Nazem Qudsi, and the Baath, since both parties were opposed to the old Kuwwatli regime. Zaim's access to power, moreover, meant the destruction of the old Republic party of Kuwwatli and the temporary arrest of Communist party activity. But it also caused a fundamental and permanent change in Syrian political alignments.

Three principal issues loomed large over the military period 1949–54 in Syrian politics. These, in turn, were to become the bones of contention between successive military rulers—Zaim, Hinnawi, and Shishakli—and civilian political groups, and eventually cause the final disillusionment of Syrians with home-grown military dictators. First, there was the question of internal political activity. Civilian groups such as the Shaab (People's) and the Nationalist parties anticipated participation in the political process through normal political activity. Much to their distress, this expectation proved unfounded when Shishakli banned all political parties in April 1952, purged trade unions, and founded the Arab Liberation movement, which he later consolidated into the Arab Liberation party to serve as a basis for his monolithic political structure. Second, there was a tendency among these army rulers to establish themselves in absolute political control, as when Zaim made himself President of the Republic by a plebiscite in June 1949. Third, there was the question of union with Iraq, an ever-present and touchy problem in Syrian politics since 1928.

Reference was made to three principal political issues characterizing Syrian politics between 1949 and 1954. One of these, the issue of union with Iraq, dated back to 1928 but continued to preoccupy the new political forces and leadership after 1954. By now, however, a dichotomy emerged in the utilization of this aspiration by Syrian politicians as an instrument of policy. It will be recalled that, generally speaking, in the past all Syrian Arab nationalists perorated on the issue, pressed it or relaxed their enthusiasm for it, depending on political circumstances. But in 1956 the issue had become a serious consideration in the minds of nationalist groups. For some, like Assali, union was naturally thought of in terms of Iraq. For the Baathists, on the other hand, union, or more precisely Arab unity, was essential to their cause. Being so unconditionally committed to Arab unity as a prerequisite to the advancement of the Arab cause, the Baathists were theoretically not committing themselves to union with any one particular country as a first step toward larger unity. It was their radicalism—in terms of an anti-Western attitude, and an insistence on the evolution of a socialist Arab political community—which led them ultimately to a rejection of the idea of union with Iraq. Akram Hourani, especially, was ultimately able to prevail on the party to adopt a more leftist view of the question, "Union with whom?" Political developments within the Arab states, as well as the policy maneuvers of foreign powers in the area (Britain, France, and the United States), worked in favor of Hourani's view.

It is interesting that all three leaders of the post-Palestine War coups in Syria were team-mates on the very first one. Colonel Sami Hinnawi, who deposed Zaim in August 1949, was in favor of union with Iraq. Shishakli, in turn, deposed Hinnawi allegedly to prevent him from leading Syria into a union with Iraq. Two of them, Zaim and Hinnawi, may have come as "modernizers" in Syrian politics but unfortunately succumbed to the well-tried medieval-Oriental methods of succession: execution in the former case, and assassination in the latter. The question therefore may be raised as to how Shishakli was able to maintain himself in power for almost three and a half years. It was surely not merely due to the elimination of his two erstwhile colleague-rivals.

Shishakli's relative success may have been due partly to certain fundamental achievements at the very outset of his political career and partly to the opportunism of most civilian political leaders. He formulated, for instance, and got adopted a new Constitution featuring some social and economic concessions to the public, which temporarily seemed to appease rising political groups such as the Baath by calling Syria "a part of the Arab Nation." Then, too, he banned politics in the army. Next, he embarked on the delicate political game of balancing the strong Peoples (Shaab) party with a majority in the Chamber of Deputies against the Baath-infiltrated army. Having used this temporary honeymoon with political parties to consolidate his position, Shishakli proceeded to ban their activity and replace them by his single state party.

The period 1950–52 in Shishakli's regime was significantly characterized by the predominance of the People's party and an attempt to curb the influence of the army. In October 1951 the latter was already being courted by the newly-formed United Front of Hourani Baath-Socialists and Assali Nationalists. Having already strengthened his constituency in the army as Minister of Defense in 1950, Hourani created a cabinet crisis by his resignation in May of that year. But by November 1951, inter-party squabbles reached such intensity that Shishakli was able to carry out what was in effect another coup, deposing the predominant Peoples party politicians on the rather flimsy charge that they wanted union with Iraq and Jordan. Furthermore, the army, which did not appreciate the Shaab's attempt to curb its power since 1950, wholeheartedly supported the Shishakli measure.

For six months, December 1951 to early June 1952, Syria settled down to a military dictatorship, followed by a Shishakli-picked Cabinet from June to August 1952, headed by Colonel Fawzi Selo and composed of independent lawyers and businessmen, to the exclusion of political parties. By August 1952 Shishakli had gradually eased himself into the position of Deputy Prime Minister—an office he was soon to use as a springboard for his final take-over in December. Having inaugurated the Arab Liberation movement the same month and suppressed political party activity earlier in April, Shishakli was ready by December to deal with the pro-Baathist army malcontents. A purge of Baathist officers implicated three leaders of the Baath—Hourani, Aflaq, and Bitar—forcing them to flee the country. The very need for the purge, however, indicated mounting opposition to Shishakli's regime and resentment of its suppression of organized political activity.

Shishakli's decline was pronounced by 1953, as indicated by

the growing opposition to his regime among both army and civilian groups. His announcement of the one-party arrangement sparked manifestations in the North—Homs, Hama, and Aleppo—which forced him to arrest all political leaders in January 1954. These drastic measures sealed his political fate with the army—the sole arbiters of Syrian political power. A military coup in Aleppo led by Colonels Mustafa Hamdun and Abdel Hamid Serraj forced Shishakli to resign and flee the country.

With the fall of Shishakli most observers anticipated a total return to the old regime—more precisely, the old pattern of Syrian politics. Those who were lulled into this fallacious inference by the return to the presidency in August 1955 of Shukri Kuwwatli, the First Arab Citizen in the U.A.R. today, soon realized that his return was not even symbolic. It was, rather, a smoke screen behind which a convoy of new elements entered the Syrian political scene led by, as could gradually be discerned, the Arab Socialist Renaissance party or Baath of Aflaq and Hourani. Its most readily identifiable political platform was a universal idea of Arab nationalism and a socialist program at home. Closely aligned with the Baath was the Nationalist group of Sabri Assali. On the other side of the spectrum, opposition came from the old P.P.S. (Syrian Nationalist party), which stood for the Greater Syria Plan. For a moment it looked as if the army, which, according to Kurd Ali in his *Memoirs,* "took action because the continual attacks made upon it inside and outside Parliament defamed and made it ridiculous," had been neutralized.[5]

As no single party could form a government, a coalition of Nationalists led by Assali, Populists headed by Dawalibi, and Independents led by Khaled Azm came to power, to prepare for elections in the autumn. The elections in September 1954 produced a significant change in the traditional equilibrium of Syrian political forces. Since no party was able to command a majority, a combination of liberal forces headed by Mamun Kuzbari, Independents, a tribal bloc, and a Socialist alliance with leftist army elements appeared in the new Chamber. The latter group formed a bloc with the Nationalists to gain the influential post of Speaker of the Chamber in the person of Akram Hourani. Significantly, also, Khaled Bakdash, leader of the Communist party, was elected to Parliament, while his party polled a large vote in the northern urban centers.

The new Chamber thus reflected the gains of the radical, pan-Arab, left-wing forces into whose hands political power gradually passed during 1955 and 1956 at the expense of conservative elements. Indeed the Peoples (Shaab) party, which had dominated the political scene between 1949 and 1952, was now utterly defeated and, for all practical purposes, disappeared from the political arena. Instead of the blocs of landed aristocrats and rich businessmen, tribal chiefs and religious leaders, there came to the political forefront the groups representing that indeterminate personality in the Middle East commonly referred to as the "intellectual," the small but growing "middle class" of professionals, artisans, civil servants, and young army officers—lieutenant colonels, majors, and lieutenants.[6]

In 1954 new patterns in political conflict appeared in Syria. The army became involved in a triangular struggle for greater political influence, at first only passively, but by 1957 as a very active participant. Both the Baath and the Communist party realized at an early stage that access to political control in Syria would largely depend on the acquisition of a military rather than a civilian constituency. This, no doubt, is a concession generally made by Middle Eastern politicians to the primacy of the army in the political process. It is at the same time a recognition of the army as the only presently available check on political authority in the absence of legal or voluntary civilian political checks.

During the period 1955–56, however, the army was not yet a forceful participant in Syrian politics. The struggle for power was still confined to the radical nationalist coalition of Baath, Nationalists, and Independents, led by Hourani, Assali, and

Khaled Azm. The army was at this stage only a recipient of the favored attention of these groups and of the Communist party. Only in 1957 did it become apparent to the political parties that the army's allegiance was crucial for control.

The young officers, especially those from the North—Aleppo, Hama, Homs—who had executed the coup against Shishakli in February 1954 represented in the view of most party leaders a source of potential power. Their success in overthrowing a previous military dictatorship, moreover, emphasized the army's continuing role as an instrument of political change and control. Prominent officers among this group were Colonel Abdel Hamid Serraj and Mustafa Hamdoun. Interestingly enough, both of these officers were also leading members of the Baath constituency in the army and later advanced to cabinet posts within its ranks.

Movement Toward Union in Syria, 1955–59

The return of Kuwwatli to the presidency of the Syrian Republic in August 1955 implied a political victory of the Nationalist-Baath bloc led by Assali and Hourani over the Independents of Khaled Azm. Thus, from the beginning, a struggle for power within the nationalist-oriented political forces had been prefigured. This rivalry gradually came out in the open by the end of 1957.[7] For example, although the first Assali government of February 1955 favored the Nationalists, Independents, and Baathists (the Ministry of Economy was headed by Fakhir al-Kayyali, Defense and Foreign Affairs by Khaled Azm, and Justice by Mamun Kuzbari), his Cabinet of June to December 1956 showed a marked preference for the Baath at the expense of the Azm forces. By January 1957, when Assali again headed a new Cabinet, it was thus obvious that political orientation was more Baathist, farther to the left, and that ascendant political groups favored closer cooperation with Egypt rather than with Iraq. In this government Assali became Minister of Interior as well as Prime Minister, while Foreign

Affairs and National Economy were placed in the hands of Baathists (Bitar and Kallas). Significantly, by this time, the old Shaab and Parliamentary Constitutional bloc had been completely neutralized, really "purged."

Internal and external forces at this time tended to produce an unstable political situation in Syria. Apart from the internal passing of power into the hands of the new coalition just mentioned, the continuous displacement of conservative forces, and the repoliticalization of the Army Officer Corps, events in the neighboring Arab countries began to affect the ever-sensitive climate of Syrian politics.

The Baghdad Pact signed in February 1955 presumably polarized inter-Arab power politics: Baghdad versus Cairo, or more specifically Nuri al-Said versus Gamal Abdel Nasser. This view, however, is an oversimplification caused at the time by the natural reaction of Egypt to the Pact. What is usually overlooked is the traumatic effect this polarization of power in the Arab world had on Syrian politics and the profound changes it caused in the Syrian political scene. Sabri Assali, for example, leader of the Nationalist group, was one of those seriously affected by Baghdad's insistent policy of alliance with the West. He had been in favor of some form of union with Iraq throughout his political career. Indeed, most Syrian politicians welcomed King Feisal's and Nuri's attempts in November 1954 for a rapprochement with the Fares Khouri Government, after relations between the two countries had been "frozen" under Shishakli. The Baath, which by this time had established a branch in Iraq with a radical nationalist following both in the army and among civilians, considered Baghdad's alliance with the West as a threat to its own position in Syria as well as elsewhere. It was already committed to an anti-foreign platform of unity, and the unholy alliances it had inadvertently concluded with more radical left-wing groups had rendered it a prisoner of the movement's momentum. As of this date, then, Syria became the possible victim of intensified rivalry between Cairo and Baghdad.

Additional factors helped orient Syria toward the Cairo camp. Republican sentiment in the country had always restrained the establishment of closer ties with monarchical Iraq. Extreme anti-Western feeling, moreover, was heightened by the subsequent Suez crisis in the summer and early autumn of 1956, the announcement of the Eisenhower Doctrine early in 1957, and the flattering overtures from Moscow initiated by Shepilov's visit to Damascus in June 1956. Undercurrents of deeper historical significance were also at work. Nuri of Iraq, for example, was himself an ex-army officer whose participation in early secret national societies such as the *'Ahd* before World War I had given him ample experience in conspiracy and the manipulation of army constituencies for political ends. He was viewed by the new radical groups, however, as the leader of an earlier stage in the nationalist struggle: the pragmatic alliance with the West, namely Britain, for the achievement of limited objectives. His continued political success and undiminishing share in power in Iraq for thirty-five years caused both resentment, on the part of younger nationalists and army officers, and suspicion of his motives.

Nuri's accession to political prominence and leadership, however, was not the result of some Arab national catastrophe, such as Palestine, but of long and arduous experience in the rather dangerous game of Arab-Middle Eastern politics. But the Palestine fiasco catapulted new elements into the political forefront of the Arab world, such as Nasser and his Free Officers in Egypt, and the Baath in Syria. As Nuri had been in the political limelight since 1914, it was inevitable that the new leadership in the Arab world should view him with suspicion at first and with open hostility later. Events were leading to an inevitable clash between a newly "Arabized" Egypt seeking to accommodate its new leadership in the North, and the long-established Arab political tradition of Iraq. Finally, in order to counteract Iraq's policy in Syria Egypt had to court the Baath and ultimately render that party her cat's-paw.

Egyptian-Iraqi conflict first broke out into the open in the

Arab League councils. Egypt's answer to the Baghdad Pact was a military defense pact with Syria signed in October 1955, calling for a unification of staff command and operations. This occurred at a time when Egypt had already entered upon the arms purchase agreement with the Soviet bloc in September of that year. Considering the nationalist mood in Syria, this new arrangement with Egypt forecast some rapprochement with the Soviet Union. In January 1957 Sabri Assali formed a Government strongly oriented toward Nasserite foreign policy, leftist sentiment, and anti-Iraq "Arabism."

The badly timed and hastily—although not unrealistically —conceived policy by Nuri and Prince Abdul Ilah of working together for the alienation and possible detachment of Syria from Egypt helped to cast the die in Syria in favor of forces favoring union with Egypt. Throughout 1957, beginning in January, the nationalist-leftist Government of Sabri Assali alleged the existence of pro-Iraq conspiracies in the country. And for the first time in February, President Kuwwatli spoke of possible union with Egypt.[8]

Anti-Iraq feeling was further intensified in Syria by allegations of an American conspiracy in the summer of 1957 and by a search for arms in Russia by Khaled Azm, the Minister of Defense. Adding fuel to the fire, alarmist reports of an imminent invasion by Turkey (a member of the Baghdad Pact and friend of Nuri's) were circulated. The net effect was, first, to create a truly popular anti-Western and therefore anti-Iraq sentiment, which was intensified as a result of King Saud's endorsement of the Eisenhower Doctrine. This created a further source of friction: a monarchy bloc (Iraq, Jordan, Saudi Arabia) versus a republic camp (Egypt and Syria). Second, it afforded the Nationalist Government a golden opportunity to purge rival or opposing political forces. Third, the army, which was still under the command of relatively moderate officers, such as its Chief of Staff Tewfiq Nizam al-Din, was now purged. The Baathist-left-wing coalition of army officers succeeded in elevating Colonel Afif al-Bizri to succeed Nizam

al-Din as Chief of Staff. The leftist army elements were indeed dissatisfied with lenient sentences passed upon "conspirators" earlier in the year. Led by Colonel Abdel Hamid
Serraj, Mustafa Hamdoun, and Afif al-Bizri, the army was now
beginning to take a more positive part in Syrian politics.

Various moves and statements by Syrian political leaders between November 1957 and February 1958 pointed to Union
with Egypt, finally announced on February 1. It is significant
that when a joint session of the Egyptian and Syrian assemblies was held earlier, on November 18, 1957, discussion centered upon a scheme for federal union. What prompted the
change in attitude that led to the type of organic Union finally
entered upon early in 1958?

The Achievement of Union

It is difficult to untangle what went on, during the months
of December 1957 to February 1958, to precipitate complete
Union. We can only suggest some possible explanations based
on the preceding analysis of Syrian politics.

President Nasser of Egypt was, as a result of the Baghdad
Pact, interested in avoiding at all costs the political and military isolation of Egypt. He kept Egyptian-led Arab nationalism alive through the Arab League, while he strove to contain
Hashemite expansion with its Fertile Crescent, Greater Syria,
and other schemes of unity. It was natural, therefore, for
Egypt to look at Syria as a potential ally, or junior partner,
in this campaign. Furthermore, the control of the North as
well as the East (Saudi Arabia and the Yemen) was essential if
Egyptian political leadership and hegemony were to be asserted and maintained.

This prerequisite to Egyptian political ascendancy was not
invented by Nasser. Past Muslim rulers in Egypt had tried to
attain such political ascendancy in the Arab world, some of
them perishing in the process. The foremost victims of this
political difficulty were the Fatimid Dynasty in Egypt between

the tenth and twelfth centuries. Indeed, during the Islamic era, particularly under the Tulunid rulers of Cairo in the ninth century, the control of Syria and preferably its annexation was a categorical imperative of Egyptian policy. Similarly the Mamelukes and later Muhammad Ali, who occupied Syria, looked askance at rival powers in Damascus or Baghdad. More recently, during 1949 and 1952–54, Egypt had occasion to fear strongly the possibility of isolation in the Arab world.

Thus Hinnawi's overtures for an Iraqi-Syrian union in August 1949 prompted Egypt to seek an Arab collective security pact. In 1954 Egypt's fears of Iraqi alignments with the West urged her to reactivate the Arab League as an arm of her foreign policy. This time President Nasser campaigned to convince both Arabs and foreigners that the defense of the Middle East could best be guaranteed under Arab League auspices. During 1955–56, motivated by the same fear, the Egyptian-operated Voice of the Arabs broadcast violent attacks against Iraq and the Western powers, both of whom sought some Western-oriented military defense accommodation with the Arab states.

President Nasser appeared at first lukewarm to Kuwwatli's early overtures, in February 1957, for a federal union between Syria and Egypt. But to the extent that Egyptian apprehension of isolation was real, it indirectly encouraged eventual accommodation with Syria. Although some Egyptians jokingly referred to the Union as one between two regions, linked by the President and Misrair, they were none the less reassured by the base Egypt secured in a territory contiguous to Jordan and Iraq.

In Syria, on the other hand, intense activity for total union with Egypt erupted suddenly in January 1958. This might have been due to the sharpening political conflict between Baath-Socialists and Communists. It is possible that civilian political elements felt they had been entangled too long in an uneasy coalition of sundry radicals (1955–57). Time had now hardened the lines of competition for power control between

Nationalists, left-wing Independents, Baathists, and Communists in this uneasy coalition. There was also the increasing personal rivalry between Sabri Assali, Khaled Azm, and Akram Hourani, the leaders of a United or Popular Front which could not last forever.

The struggle soon narrowed itself to two camps: Baathists, willingly or forcibly supported by the Assali group of Nationalists, versus Khaled Azm Independents, who were supported by Communist elements.[9] The struggle between these two groups became critical when it shifted to the army and some kind of political upheaval became imminent. By January 1958 a decision in the conflict between them could be reached only by an outside arbiter. Iraq, nearby, was about to recapture the initiative for Arab unity by suggesting conferences to discuss federation; this move sharpened Syrian domestic rivalries. The turning-point in this political conflict was reached in mid-January when a caravan of Syrian cabinet members, including the Baathist Foreign Minister, Salah Bitar, and the head of military intelligence, Colonel Serraj, began to arrive in Cairo. This was preceded by military talks conducted in Cairo by General Afif al-Bizri, Syrian Chief of Staff, and on January 31 a Syrian delegation arrived in Cairo to negotiate actual Union, which was officially proclaimed the following day.

It is difficult to assess the exact role of each of the above-mentioned groups in this final step. One suggestion is that the Baath, having entrenched itself in the control echelons of the army and successfully worked up political sentiment in the country against Iraq, was able to outmaneuver the other groups in favor of Union with Egypt. Fulfillment of this aspiration was in many respects essential to the Baath's continued predominance in Syrian politics. Another suggestion is that the radical-nationalist groups that succeeded Shishakli in political leadership in 1954 had, by their declarations and actions, raised the expectations of the now less apolitical Syrian public beyond any measure of their ability to fulfill them. They could thus choose to pursue a gradual orientation farther left to the satisfaction of the Communist party, or to permit the reintroduction of Iraqi influence, or to settle for another short-term military dictatorship. Union with Egypt was, if nothing else, a form of Arab unity—a vague though psychologically potent mass elixir, which in 1957–58 appeared to have some practical value.

Still another hypothesis is that the nature of the Syrian political community requires the presence of an outside arbiter to impose a measure of stability on its politics. In contrast to a relatively united Egyptian nation, Syria has traditionally lacked national, let alone political, unity. Its primitive communications never permitted any high rate of internal mobility. Politically this meant the rise of a landed-aristocratic oligarchy which ruled in Damascus roughly from 1930 without ever facing the problems of political assimilation in the countryside. But it also meant, twenty years later, the displacement of this traditional ruling class by a new one, causing instability. The displacement was unfortunately not accompanied by political education of the community or by the development of greater political homogeneity. Under the new radical group of intellectuals, professionals, army officers, and other urbanized elements, the problems of communication for the diffusion of authority and, hopefully, dispersal of power were never faced or solved. Thus the tribal Syrian in 1957 or 1958 could still trust his Amir and the 20,000 rifles at his disposal rather than concede legitimacy to Damascus. An impasse was reached in the late 1950's whereby a new radical power elite, having displaced the traditional one, still found itself without much in common with a fragmented nation.

The absence, moreover, of any link between the ruling oligarchy of landowners and merchants and the rest of the country in the period 1945–49 deprived the Syrian nation of the basis of minimum agreement on certain fundamentals like the nature of authority, sovereign power, legitimacy, and economic structure. The absence of voluntary political activity on the rural and small-town level deepened this chasm. The rise of new power groups to challenge the established one was therefore inevitable. In Syria it could have been one of many groups. It could not be a proletarian power elite, because a labor force and labor organization were only incipient. It could not be a tribal power elite (although tribes constituted about 20 per cent of the Syrian population) because tribal chiefs were easily identified with the landowning group. Neither could it be a religious elite, despite the Muslim Brotherhood's relative success under Sheikh Sibai in Syria between 1944 and 1950, because of the lack of an organized priesthood and the impact of competing cultures in Syria, as well as elsewhere in the Arab countries. The field therefore was narrowed down once more to the urban forces.

Lack of communication between the ruling groups in Damascus and the rest of the country was accompanied by a rigid power structure. Rising groups of educated, professional, and other persons were often excluded from the ranks of the ruling class. The social-economic-political status of these new groups was as a result much lower than what their members thought their qualifications and ability entitled them to. In the early years between 1946 and 1949, the army group was, of course, too new an organization to compete for power efficiently. It did, however, find itself later in alliance with the frustrated new classes seeking to share in power. This alliance represented by 1949 the middle group between the ruling oligarchy long in power and the politically inept and apathetic masses. Occupying key positions in public communication as lawyers, civil servants, journalists, writers, and teachers, the new groups were able to spread their ideas in the army and the countryside. The ultimate breakdown of civilian authority in 1949 brought military rule in cooperation with some of these new groups.

A series of hypotheses may be formulated at this stage on the apparent acquiescence—and on the surface, enthusiasm— of the Syrian public for Union with Egypt, although union with Iraq was a longer-cherished aim of those who preached Arab unity.

One hypothesis is that during the inter-war period political experience in most of the Arab states, including Syria, was limited to a struggle for complete independence from foreign control. Political parties were born in this struggle, and managed to rally the majority of the population behind them against the imperialism of the West. Usually one strong popular party monopolized the national struggle in its early stages. It was fairly representative of a nation agreed on seeking independence without any particular attention to internal problems and interests. In Syria the leadership of this national movement represented the old National bloc of landowners and merchants. Any other parties that emerged at this stage were splinter groups from the major one, usually motivated by personal rivalries rather than by ideological differences. These parties were feudal in their methods of operation, and authoritarian at the top, since the leader and his executive group were all too powerful. The power elite, in other words, remained inimical and inhospitable to new aspirants to political office and leadership.

Twenty years later these parties in Syria, originally established for the limited purpose of achieving independence, had outlived their usefulness. The trouble began when they continued to exist after independence had been achieved in 1946 without changing their basic character. By excluding the new group of intellectuals, professionals, and army leaders they failed to meet the new demands and political challenges of the postwar years. Their inability to mold public opinion, their exploitation of a large rural community, and the peculiar electoral laws devised to keep their members in power resulted in loss of public confidence in them. Beginning in March 1949, the leaders of these parties were swiftly removed from power by a series of military coups d'état without serious repercussions in the countryside, for the political groups represented by the older elite lacked a country-wide constituency.

Another hypothesis is that existing institutions in Syria gave no scope for organized voluntary participation in politics by the general public. The new emerging groups—intellectuals, army officers, and professional men—like the old power elite, discounted the voice of the peasants in the making of policies. They did, however, from the very beginning appreciate the importance of the peasantry as a "guided" mass following. In propitious moments the masses, who had never seriously considered themselves as a constituency of the ruling class, could be reached by the appeal of an extremist ideology. Having assisted in the displacement of the old oligarchy by a new and more radical one in 1949, 1954, and 1957, the masses reverted to their old position as "objects" of politics.

A third hypothesis, therefore, is that Union with Egypt came about as the result of a political struggle in Syria that was limited to the conflict between old and new power elites without much active participation by the public—some may argue, against its wishes. But the Syrian populace is fast surprising its leaders by an increasing awareness of political facts and aspirations. Hence a corollary proposition is that continued instability in the country was disconcerting to all classes of Syrian society. Any possibility of relative stability and a damper on political extremism was highly welcome. Union with Egypt offered such a possibility.

Consequences of Union

On the basis of the preceding discussion of Syrian politics leading to Union with Egypt, one must assume that the Egyptian military regime faced a very difficult task in Syria during the first year of the U.A.R.'s existence. Though both were Arabic-speaking, the two countries had different economic and social structures and lacked a common frontier. They were, in fact, separated by the state of Israel, which was still technically at war with them. Syria, moreover, as the Northern Region of the U.A.R., had a common frontier with the unfriendly Hashemite Kingdom of Iraq during part of the first year. This proximity might conceivably have caused the subversion of the Union in Syria. Later Syria found herself on the border of an Iraqi Republic ruled by General Kassem, the foremost rival of President Nasser for Arab leadership.

At the beginning, Union was obviously not going to affect Egypt to any great extent. The fact that Syria had asked for the merger had a variety of repercussions, the most serious being economic and political. Syria had actually prospered between 1946 and 1957 on a free economy largely based on the profitable cultivation of grain, a small but highly successful textile industry, and a commission transit trade with Lebanon and Iraq. An open and free currency market had given Syria merchants a sense of freedom in trade. This contrasted sharply with the tightly controlled Egyptian economy, where the government had been the nerve center of all export-import trade, construction, capital investment, and major production. Private activity in any of these fields in Egypt was circumscribed by a multiplicity of state controls.

A humorous but significant illustration of this disparity in economic systems, policy, and practice was provided the writer in Damascus as late as February 1959. The Syrian capital was on February 21–22 preparing to receive the President of the Republic and his guest, Tito of Yugoslavia, for the celebrations of the first anniversary of Union. In the lobby of the Semiramis Hotel a variety of Egyptian officials, journalists, artists, and security officers had just arrived for the event. Their first preoccupation was dashing off to the nearest pharmacy to stock up on large boxes of Aspro, the famous British-made substitute for Aspirin. In short, Syria still had available such hard currencies as sterling and dollars to buy Aspro, which had not been seen in Cairo since 1957. This is not intended to give the impression that, in the absence of Aspro, Egyptians had no protection against headaches; the writer himself man-

aged very well with one-piaster packs of Egyptian-made As-
pirins. One must conclude that the need for that particular
brand of Aspirin was more psychological than physiological.
But the incident does show how attached a generation can
be to a commodity produced by the technically superior West.
They did not seem to realize that the absence of foreign drugs
was the greatest impetus to the expansion and improvement
of pharmaceutical production at home.

Nor was Union once entered upon—even though reluc-
tantly—to be scorned by Egyptians, for they were tacitly accepted as the senior partners in the venture. President Nasser
and his policy, for better or worse, were identified if not
equated with the "revolutionary" tendency in Arab politics.
And revolution, according to radical nationalist doctrine, had
become by 1957 the accepted instrument of change. Egyptian
officialdom, moreover, could look forward to new positions of
administrative and policy control in the newly acquired Northern Region.

Between February and October 1958 the two regions were,
at least on a day-to-day basis, administered separately. There
was reasonably enough no immediate rush to unify all aspects
of governmental activity and policy-making by sweeping legislation. Syria was largely left in the hands of the pro-Baath
group, headed by Colonel Serraj, together with a Baathist-
infiltrated administration.

The political predominance and ascendancy of the Baath in
Syria after Union was to be expected—Baath leadership expected it too. Thus Michel Aflaq was privately claiming in
1958 that President Nasser had adopted Baath principles and
policy in his call for Arab unity since 1956. The Baath,
furthermore, according to Aflaq, had provided the necessary
support and political machine in Syria during the first months
of Union. What was interesting, however, was the refusal of
the Baath to fade away as an organized political party in Syria,
President Nasser's March 1958 decree to the contrary notwithstanding. One reason for this was that Baathists soon became

distressfully aware that President Nasser had used their party and its platform as convenient arms of foreign policy but prevented the Baath's formal organization and activity at home. This Baathist allegation has some basis in fact when one considers U.A.R. policy toward Iraq from July to November 1958. Indeed, Baathist leadership went so far as to contend that the experience of previous army-led coups d'état in Syria (1949–54) had shown that the army's success in Egypt was largely due to its adoption of a popular cause: the Baathist-propagated philosophy of Arabism and unity.

Baathist reluctance to discontinue party activity derived also from the party's realization that the Army Officer Corps in Egypt, and possibly Syria, was beginning to transform itself into a political ruling group with identifiable interests which it sought to translate into public policy. The Baath was unwilling to permit the army to monopolize political life. One might argue that the Baath should have been satisfied with the attempt to create in the U.A.R. a National Union which would ultimately supersede all other parties. In 1958, however, and apparently thereafter, the Baath was highly dubious of any monolithic structure intended to regiment political attitudes and replace the voluntarily organized nationalist parties. The Baath argued that in the highly centralized National Union control would be exercised by the Free Officer cadre. Debate, criticism, and free expression would consequently become extremely limited. Moreover, the hierarchy of the National Union was evidently to be staffed largely by army personnel who lacked any long experience in political organization; hence its appeal to a highly motivated political group like the Baath was slight. Nor, in February 1958, was the Baath eager to accept the army officer class as the only elite group capable of leading the Arabs to a better political and economic future.[10]

The Baath's leaders, and most of its members, were not altogether in agreement on the advantages or disadvantages of Union without reservations. Although they viewed the early economic discomfort in Syria as only a temporary consequence of Union, they felt the pressure of public discontent in certain quarters. Undoubtedly they were seriously disturbed by the fact that the formation of the U.A.R. was not quickly followed by larger Arab unions; there was no bandwagon for unity. This they came to consider a serious flaw in the practical application of their "unified" theory of Arab problems and politics. Their disillusionment was made more bitter when, in 1958–59, they were being successfully challenged and fought in Iraq, quietly combated in Lebanon, and openly jailed in Jordan. Finally, in December 1959, Baath leadership was unceremoniously removed from at least the formal political structure of the U.A.R.

It was possible at the beginning of 1959 to observe in Syria three major political rifts. First, there was the gradual split in the Baath ranks between the Hourani forces and the Aflaq followers. The former had hastened to subordinate the Syrian role in the Union for a guaranteed share in governing. Hourani, for instance, was appointed Vice-President of the Republic both in March and in October 1958. The more ideologically inclined Aflaq group was hesitant to compromise fundamental Baathist principles, including insistence on a freer political process. The latter group can hardly claim any direct share in power at any time since the Union between Egypt and Syria took place in February 1958.[11] A second dent in the Baath's solidarity was made by the influential role of Colonel Serraj and the army. As Minister of the Interior almost continuously since Union, Serraj had under his control the total apparatus of the security forces. Depending on his very close personal ties with President Nasser and his intelligence service at home, he was able in effect to rule Syria without the help of the Baath—a potentially rival political group. A third difficulty arose when the economic and political dislocation consequent upon the Union resulted in discontent among some sectors of the Syrian community. Thus two major sources of discontent during the first year of Union were the rigid control exercised by the Serraj administration and the application of the Agrarian Reform Law for Syria passed on October 1, 1958, together with the abolition of special tribal legislation and jurisdictional autonomy. Both of these measures caused greater discontent in Syria than in Egypt.

We have seen how agrarian reform was adopted early in the revolution in Egypt both as an economic-social measure and as an instrument of desired political change. As for tribal legislation, Egypt required none in the absence of any sizable tribal element in its population.

Syria, on the other hand, presented a somewhat different situation. The Egyptian rulers argued that the Agrarian Reform law was aimed at the destruction of the economic-political power of the landowning class, and the achievement of a more equitable distribution of income. Many Syrians argued, however, that there was much unused State Domain land which could first have been distributed for the benefit of peasant farmers without touching privately owned large estates, and therefore without affecting the level of agricultural productivity for a few years.

Resentment over the tribal question was deeper. Tribal chiefs who had long enjoyed a certain autonomy within their own communities were suddenly expected to relinquish their independence to a central authority. As traditional fundamental values are usually difficult to legislate out of existence, the tribal question will remain a problem for some time to come.[12]

Finally, the first year of Union was still plagued by uncertainty and mixed loyalties. Many Syrians, especially in the Aleppo district, may still have been inclined toward closer union with neighboring Fertile Crescent countries (Iraq and Jordan) as a more practical step toward greater Arab unity.

President Nasser and his Egyptian colleagues were, it seems, fully aware of these difficulties and, perhaps, of many more. The reorganized executive structure of the U.A.R. government decreed in October 1958, and discussed below, is an indication of an effort to meet the situation, for seven months after Union, it appeared that Syria and Egypt were so far away from a genuine organic union as to permit a reorientation among Syrian political groups, which did not preclude separatist sentiment. It was soon apparent to the Egyptian rulers that, left to their own devices, Syrian political groups were prone to continue their indulgence in extremist politics. Furthermore, Syria's proximity to Iraq encouraged separatist factions, and the clandestine operation of the highly organized Syrian Communist party was exacerbating the situation resulting from economic and political dislocation due to Union. Between November 1958 and March 1959, the indeterminate and anomalous political situation in Syria required the full tactical capacities of the Egyptian military regime.

In an address to the Annual Conference of Cooperative Unions in Cairo on November 27, 1958, President Nasser subtly alluded to the Aref-Kassem rift of November 5 despite the absence of comments about it in the Egyptian press until January–February 1959. There was, however, an implicit warning to Kassem in Nasser's statement, "Arab nationalism cannot be genuine if it embraces one Arab country without the others."

During the second and third weeks in December 1958 the situation in Iraq was deteriorating rapidly. Baathists and pro-Nasserites were being jailed along with Rashid Ali Geylani, while many officers of Aref's following were being cashiered. Others were escaping to neighboring Syria. It soon became apparent that Cairo was worried about the possible effects of the Iraqi situation on Syria.

On December 23, 1958, President Nasser delivered his Victory Day speech in Port Said. It marked a major shift in U.A.R. politics, whose impact cannot yet be fully assessed, and at the same time it reflected the political problems facing the first year of Union with Syria. In this speech the President directly and openly attacked the Communist party as well as other separatist elements in Syria which were undermining Union.[13]

Developments throughout December 1958 showed that President Nasser was seriously concerned about the intensified activity of the Communist party in Syria, which was simultaneous with the deterioration of relations between Iraq and the U.A.R. The attack on the Syrian Communist party in the December 23 speech was not, therefore, merely for home consumption. It was absolutely necessary to stem the tide of anti-Union sentiment in Syria resulting from (1) disillusionment with Union as such, (2) economic difficulties caused mainly by a trade boycott imposed against Lebanon and Iraq, and (3) the general reaction of Syrians to a combination of direct control policy from Cairo and the rigid administration at home of Colonel Serraj, proconsul in Damascus.

A special Emergency Committee was appointed by President Nasser on December 24, 1958, consisting of Abdel Latif al-Boghdadi, Zakariyya Muhieddin, and Akram Hourani, to "supervise executive policy in the Syrian region." This committee, referred to by some observers on the scene at the time as the "Committee of the Three Wise Men," was hastily dispatched to Damascus for the publicly announced purpose of "planning economic development and growth in the northern region." It had an important undeclared mission: (1) to counteract divisive and discontented political elements in Syria now fomented and possibly led by Communist groups, and (2) to prevent, if possible, any further alienation of the Syrian public by investigating the policy and tactics of Colonel Serraj, as well as the political orientation of army personnel in Syria generally. The real task of the Committee was a difficult one: the achievement of some sort of political integration between the two regions of the Republic.

The composition of this Committee was significant. It featured two Vice-Presidents of the Republic, one of whom, al-Boghdadi, had been in charge of the politically powerful Planning Ministry. Akram Hourani, as head of the disbanded Arab Socialist Renaissance party and Syrian Vice-President of the Republic, headed at that time the U.A.R. Ministry of Justice as well as practically every legislative committee charged with devising uniform legislation for both regions of the

Republic. Zakariyya Muhieddin was the able, diligent, but very quiet U.A.R. Minister of the Interior, whose efficient security forces and alert intelligence bureaus kept watch over the internal political scene. Moreover, both al-Boghdadi and Muhieddin were members of the Free Officers Executive in Egypt.

An intensive campaign against the Syrian Communist party followed immediately in the Egyptian press, while the *Ahram* carried daily telegrams from Syrian groups to the President expressing their solid support against "all enemies of Union." This press campaign concentrated for a while on two major themes: (1) the anti-Arab, anti-nationalist character of the Communist party in Syria, and (2) the justification of U.A.R.-U.S.S.R. friendship in the face of anti-U.A.R. Communist policy in Syria and Iraq.[14] Egyptian journalists were also pre-occupied with coining new terms to identify the threat to the nationalist cause. *Shu'ubiyya* or separatism, referring to the nature of the Communist party in Syria and Iraq, now became a key term in the contemporary Cairo and Damascus political vocabulary.[15]

As it is not possible to test empirically the popular support for President Nasser in Syria or Egypt today, three propositions are offered merely for future validation or rejection. The first proposition, suggested earlier, is that that Union was not unanimously desired by the Syrian public, but was largely the outcome of political conflict confined to identifiable political groups. Events in Iraq in November–December 1958, which led to an open rift between pro-U.A.R. Aref-led nationalists and the Communist-supported Kassem forces, inevitably undermined the placid acceptance of Union by Syrians. Divisive and separatist propaganda in Syria therefore became possible.

A second proposition is that the army-supported regime in Egypt and Syria could not permit a continuation of Syrian politics. More rigid control from the top became an accepted extension of U.A.R. policy in Syria as evidenced by the three-man Committee of December 24, 1958.

A third proposition is that the Egypt-supported military group in Syria, headed by Serraj, was able to displace the existing political cadres of leadership which had originally helped to bring about Union with Egypt. A statement by Colonel Serraj to the *Ahram* of Cairo on December 26, 1958 supports this proposition. He referred to Union as being "a matter of life and death for the Syrians."

A major ideological change in policy orientation became necessary. The Communist party in Syria, Iraq, and other Arab countries became, according to the official view of the Egyptian rulers, the major ally of reaction (*ar-raj'iyya*), separatism, and, therefore, Zionism. The attempt to identify this image of divisiveness had become by March 1959 a major task of all communications media in the U.A.R.

The U.A.R. Executive Structure

On October 8, 1958, eight months after the Union between Egypt and Syria, President Nasser announced by official decree the reorganization of the United Arab Republic's government. The short-lived Arab National Assembly of February to April 1958 was a thing of the past, parties were formally dissolved in Syria, too, and the U.A.R. settled to government by "decree of the Executive-in-Council."

Originally, the suspended Egyptian Constitution of June 1956 had offered a presidential rather than a cabinet form of government. In practice, however, it was a formalization of the legislative-executive power of the early Revolutionary Command Council (1952–56), as reorganized, reshuffled, and purged between 1952 and 1956. The reorganized structure of October 1958 represented a further strengthening of presidential control while at the same time it brought Syrian elements into the government. It also reflected a deliberate limitation of ministerial responsibility in favor of direct and personal obligation to the President.

After the formal ceremonial declaration of Union by Presidents Nasser and Kuwwatli, Premier Sabri Assali officially released the resolution of both Councils of Ministers to the effect that the new Republic would have a "democratic presidential regime." The President was to have full executive powers, choosing and appointing ministers responsible to him. On February 4 Nasser decreed the dissolution of all political parties in Syria, a measure which, as we have seen, was not accepted as placidly there as it had been in Egypt five years earlier. The following day Nasser decreed seventeen fundamental provisions to serve as the temporary Organic Law of the U.A.R.

The provisional Organic Law designated Syria and Egypt as the two regions comprising the U.A.R. (Art. 10). It provided that the two administrative structures, as they existed at the time of union, would continue for the time being, and the existing laws of both countries would remain in force temporarily (Arts. 9, 13, 14). It also set February 21, 1958, as the date for the plebiscite on Union and the choice of a President (Art. 17). In the election almost all the votes cast, 6,000,000 in Egypt and 1,250,000 in Syria, went to President Nasser. By February 22 Foreign Affairs, War, and Education had been integrated into three Central U.A.R. Ministries.

On March 6 a provisional Constitution and a new Central Government for the U.A.R. were formally announced. The seventy-three Articles of the Constitution clearly strengthened executive power; two additional decrees on March 12 conferred on the President all powers afforded by legislation already in force in both regions of the Republic. The membership of the first Cabinet, however, was of interest. Out of thirty-four members (excluding the President) twenty were Egyptians and fourteen Syrians. Among the Egyptians, nine were army officers, and among the Syrians four. Of the fourteen Syrians nine were Baathist or Baathist sympathizers. The Baath, in other words, was indispensable for the first difficult period of Union in Syria. The portfolios of War, Foreign Affairs, Education, Industry, and National Guidance were held at the outset by Egyptians.

In the Syrian Cabinet four known Baathist civilians occupied the posts of National Economy, Treasury, Planning, and Public Works. Only two ministers, of National Economy and Public Works, retained the portfolios they held in the independent Syrian Cabinet immediately before Union. Both were Baathists. Two others from the pre-Union Syrian Cabinet moved to the Central U.A.R. Government as of March 13, 1958. It should be noted that not a single Syrian army officer was appointed to the U.A.R. Central Cabinet at that time, and that among the three Syrian civilians on it, two, Vice-President Akram Hourani and Minister of State Salah Bitar, were Baathists, while one, Vice-President Sabri Assali, was a Nationalist.

The Presidential decree of October 8, 1959 described the new executive structure of the U.A.R. as consisting of one Central Cabinet and Executive Cabinets, or Regional Councils of Ministers, for both the Egyptian and the Syrian regions. Another decree named the two chairmen of the Executive Cabinets and simultaneously appointed them to the rank of Minister of State in the Central Cabinet.

The Central Cabinet listed nineteen ministers with portfolios, plus two Ministers of State. To these should be added the two chairmen of the regional Executive Cabinets, making a total of twenty-three. Of these fifteen were Egyptian and eight Syrian. Of the fifteen Egyptians eight were army officers besides the President, and of the eight Syrians two were army officers, making a total of ten army officers in the Central Cabinet.[16]

The Egyptian Regional Cabinet listed fourteen ministers besides the chairman. Among these, ten held Cabinet posts for the first time. Of these ten, five were army officers, holding the key ministries of Interior, National Guidance and Culture, Social Affairs and Labor, Industry, and Public Health. In the Syrian Cabinet, among fourteen ministers (including the chairman) there were seven new faces. Army officers held the key ministries of Interior, Social Affairs and Labor, Agrarian Reform, and Municipal and Rural Affairs.

Thus there was a total of fifty ministers in the three-cabinet government of the U.A.R. Nineteen of these had never held cabinet posts before in either Egypt or Syria. Eighteen (including the President of the Republic) had a military background; six were lawyers, five engineers, five economists, three medical doctors, three agricultural experts (engineers, horticulturists, etc.), two university professors, three religious men and financiers, and five could not be classified.

In contrast to the composition of previous cabinets in the Arab countries, it is significant that members of practical professions such as engineering, economics, and agriculture outnumbered lawyers.

The earliest indications of a major change in the organization of the U.A.R. government came around September 20, 1958, when the semi-official daily *al-Gumhuriyya* talked in general terms of the serious problems that were being faced by the Republic in planning policy for the two regions. It hinted at the inadequacy of separate cabinets for Egypt and Syria without some kind of central coordinating and supervisory agency. It also complained of the lack of an over-all body responsible for policy affecting the U.A.R. as a whole. At the same time rumors of subversive plots against the state in Syria were being publicized as by-products of possible Iraqi machinations. Coupled with serious economic problems in the North, these reports seemed to represent a semi-official announcement of the President's intention to take drastic action to meet mounting political difficulties, especially in Syria.

In the official announcement of the reorganized U.A.R. government, a full-length explanation was provided. Briefly, the President desired to strengthen Union through uniform legislation and executive action, in order gradually to evolve a unified policy for both regions, especially in the critical areas of agrarian reform, industrialization, economic planning, finance, and education. He felt, it was reported, that the absence of a central cabinet made it difficult to plan policies or to execute them quickly and smoothly. A reorganized governmental structure as decreed on October 8, 1958 was therefore, in his view, imperative for the social and economic revolution required to stimulate progress. Another of the President's concerns was that of defining responsibility concerning problems affecting the U.A.R. as a whole.

One might discern three basic difficulties during the first year of Union which were decisive in bringing about the new executive structure of the U.A.R.: (1) the difficulty of establishing uniform legislation; (2) the inability clearly to define responsibility in government; and (3) the lack of proper control and supervision over the execution of presidential policy in both regions.

Under the October 1958 arrangement all departments came to have three ministers—an Egyptian, a Syrian, and a central U.A.R. minister—except War and Foreign Affairs, which had Central Ministries only. Foreign Affairs, however, had two deputy Foreign Ministers, one Syrian, the other Egyptian.[17]

Before attempting any critical analysis of the October 1958 plan to reorganize the U.A.R. government, it would be well to describe the formal relations established by the decree between the Regional Councils of Ministers and the President, as well as the functions of the various Cabinet committees.

The decree designated four major ministerial committees to serve the Central Cabinet: legislative, executive, economic, and general services. General policy for both Egypt and Syria was to be planned by the Central Minister concerned and submitted to the appropriate committee in the Central Cabinet for discussion before going to the President for final decision. This was to be handled by the Legislative Committee in the Central Cabinet. Recommendations of Regional Cabinets were to go to the Executive Committee first via the Secretary-General of the Central Cabinet. This did not mean, however, that Regional Cabinets would not be able to send their recommendations directly to the President.

It should be noted, moreover, that the Central Cabinet Legislative Committee was to have subcommittees on legislation, finance, and the budget. Its Executive Committee was to deal primarily with Presidential decrees, orders, administrative promotions, and related matters. Its Economic Committee was to be concerned with the general planning of economic policy for the U.A.R.

More interesting was a provision in the decree for the duplication of the four Cabinet committees in the President's Office (*maktab ri'asat al-gumhuriyya*). These were to be "Advisory Committees" to the President and came under the direction of the Minister for Presidential Affairs or one of the three Vice-Presidents of the Republic. Usually the latter would also head the various Central Cabinet committees.

Although there were to be Executive, Economic, and General Services committees in each of the Regional Cabinets, neither was to have a working legislative committee. This seemed to indicate that legislation was to be confined to the Central Cabinet, which, in turn, would supervise its execution by the appropriate Regional ministries. But all four committees of the Central Cabinet were made responsible to the President. The same applied to Regional Cabinet committees. By Presidential decree of October 26, 1958, all central and regional ministers were made formally responsible to the President. The respective chairmen of the Regional Councils of Ministers were also appointed Ministers of State in the Central Government, putting forth the recommendations of their Councils to the President and participating in general policy planning.

Members of these Cabinets were not responsible to any legislature. The people were presumably to be "represented" by Nasser through a transitional constitution, while ministers were to be individually responsible to the Head of State.

On July 8, 1959, elections for members of the provincial and local committees of the National Union were held in Egypt and Syria. This was the first time the electoral process was used in the U.A.R. since the Plebiscite for Union and the President of the U.A.R. on February 21, 1958. Although elections were held, a National Assembly was not to meet until successful candidates for local and provincial Committees of the National Union began to perform their separate functions, and until the government selected from among these successful members of the one-party structure those who would sit as members of the National Assembly scheduled to meet in February 1960.[18]

The operation of the government was complicated by the breakdown of ministerial responsibility within Regional Cabinets, between two or more functioning ministries, and within a ministry. This is a rather curious situation, and is best explained by an illustration. The Minister of *Waqfs,* for instance, although presumably working through Executive Cabinet and Central Cabinet committees, was according to the October 1958 decree also directly responsible to the President and may have had direct access to him on certain problems. In effect, he was not really responsible for his performance and policy to anyone except the President. Such a minister tended to become immune to criticism from his own ministry and from other ministries. The fact that so far no ministry has had to face a legislative body has further freed them from the necessity of justifying or explaining their policies to the public or its representatives. A more dangerous aspect, however, was that any ministerial abuses of power might continue unchecked unless they were detected by the President himself. One instance of the tragic results of such procedure was witnessed in Cairo in 1959.

The structure of the new cabinet system decreed in October 1958 suggested that Nasser had made both administrative and political gains. He had been able to reorganize the execution of U.A.R. policy in both regions with little friction, and to replace many of the older members of the Free Officers Movement with new men (in part by extending a peculiar spoils system to include Syria). It will be recalled that by the end of 1954 Nasser had achieved a complete take-over of policymaking from a mixed civilian-army cabinet, when practically all Revolution Command Council members were given cabinet posts. More significantly, in 1958 he was able to appease and indirectly to control Akram Hourani, the fiery leader of the Syrian Baath party (which refused to be effectively dissolved) by making him Vice-President of the Republic and Minister of Justice. The Number Two man of the Baath, Salah al-Bitar, was appointed to the post of Central Minister for National Guidance and Culture. In December 1959 both men were removed at a propitious moment.

It is also clear, from the 1958 formal structure of the U.A.R. government, that general policy has been so far planned by the Central Ministers for both regional Executive Councils. Such policy has usually been submitted to the appropriate committee in the Central Cabinet for discussion before going to the President for decision. But it must be pointed out that before arriving on the President's desk, many of these proposals of policy have been presumably "filtered" first through the duplicated ministerial committees to be found in the Office of the Minister for the Presidency. The Central Minister by the October 1958 decree came also to supervise the execution of decreed or approved policy in both regions.

Certain characteristics of this executive structure are significant. The resignation of the Chairman of an Executive Council of Ministers for either region of the Republic would not affect the status of the other members of the Council. The decrees establishing the new cabinet structure were, however, vague on the settlement of disagreements arising between Executive and Central Ministers. This may have been due to the fact that one of these decrees made Executive Ministers responsible to the President, and gave them direct access to his office.

The argument at the time that it was necessary to have parallel Syrian and Egyptian cabinets was cogent. Neither Egyptians nor Syrians were yet familiar enough with problems of both regions. There was need for central control, especially in matters of defense, foreign policy, and, to some extent, education. Indeed, there was no unification of currency, no uniform customs procedure, no completely uniform economic measures applying to both regions. It was hoped that this would be achieved by the end of 1960. Geographic detachment further dictated separate regional cabinets.

Politically, this arrangement was commendable, indicating the increased political maturity of President Nasser; for it was a way of satisfying the politically articulate and, to a great extent, representative elite in Syria by political appointment and a share in governing even though on a regional level. One may observe that President Nasser has been trying to make his governing class more flexible by permitting a certain amount of mobility which brings other groups into the power complex.

Various interpretations for the basis of selection of members of the October 1958 executive structure have been put forth by Egyptians. One is interesting, novel, and naïve. Yet it is fairly representative of native rationalizations of U.A.R. politics current in 1958. In an editorial in *Akhbar el Yom* (Cairo, October 8, 1958) Mustafa Amin argued that the basis for selection or recruitment to the Cabinet was "revolutionary": only those who believed in the Revolution could have been recruited. Whether President Nasser had known them in the past was irrelevant. And as the Revolution was no longer identified with Nasser as an individual, their being for him or against him was immaterial so long as they were qualified. Personalities were not important. A contrast was indeed drawn, in this interpretation, with patronage appointments in the past.

The interesting contradictions in this interpretation come to light when one looks at the first general elections in Egypt, on July 3, 1957, and the elections in the U.A.R. on July 8, 1959. Because of the absence of political parties or groups and the general political "vacuum," candidates neither represented political parties nor stood on different platforms. Personal and professional qualifications became the major criteria in election campaigns, buttressed by general slogans of domestic policy (such as industrialization, social and economic advancement, the "principles of the revolution," and Arabism). Moreover, candidates were initially screened by a Presidential Committee to determine their standing with and loyalty to the regime.

Ihsan Abdel Quddus, a leading political commentator, in the

December 23, 1958 *Rose el-Youssef* thus justified the new organization plan for the Executive on three counts. He argued that (1) the lack of "partisanship" in the U.A.R. necessitated planning; (2) the anti-party concept of government that was being evolved in the U.A.R. since 1952 extended naturally to the creation of the new Executive; (3) the "planning of interests" as a basic tenet in the new "socialist democratic" philosophy of the Revolution required a non-politically oriented Executive.

The total effect of the reorganized Executive apparatus of October 1958 in the U.A.R. may best be described by some working hypotheses. The first is that the reorganization was designed to extend further the political control of the President into the Syrian region. Another is that the regime, which until that time had largely depended on the Armed Forces for its internal support, felt that it was gradually gaining mass acquiescence, if not support, but that it had yet to achieve the active support of political groups or of an emerging party organization, necessary for its long-term success. The National Union had only just begun its activities. A third possibility is that the reorganization permitted the President to proliferate government committees as the need arose for his direct institution or supervision of special programs or policies. The practice of "government by committee" was thus becoming more commonplace in the U.A.R. It appeared to serve equally well as an instrument of direct control by the President—the Central or Regional Cabinet Ministers notwithstanding—and as the best way for the acceleration of industrial, economic, and social programs. Until this writing, however, the whole system has contributed to greater regimentation in government activity while supporting tight presidential control.

This control system may be further examined in the light of cabinet changes from October 1958 until this writing. A presidential decree (March 6–13, 1958) established the executive structure for the October reorganization. It provided for separate Egyptian and Syrian Councils of Ministers, and for four Vice-Presidents of the Republic, two of whom were Syrians:

Akram Hourani and Sabri Assali. The latter, a Syrian Nationalist, headed the Syrian Cabinet immediately preceding Union. Indeed, one of his former Cabinets had discussed Union as early as January 1957.

The difficulties confronted during the first eight months of Union, February to September 1958, led to Nasser's attempts at reorganization in October. Assali, who appeared as one of the leading architects of Union from January 1957 to January 1958, was not selected to serve in either the new Central Cabinet of the U.A.R. or the Regional Cabinet for Syria. The last phase of his career is an example of the awkward position in which many Syrian political leaders found themselves as a result of Union.

Toward the end of September 1958 statements by Fadhil Jamali of Iraq during his trial for treason in Baghdad seemed to implicate Sabri Assali's position with regard to union with Iraq or Egypt. The *Ahram* of Cairo (September 27, 1958) reported one of Jamali's statements: "Sabri Assali used to criticize the policy of the Iraqi government in the past in suppressing the people, and its dependence upon Sheikh Maaruf Dawalibi [Syrian Populist] and other personalities for the extension of their influence in Syria. If Iraq were serious about unity with Syria it should have depended on him, because of his sincere belief in union [with Iraq]. Although he could not guarantee immediate success, he would dedicate his life work for the attainment of this national objective. Even though his relations with President Kuwwatli were good, he disagreed with him in following a pro-Saudi policy regarding the question of Arab unity and will continue to strive for unity [with Iraq]."

Although one may have misgivings about Colonel Mahdawi's "revolutionary court" in Baghdad in 1958–59, the very mention of Sabri Assali's name required some explanation. Assali was at the time Vice-President of the U.A.R. for liaison with the Syrian Region. By October 7, the day before President Nasser's announcement of the new U.A.R. Executive structure, Assali issued a public statement explaining his position. At the same time he tendered his resignation pending the report of a

Presidential Committee that had just been appointed to investigate the allegations made in the Baghdad trials.

The Assali statement is a most interesting document which reflects in many ways the tenuous status of Arab politicians when the power structure is dominated by the military, and when political orientations change with political events. It also suggests the impact of Syrian-Egyptian Union in sharpening the conflict between the U.A.R. and Iraq.

Assali based his apology on one aspect of Syrian politics, namely, that during the Mandate (1920–45) and after independence (1946–54) all Syrian politicians and political leaders—including Baathists—were at one time or another involved in some scheme of unity with Iraq. "Union of Syria and Iraq," he asserted, "is an old subject dealt with by all political parties and governments [in Syria]." His argument, however, went on to distinguish between Syrian policy regarding union with Iraq before the Baghdad Pact in February 1955 and after. In this connection he (1) admitted his active advocacy of some form of unity with Iraq before 1955, (2) admitted his efforts as official delegate of Colonel Zaim in 1949 for the conclusion of an Iraqi-Syrian military alliance, and (3) asserted his meeting with Fadhil Jamali in Brumana, Lebanon, in June 1954 to discuss unity schemes, as was alleged during the Baghdad trials.

Assali's name did not appear on the new cabinet lists of October 8, 1958. He went back to the private practice of law in Damascus, having unavoidably invited the suspicion of the authorities. With Assali's separation from the councils of government, Akram Hourani remained between October 1958 and December 1959 as the only Syrian political leader in power, along with some Syrian army officers.[19]

It will be interesting to follow Syrian reaction to the expected increased political regimentation from Cairo and the gradual institution of a controlled economy throughout the Republic within the next few years. Both of these policies may seem standard enough to Egypt and the Egyptians, but they are quite alien to the less placid Syrian in the North.

Part III
Theoretical Considerations

7. Problems of Political Leadership: Islam, Nationalism, and Arabism

THE USE of traditional symbols by leaders of newly independent states to achieve consensus in their political communities is fairly common in these days. The professed aspiration of these leaders to modernize their societies does not preclude their manipulation of traditional symbols for the maintenance of order in a period of troubled transition. Often, therefore, the student of politics in these states finds that formal alterations in the institutions and functions of government do not necessarily reflect basic changes in structures or underlying concepts. Nor do they necessarily affect appreciably the conception, use, or allocation of power.

When members of the military establishment acceded to political power in some Middle Eastern states in the past decade they announced their intention of "modernizing" their societies. This aspiration raised a variety of questions interesting to the student of Middle Eastern politics. What ideology, what political system, was the new leadership proposing? The desire of the new military rulers to "modernize" implied that their societies were still steeped in a complex of tradition-

An article adapted from this chapter appeared in the March 1961 *American Political Science Review* under the title, "Dilemmas of Political Leadership in the Arab Middle East: the Case of the UAR."

bound relationships and structures. The relation between the new military leadership, which claims that it wants a departure from the traditional past, and the Islamic religious-traditional background of society should be a primary consideration in any analysis of this new leadership.

Military accession to power in these states also compels the student to consider the aspiration of the new leadership to provide a secular formula for national identification, recently manifested in the concept of Pan-Arab nationalism, or Arabism. The relation between the leadership provided by the Army Officer Corps and these preoccupations of national endeavor in the Arab states of the Middle East is of particular significance in the case of the ruling group of Egyptian army officers, because Egypt has only recently begun to identify its national interest and destiny with that of Arab nationalism and Arabism.

The importance of the traditional religious element, Islam, to the study of the army in politics stems from the desire expressed by army officers who recently came to power in the Middle East, especially Egyptian officers, to "modernize" and reform their society along "secular lines." At least since 1956, the Egyptian military rulers have announced their intention of creating a new "socialist, cooperative, democratic" society based on industrialization, and social and economic reform generally; in brief a new modern society from which will emerge a new political order. What role Islamic tradition will play in the forging of this new order is one consideration. How the army rulers have viewed the role of Islam and the importance of its tradition is another.

The military rulers of the U.A.R. have been faced with the difficult task of devising a secular formula for national identification and orientation, to replace the traditional one of Islam. Although considered to belong to the most modern secularly oriented national institution in Egypt, the officers in power today continue to use Islam and the traditional ethos of the Egyptian community as instruments to legitimate their authority and to command the allegiance of all classes in a still undifferentiated public. At the same time, their use of traditional symbols has permitted the army rulers to attain a certain degree of political consensus among the masses without, however conceding to them any great measure of participation in the political process and the making of policy. Second, the U.A.R. leadership in the coming decade must work out its relationship to Arab nationalism, especially in its more recent expression of Arabism.

The Army Officers and Islam

In November 1954 the Egyptian government, controlled by the Free Officers Executive, which at the time was organized as the Revolutionary Command Council, decreed the establishment of the Islamic Congress (*al-mu'tamar al-islami*). Significantly, this decree was promulgated at a time when the struggle for power between the revolutionary army officers and the Muslim Brethren was in its final stages.[1]

The aims of the Islamic Congress were outlined by the decree as the educational and social welfare of all Muslims; the translation of the compendiums of Islamic traditions into Asian and African languages; the initiation of studies on the economic problems of the various Muslim countries preparatory to the increase of commercial and trade relations between them; the propagation of the message of Islam in Africa and Asia; the teaching of Arabic and the publication of the Holy Koran for wider distribution among Muslims everywhere; the establishment of cultural centers in Jerusalem, Indonesia, Somaliland, and Northern Nigeria; and the creation of a central office for the guidance of Islamic youth.[2]

Legally, the Islamic Congress was designated by the 1954 decree as an agency of the presidency of the Republic. Thus it came under the ultimate supervision of the President. Administratively the Islamic Congress was headed by ex-Colonel Anwar es-Sadat, who was appointed Secretary-General, and who was advised by a rather conservative panel of Islamic scholars. Although the aims of the Congress as outlined above appear to be of wide scope, it has so far concentrated its activities on Egypt's relations with other Islamic countries, especially Northern Nigeria and Somaliland. It maintains an extensive scholarship program for Muslim students from other countries wishing to study at the Azhar University or the secular state universities of the U.A.R., as well as programs of medical aid to backward Muslim countries, and it has provided teachers for their schools. The apparent discrepancy between the originally outlined aims of the Congress and its actual program is due to the hesitation, mixed with suspicion, of other Muslim rulers or heads of state to participate extensively in its activities. They have feared that the Congress was basically an instrument devised by revolutionary officers in Egypt for political action abroad.

Within the U.A.R. itself, the Islamic Congress has not been particularly active. Nor has enthusiasm for it been widespread among Egyptians or Syrians. Its establishment, however, did have some impact on the relation between the army officers in power and the majority of an Islam-conscious public, insofar as it reassured the latter of the army's desire to uphold, and even promote, the message of Islam and the solidarity of Islamic peoples in the Middle East and elsewhere. It helped to promote the idea in the minds of the people that defense of the faith is not the exclusive prerogative of conservative religious leaders (*sheikhs* and *ulema*); army officers can also perform this role. In more practical terms, the concern of an army junta with Islamic welfare represented a broad-gauged measure to placate fundamentalist fellow travelers of the Muslim Brethren when the latter organization was dissolved in October 1954 following its implication in a plot to assassinate Gamal Abdel Nasser in Alexandria.

While in no way indicative of the concern of the ruling army officers over Islamic political institutions or aspirations for the establishment of an Islamic State, the Islamic Congress profitably emphasized for public comfort the junta's respect for the Islamic heritage. The Free Officers leadership understood from the beginning the importance of Islam as a link between their movement and the majority of a tradition-bound public. In the absence of any other strong or fully developed political link, the religious-national bond of Islam appeared to the army rulers the most efficacious for political purposes and communication with the masses.[3]

Contrary to the view held by many Westerners, the average Muslim in the U.A.R. today is not concerned with the establishment of an Islamic state in the religious-legal sense of the term. Today the average Egyptian or Syrian claims to be more concerned with an efficient state. There was, for example, no objection to or agitation against the recent legislation in Egypt and Syria abolishing Islamic or *sharia* courts. Similarly, decrees which rendered a woman's testimony equal to a man's were accepted quietly. Yet the political appeal to an Islamic sense of community and loyalty is still potent. Thus, while abolishing courts of religious jurisdiction, the U.A.R. government required all schools in the Republic to provide religious instruction. The assumption of political office continued to be ceremoniously legitimated by the *bay'a,* or traditional Islamic oath of allegiance by the people to the ruler. All official government correspondence was prefaced by the opening verse in the Holy Koran, "In the name of Allah the Beneficent, the Merciful" (*Bism illah ar-rahman ar-rahim*).

Much has been said about the all-embracing character of Islam and the dilemma faced by modernizing Muslim rulers, who wish to maintain a modern state and administration and at the same time to perpetuate an Islamic tradition. It is still difficult for any ruler in the Middle East today to reject completely or legislate out of existence the Islamic heritage, regardless of the inroads a foreign culture may have achieved. Significantly, though, President Nasser has not been inclined to revive, let alone strengthen, Islamic institutions. Nor were his predecessors able to reform them in the light of modern necessities. In a sense, the "Islamic myth" has failed to produce a stable and strong Arab, Egyptian, or Syrian political community. Its replacement by a secular national formula has appeared necessary in the last decade. But the new ruling class of army officers in the U.A.R. has been faced with a maddening paradox: the need to appeal to the "Islamic myth" of communal and cultural identity in order to work for the achievement of a new formula to supersede it.

The use of Islam as an instrument of policy by the rulers of the U.A.R. is undeniable. Not only does Islam constitute one of the traditional bases of legitimacy, but it also serves as an effective arm of foreign policy. It is, however, strange for a government to promote a supranational identity when it is trying desperately to create a national consciousness. Or is the only valid and possible nationalism open to the Arabs an Islamic one? Wilfred C. Smith's thesis in *Islam in Modern History*,[4] that there is a special relation between the Arabs and Islam in the sense that the Islamic element is paramount in Arab national consciousness, is a plausible one. But this relation multiplies the national problems of modern leadership in the U.A.R. To become permanent, the secular nationalism of the army ruling group must be religiously accepted by the masses. Islam and its traditional nexus unavoidably influence such political issues as social order and control, leadership and the formulation of public policy, national goals and interests; for regardless of the terms in which the attempted secular national myth is couched, it acquires religious momentum as it penetrates the masses. In Egypt, particularly, where does the use by the army rulers of the Islamic-Arab premise in national development leave the Egyptian consciousness of a folk nationality antedating Islam? With the exception of the brief Fatimid period (963–1170), Egypt cannot proudly associate itself with Islamic glory. Then, again, the Islamic factor in nationalism is both exclusive and inclusive. It leaves outside the pale the non-Muslim Egyptian and Syrian; and it includes the vast majority of Middle Eastern Arabs.

The army rulers of the U.A.R. have perhaps been justified in using Islam as an instrument of national policy. Other societies and states have used and continue to use their religious heritage for national purposes, apart from the legitimate contention that religion does provide a fundamental type of social integration even in the most developed political systems. Political power and authority in the Middle East are still associated and, in some instances identified, with the religious tradition in the sense that religion is still a major source of loyalty and consensus in a community. So long as the Middle East was organized in empires and dynasties within which religious communities carried on an autonomous existence, the problem of political stability was not a serious one. But the eventual confrontation, if not serious clash, between secular nationalism and Islamic fundamental and communal particularism produced a major crisis as yet unresolved. The concept of the nation-state introduced into the Arab-Islamic area by preachers of the secular nationalist gospel was a decided novelty which, so far, does not seem to be the final political form agreed on by all Arabs or other Muslims.

Religion and politics have overlapped throughout the history of Islamic nations. Politics, however, usually dominated religion. Ibn Khaldun, who recognized the predominance of politics over religion in the affairs of Muslim states, has presented us with an incisive criticism of the institutions of the caliphate in his *Prolegomena (Muqaddima)*. The earliest factionalism in Islamic history was motivated by political considerations, as is plain in the first Sunni-Shia schism under the Caliph Ali. Indeed, one may safely assume political motives in most of the doctrinal and sectarian differences in medieval Islam.[5]

President Nasser of the U.A.R. was thus justified in his *desire* to separate politics from religion. He once admitted, "When you mix politics with religion, politics will still dominate." He has further been aware that the Muslim community, as a community of believers (*umma*), has lost much of its solidarity by

fragmentation under the impact of modern forces. The proliferation of largely Muslim nation-states in the past fifty years,
the hardening of geographical-national boundaries between
them, and the influence of modern economic and social institutions have created wider chasms in state-national and class
loyalties. But when President Nasser, or any other contemporary
head of an Arab state, speaks of divorcing politics from
religion, he usually means the administration of the state and
the functions of government. He does not necessarily imply
adoption or implementation of completely secular political
concepts, such as the nation, authority, and citizenship, independently of the Islamic cultural complex and faith. Except-
ing a small percentage of the urban population in Egypt and
Syria, both societies are largely folk-structured and religion-
oriented, especially the 5,000-odd villages in Egypt, where
Islamic forces continue to mold and guide individual as well as
corporate life. The integrative role of Islam is so pronounced
in the bulk of U.A.R. society that government institutions introduced to regulate certain aspects of rural life (such as health,
agriculture, compulsory schooling) have, until recently, made
slow progress in breaking down, let alone superseding, traditional behavior. Little wonder then that some Arab thinkers
can still assert that an attachment to the Islamic faith and spirit
is necessary for the future development of Arab societies. Without this, they argue, the prospects would be barren.[6]

One may argue that increased material changes and wider
access to the fruits of technological civilization will inevitably
break down the folk-religious base of the community. If this
argument is correct, then the rate of this change must be very
slow in Egypt at least. Most villagers have indeed begun to
imitate city-dwellers in their use of more material goods. But
their basic attitudes toward community life and social relations
have not changed appreciably.[7] President Nasser is soberly
aware that it is a long step from the villager's ready folk-
religious identification as one among the *ummati'l-muslimin*,

or community of Muslims, to active membership in a "democratic, socialist, cooperative" society.

The problem, therefore, which has so far faced the army
rulers—as the self-styled, and perhaps the only available, agents
of social, economic, and political change—is not *what* new
national ideology to foster, but *how* to devise one. They could
not very well reject Islam the Faith; nor could they revert to
pure Egyptianism, for they now claim an interest in and a
message for the larger Arab political community. If, as Wilton
Wynn claims in *Nasser of Egypt: The Search for Dignity*,[8] they
"yearn for independence and dignity," the army rulers cannot
escape the fact that the only dignity and glory Arabs ever knew
was under the banner of Islam. A nationalist interpretation of
Islam presents itself as a ready alternative to the new army
leaders. It is often nationalist Islam, indeed, which appears
as Arabism, *al-'uruba* and *al-qawmiyya al-arabiyya*, today. But
such an interpretation or use of Islam is also embarrassing
because nationalist Islam has been humiliated partly by prolonged European domination in the past and partly by the
more recent defeat in Palestine.

Within the U.A.R., the military regime has been trying to
curb the political influence of Islamic religious leaders. Their
policy in this respect has not been as drastic as that of Ataturk
in Turkey thirty-five years ago. In Egypt, for example, the
Nasser government has brought the Azhar University hierarchy
under more rigid state control. Under the previous regime in
Egypt, the Azhar *sheikhs* were able to exert a good measure of
political influence and control in the affairs of state through
their convenient alliance with the Palace. Religious and mystic
orders, *tariqas*, which claim some three million followers and
sport a variety of saints and cults, have also been recently
brought under more rigorous state control.[9]

Unable, though, to disassociate themselves completely from
the religion, the army rulers saw fit to utilize it as a ready
medium of communication with the masses for the transmis-
sion of their interests and policies. The Friday Sermon, a

traditional institution whether in mosques or on the radio, has become since 1955 a didactic technique as well as a vehicle for the expression of "revolutionary" policy. President Nasser's famous November 9, 1956, mosque address, soon after the Suez attack by Anglo-French forces, was representative of this technique. This particular address re-fused in the person of President Nasser the religious and political leadership of the Islamic community in the face of a common infidel enemy. But the speech also reflected the re-fusion of nationalism and Islam. As Anwar es-Sadat postulated on September 26, 1959, during the Islamic Congress celebration of the Prophet's birthday, "the Islamic idea arose on the basis of *tawhid,* or the oneness of God, in order to unite the Arabs in one strong nation."[10]

Students of the Arab Middle East have often contended that secular nationalism in the area was led by a highly Westernized elite. If one accepts the thesis that the Army Officer Corps is the most cohesive Westernized group in Arab society today, one must argue that it is the natural leader of secular nationalism. Unfortunately, like that of other less forceful Westernized elites in Arab countries, the army rulers' following today remains largely un-Westernized and stubbornly traditional. On closer observation one even finds a certain contradiction in these terms when applied to the members of the Army Officer Corps in power today. Many of the cabinet members in Egypt, for instance, especially among the army officers, still subscribe to a religiously conservative and traditional view of life. In a recent interview with the *Rose el-Youssef* magazine, the Minister of Social Affairs for the Egyptian Region of the Republic, and ex-army officer, emphasized his attachment to the integrative force of the religious tradition. Socially speaking, very few of the original members of the Free Officers Executive still in power can be said to have a Western outlook on life. The Western model is not, however, the only one available today for emulation or greater achievement. Two more recent models loom large in their area of choice: the Soviet and the Chinese-Asian. Whether the commitment of the army leaders, as the foremost agent of change in the U.A.R., to "modernize" will mean their use of the Western model or one of the other two remains to be seen. They may, on the other hand, develop their own model.

It was suggested earlier in this chapter that fundamentalist Islam insisted always on an active relationship between religion and politics, so that any nationalist ideology cannot escape its limitation by the faith. This relationship between Islam and nationalism explains in part the success of the Muslim Brethren in the 1940's. But even today the Army Officer Corps and its leaders encourage a dual development in national endeavor: (1) the acquisition of technical and political training inspired mainly by Western standards, and (2) a continued attachment to the ethical-educational benefits of Islam, so that the use of religious symbols by the army rulers of the U.A.R. is an integral part of any nationalist program. Until the army leaders can arrive at some agreement over fundamentals and goals for the nation based on a secular formula, Islam will continue to serve, in many respects, as the basis for minimum agreement among members of the political community. One may properly question this device by an Egyptian ruling group when one realizes that Egypt among all other Arabic-speaking countries has had the longest existence as a nation, independently of Islam. It was Pharaonic, Ptolemaic, Roman, and Arab-Islamic. The latter stamp, many argue, has been the one with the strongest imprint. Today, the military rulers argue that despite a pre-Islamic national identity, Egyptian national consciousness has been saturated and mostly guided by its later Islamic faith.

The Army Officers and Arab Nationalism

History, geography, and politics have made Egypt, the country accused by other Arabs of being least Arab, the center of Islamic consciousness and the leader of Arab nationalism. Modern nationalism in the Arab countries, even Arabism today, did not arise or gather momentum outside the religious-cultural complex, George Antonius to the contrary notwithstanding.[11] Although one may argue that the religious base of legitimacy has been undermined in the Arab countries, in the sense that an Abdul Hamid was not readily acceptable as a Caliph at the turn of the century, or that a Farouq was later ridiculed for having similar ambitions, a complete secularization of the basis for political leadership could still prove the undoing of many rulers in these countries. The army rulers in Egypt have grasped the truth of this maxim from the outset. Thus, if Damascus and Baghdad claim pre-eminence in Arabism, it was and still is in Cairo that its advocates can expound and nurture it. Although Mecca and Jerusalem may represent all that is holy in Islam, it was and still is in the Azhar University at Cairo that religious thought, teaching, and orthodox Muslim pronouncements are molded and diffused. Cairo may not have been the birthplace of Arab nationalism or Arabism, but it manages to represent better than Damascus, Baghdad, or Mecca all that Arabism presumably aspires to. Whereas the traditional insularity of Egypt precluded her early leadership of Arabism, her position as the cultural and intellectual center of Islam permits her today to be effectively Pan-Arab. This privileged position of Egypt has been argued by such an eminent advocate of Arabism and Arab unity as Maître Michel Aflaq, when he said that in spite of Syria's earlier leadership in the cause of Arab unity, certain conditions in Egypt—greater political independence and freedom, and a wider awareness of social and popular demands on the part of the army rulers—rendered her better suited to lead the cause. He further claims that the disaster in Palestine caused Egypt to abandon her old isolationism.[12]

To avoid isolation, Egypt has had to evolve an Arab-oriented policy since the Second World War at least. This policy acquired a minimum of three facets. (1) Egyptian rulers even before Nasser always sought to contain Hashemite expansion and consolidation in the North. This explains, in part, Egypt's traditional opposition to the Fertile Crescent and Greater Syria schemes of Arab unity, both of which were inspired and dominated by the Hashemites. (2) For the time being, Egypt has been able to thwart or at least contain these schemes through the acquisition of a base in the North, in the heart of the proposed Great Syria and Fertile Crescent schemes of unity—Syria itself. A previous attempt by Egypt to maintain a balance against the Hashemites through an alliance with Saudi Arabia was not as fruitful. (3) Egypt feels constantly pressed to maintain her pre-eminence if not leadership as spokesman of the Arab states by striving to dominate Arab League councils and politics.

The need for Egypt to control or at least influence some segment of the Arab nation to the north has some basis in historical precedent. Today, however, there is another explanation for Egypt's seeking to lead Arab nationalism or Arabism: there is a positive identification of Egypt by the Arab public at large as the "revolutionary leader" of all Arabs seeking political, economic, and social emancipation. Thus Habib Jamati, writing in a special issue on Arabism of the monthly *al-Hilal,* can assert, "Egypt is today at the head of this Arab family, which, stretching from Morocco to the Persian Gulf, has awakened to the goals of freedom and independence."[13] The postwar recession and, presently, absence of direct Big Power control or influence over most of the Arab states is an added temptation for Egyptian leaders.

As an instrument of policy and popular means of communication between the officers in power and the masses, Arabism is not essential for legitimating the political power of the military in Egypt proper. Union with Syria in 1958, however, catapulted Arabism into an efficacious formula by which the Egyptian army rulers could transfer their leadership into a Syrian national context and secure a measure of popular allegiance. Arab nationalism, *al-'uruba* or *al-qawmiyya al-arabiyya,* was the most forceful symbol representing popular aspirations. The army officers ruling Egypt recognized it as a source of strength while the people in Syria appeared to hail it as an essential prerequisite of change. Since 1955, the Free Officers in power in Egypt have intensified their efforts to present their revolutionary movement as an expression of the movement for Arabism. Anwar es-Sadat, often the spokesman for the junta, asserted in March 1957:

and there was nothing behind our coup other than Arab nationalism . . . which awakened a new historical development. . . . We must nurture this link between the peoples of the Arab nation . . . for when the revolution occurred in Egypt it rendered the Arab nation one nation, sharing one history and claiming one destiny.[14]

During the same month President Nasser, addressing a rally of Palestinian students after the Israeli withdrawal from Gaza, emphasized Arabism as the major political and social weapon in the hands of the Arabs. He said on this occasion:

Nationalism [al-qawmiyya] is the arm which protects the Arab nation from imperialist plots. It is the nation's weapon for securing the future. Nationalism is the means by which we can retrieve the rights of independence and freedom.

It appears therefore as if the term "Arab nation" has recently become essential in Arab nationalist vocabulary. The term presumably refers to all the Arabic-speaking countries and implies their essential unity as a cardinal aspiration of all Arabs. All other slogans of Arab nation-states, especially Egypt, such as "positive neutralism" (al-hiyad al-ijabi), "revolutionary society" (mujtama' thawri), "democratic, socialist, cooperative society," represent necessary tactical measures for the establishment of the Arab nation, al-umma'l-arabiyya.[15] In Egyptian usage, Arabism may conceivably imply more traditional aspects of Egyptian policy. The Egyptian Free Officers undoubtedly view their movement as the model for liberating movements in all the Arab countries. Their interest in universalizing or implementing the model elsewhere has frequently brought against them and their leader, Nasser, in recent years the charge of expansionism. The brief success of the Nabulsi-led government in Jordan during 1956–57, and the early stand of the opposition in the Lebanon during the May–September 1958 crisis, prompted other Arab rulers to interpret the Arabism espoused by the Egyptian military rulers as a convenient tool for the extension of Egyptian hegemony over the neighboring Arab countries. Indeed, Iraq, the youngest republic among the Arabs, also the creation of a native Free Officers group conspiracy, now comes forth with a divergent interpretation of Arabism; perhaps one that implies, if not stipulates, Iraqi leadership and hegemony.

Although it would be unfair to underestimate the genuine *sentiment* for Arabism among the politically conscious Arabs everywhere, and their often intense desire for unity, one cannot honestly overlook the instrumentalist role of Arabism for the promotion of strictly national interests. The army officer groups now in political control of the most advanced Arabic-speaking countries, the U.A.R. and Iraq, are unlikely to agree on a common understanding of Arabism through political compromise. As the content of current nationalist ideology is developed by competing army juntas, Arabism itself becomes a competitive idea. Thus there is the Arabism of Baghdad, emphasizing local national development, which is diametrically opposed to that of Cairo; whereas the Arabism of Amman views both of these as late-comers and covetous. The attempt to define a Lebanese variety of Arabism is risky. If Arabism implies a desire for unity with other Arab states, Lebanon's case, even after the 1958 crisis, has not shown it.

If anything, Arabism seems to be a *sentiment* which develops most rapidly in areas where "revolutionary" change is fomented or is imminent. Some of the Persian Gulf and southwest Arabian coast principalities may conceivably fall in this category in the near future. Yet Arabism remains juxtaposed with a growing state-national sentiment in individual Arab countries that have achieved independent status.

The ready identification by some Arabs of the Nasser-led Free Officers in Egypt with the leadership of Arabism is partly due to the sensational success of the army movement in estab-

lishing itself in Egypt and its subsequent gains (or luck) in
dealing with the Big Powers. The overthrow of a foreign
dynasty, the achievement of freedom from foreign domination,
and the beginnings of a social and economic reform program
in Egypt have captured the imagination of many Arabs elsewhere who are politically and economically frustrated and
who seek emancipation and, as they put it, "dignity." This
response to the bid of Egyptian Free Officers for Pan-Arab
leadership was possible only so long as no other similarly successful military conspiratorial group appeared on the Arab
political horizon. The presence today in Iraq, however, of
another army-led movement and government in the Arab
world, which was able to overthrow a monarchy and a regime
notorious for their adeptness at total control, no longer permits
a monopoly of the interpretation of Arabism by the Egyptians
or Syrians.

Arabism or *al-'uruba,* today, thus seems exposed to various
levels of interpretation. It means different things to different
groups. To the intellectuals, Arabism evokes an ideological
concept which will be eventually embodied in a structure to be
known as the "United Arab States of the World." A leading
Arab journalist can thus seriously assert that Arabism is the
highest aspiration of all Arabs, as well as of their respective
governments. By Arabism he means its ultimate form and
structure: Arab unity. At one point this journalist glibly compared the period 1860–65 in American history to the present
stage of evolution of the Arab states.[16] To the masses, on the
other hand, Arabism often means the recapture of old Islamic
unity and power. Until very recently, Arabism to the masses
meant the power of the Muslim community (*quwwat al-mus-
limin*) and its dignity, but not much else. Under the impact of
military regimes bent on making nationalism mean more than
mere slogans, the masses may begin to associate local nationalism as well as Arabism with concrete material and other needs,
desires, and aspirations. To provide a practical meaning and
content for Arabism is therefore a major political task of the
military regime in the U.A.R., especially now that the cham-

pions of Arabism, the Baath party, are in political eclipse.[17] President Nasser and his inner core of Free Officer colleagues now associate Arabism with the revolutionary goal of a "democratic, socialist, cooperative" society.

The central role of the army in the general evolution of Arab nationalism is not a new or sudden development. Indeed, the concept of the army outside politics is unknown to the last two generations of Arabs. It is also quite alien to the Islamic tradition and state. The successful warrior in Islam, especially a prince of armies, was usually rewarded by the ruler with high political office. Whereas the rise of modern Arab states since World War I has been associated with dynastic leadership in the case of Egypt, and tribal-personal-religious leadership in the case of Sherif Husein and his sons in the Hejaz, Iraq, Syria, and Jordan, the beneficiaries of the Arab independence movement in terms of political power and control have been the members of the rising native military establishment. Thus army officers who formed the nucleus of Sherif Husein's and Feisal's political leadership maneuvered themselves into political office in Iraq and Syria during the inter-war period. Indeed, the 'Ahd, one of the earliest conspiratorial nationalist societies among the Arabs before World War I, was mainly an organization of Arab officers in the Ottoman army. It was led by such famous revolutionaries as Major Aziz Ali al-Masri and Salim al Jaza'iri. The early politics of independent Iraq in the 1920's and 1930's were dominated by Arab ex-officers in the Ottoman army, among them such members of the 'Ahd as Nuri al-Said, Jaafar al-Askari, and Taha al-Hashimi.

It is difficult to assess the final character of Arab nationalism as interpreted by the military regime in the U.A.R. or elsewhere in the Arab world. This is due partly to the fact that the assertion of Arabism and Arab national endeavor in general is associated with Islam. If Islam is and has been a basic component of Arab nationalism, will the new leadership of the Army Officer Corps replace it by a secular formula? Undoubtedly, Islam has always lent an aura of representativeness to those national leaders willing to link the Arab nation and its struggle for political freedom and unity with the Islamic cultural framework. For example, as contemporary an Arab nationalist as Munif al-Razzaz opens his remarks in *Maalem al-hayat al-arabiyya al-jadida* by asserting that "this force which was released fourteen centuries ago to realize itself and its potentialities and to fulfill its message has not lost any of its vitality and spirit." The connection between Islam and the Arab thrust outward from the Arabian peninsula is here unmistakable. Michel Aflaq, a Christian Arab, on the other hand, gives religion a place in this movement but, for obvious reasons, underplays its significance. He overlooks the possibility, however, that without religion, very little seems to be left because the Arab Middle East as a whole has known an independent and flourishing existence only when Islam was in the ascendant. What these and other writers generally gloss over is the question: was the Arab nation ever really *one* nation even under Islam? The history of schism and revolution soon after the Prophet's death in A.D. 632 argues against the existence of one Arab nation at any time.

Perhaps Munif al-Razzaz among contemporary Arab writers has come closest to describing adequately the forces which many Arabs claim produce tension in the Arab community today. He listed three: (1) an internal force, represented by the sacred message of Islam, which pushes the Arab community forward to unity; (2) a reactionary force, represented by the recent experience of autocratic rule in the Arab world; and (3) a force representing the exogenous influences of imperialism and foreign domination. The latter force obstructs the Arab community's efforts to achieve unity.

One can suggest a fourth and different source of tension in the Arab world today. Most contemporary advocates of Arabism argue the necessity and inevitability of one Arab nation on the basis of "common feeling and thinking" among all Arabs today, the existence of a uniform language, and the sharing of similar historical experience by all Arabs over a long period. Much tension today, though, results from the disparate levels of leadership in the Arab world, the existence of separate nation-states, and a difference, if not a clash, between the interests of local ruling groups. It is not unforgivable to reiterate the obvious chasm separating the political orientations and interests of North African rulers (Morocco, Tunisia, and Libya) from those of the United Arab Republic or the Republic of Iraq. The diversity of political institutions and forms of government, and the difference in levels of economic and social achievement among the various Arab states today, further complicate the issue of Arabism's validity for all Arabs, let alone its acceptance by them. The one component which remains readily identifiable and palatable to all Arabs in spite of practical differences of policy among their rulers is Islam. An Arab anywhere in Morocco, Saudi Arabia, or Iraq accepts Arabism more readily if it is equated or linked with Islam. It is not at all certain, however, that he would accept it as enthusiastically were it couched in terms of U.A.R.-led and interpreted Arabism, or Saudi Arabian-inspired Arabism.[18]

One must settle then for the hypothesis that Arabism for the present and the near future at least will remain intimately connected with Islam; that nationalism will continue to be at once parochial and Pan-Arab. More important, though, is the hypothesis that nationalism and nationalistic Arabism will remain for some time to come a *competitive* concept. Cynicism, on the other hand, would argue that Arabism will cease to be competitive when one or another of the military ruling groups in Arab countries succeeds in imposing its hegemony over the entire community of Arab states. So long as the members of the Arab political community, or Arab nation, are not agreed on the representativeness of different rulers, especially military rulers, with regard to Arabism, a competition for the allegiance of Arabs generally becomes inevitable. For the same reason, Arab unity, another aspect of Arabism, remains problematic.

Arabism as a belief may constitute a great source of social power. But when it is advocated by different leaders, expressing opposite interests in the short, if not the long, run, its social power is dissipated. Although we may concede that most Arabs today subscribe to Arabism, to the worth and desirability of its goals—among them Arab unity—they are not all agreed on its leadership. Their leadership orientation, on the contrary, has changed many times in the modern history of Arab nationalism. At one time it was the Sherif Husein of Mecca and his Hashemite family concentrated in the Fertile Crescent lands. Arabism and its followers gravitated toward Hashemite leadership until the outbreak of the Second World War. Later, in the 1940's, the leadership of Arabism gradually shifted to Egypt and its non-Arab Muhammad Ali dynasty. Until 1950 this leadership was shared by ruling monarchs and conservative politicians elsewhere in the Arab world. The failure of this Arabist leadership to safeguard and promote the Arab position in Palestine not only discredited it but indirectly brought about its downfall. Members of the Army Officer Corps in the military establishment emerged as the "revolutionary" leaders of Arabism.

But one must observe carefully the process and pattern of elimination in the multiplicity of Arabist leadership from 1950 to the present. Elimination is not quite an accurate description of this pattern, because there is no guarantee that once a leader is eliminated he will not reappear. Soon after the Palestine War of 1948–49, for example, some of the earliest advocates of Arab unity—the late King Abdullah of Jordan, the Wafd party of Egypt, and the old Nationalists in Syria— were eliminated. Between 1952 and 1958 the government established in Egypt by the Free Officers movement was easily identified by the Arab public as the leader of Arabism. This was not only because this regime purported to be "revolutionary," but even more because it became the main target of attack by Israel and the West—two of the most popularly accepted common enemies of Arabism. Syria, on the other hand, could no longer claim the leadership of Arabism after its Union with Egypt in February 1958. The emergence of the Iraq Free Officer regime in July 1958 revived Iraqi claims to the leadership of Arabism after they had been in abeyance under Nuri al-Said between 1955 and 1958. Indeed, the effect on Arab politics of the army's seizure of power in Iraq has been wider than most students of Arab nationalism are willing to admit: it has reintroduced into the competition for leadership perhaps such lesser candidates as King Husein of Jordan and King Saud of Saudi Arabia.

Now that the Egypt-controlled military regime in the U.A.R. has espoused Arabism, in addition to Egyptianism and Afro-Asianism, as a tenet of its revolutionary philosophy, it must translate it into policy. That it uses Arabism as an instrument of policy is clear. That Arabism is at the present time an articulated interest of the Nasser-led military regime is also clear. But whether the average Egyptian accepts the achievement of the goals of Arabism as a political task of the collective Arab political community is not so clear. This is not to say that the average Egyptian would disdain or reject the realization of the program of Arabism under Egyptian leadership. But if any sacrifices are to be made in its cause, there is no indication, let alone guarantee, that the average Egyptian is ready to make them.

The military regime in Cairo does not face serious problems of Egyptianizing its citizenry or making them nationalistic. It may, however, find it a more exacting task to Arabize them in terms of the concept of Arabism used here. Some serious problems are involved in this connection. To make the Syrian citizens of the U.A.R. Arab nationalists may prove a comparatively easier task for the military rulers than that of tackling a national community which has been Egyptian for almost seven millennia. The Arabization of the Egyptian political community, on the other hand, may require either the replacement of the Egyptian folk and national sentiment and identity by Arabism, or the forceful superimposition of the latter as an adjunct of the former. Although the military governors can recognize the values and the political and strategic virtues of Arabism, the latter does not appear as crucial to most Egyptians. The cogency or urgency of Arabism, as a defensive and offensive weapon in the hands of the Egyptian state and power elite, is not widely understood by the Egyptian masses. Arabism, after all, implies an *inter-*

nationalism among the Arabs at least for which the Egyptian traditionally has lacked sympathy. The *"bilad barra"* ("the countries outside") concept of the average Egyptian applies to the Arab countries outside Egypt as much as it does to far-away places. One clear advantage remains in popularizing Arabism to the Egyptian masses: linking it to Islam, one might almost say, Islamizing it, since its imperial overtones cannot be openly advocated.

To list all the identification tags the military regime wishes to issue to all citizens of the U.A.R. is to render the regime's program for Arab nationalism and Arabism less realistic. If an Egyptian is to share in Egyptianism, Arabism, and Afro-Asianism, one wonders whether he would not prefer to settle for what comes naturally: being an Egyptian. This he always was. Although he has spoken Arabic for almost thirteen centuries, he was never really aware of an Arab nation in the modern sense of the term. But he has always been aware, perhaps vaguely, of a Muslim community, and possibly a Muslim nation. Indeed, the rise, spread, and conquests of Islam extended abroad the language of the earliest Muslim elite: Arabic. This Arabic-speaking elite was and remained a minority that was soon overthrown politically by a conglomeration of non-Arab Muslims.

There are today many Arabic-speaking nation-states. *The* Arab nation has yet to emerge. If the present military regimes are able to kindle the desire for the achievement of an Arab nation, one cannot deny that the effort is necessary preparation for its formation, regardless of the methods to be used in achieving it or the final form that it may take. But what one is left with today is a vague feeling of Islamic community. Should the "modernizing" military rulers of the Arab countries strengthen this feeling in order to create *an* Arab nation or *the* Arab nation, or should they discourage it? Islam without Arabism has been and is possible. Can there be Arabism without Islam? To resolve this issue is no mean political task for any ruling group, including the army.

8. The Army Officer Corps and the Pyramid of Power*

SOME AUTHORS writing about the contemporary Middle East include in their works a section entitled "What Does Nasser Stand For?"[1] They differ in their prejudices and personal inclinations, but very few of them succeed in answering the question. This is not, strictly speaking, the authors' fault, for it would be difficult to extract a definitive answer to this question from Egyptians or Syrians in general, and members of the Free Officers movement in particular.

After examining the literature on the subject, official and unofficial, emanating from Egypt and Syria, one concludes that the military rulers of the U.A.R. today are a nationalist-revolutionary group of ex-army officers bent on maintaining the independence of their country while desiring to modernize it through industrialization and other means. The term "modernization" has been variously used in recent Western literature on non-Western countries; in this context it refers to the efficiency of political organization and action rather than to modern political and social ideas, philosophy, and institutions.

---

* The propositions suggested in this chapter are based largely on the views and reactions of Egyptians and Syrians to the military regime. They also depend heavily on current published materials especially from Egypt.

211

It is apparent, for instance, that the army-dominated power elite in the U.A.R. has, so far, desired an efficient state organization, a properly functioning state system, and an effectively performing citizenry. It is not readily apparent so far, however, whether the military regime also aims to encourage the emergence of a highly articulate and mobile citizenry with access to all the political and social appurtenances of a modern free society. Indeed, there is some evidence that on the scale of national values being devised by the regime priority has been given to efficiency, performance, state responsibility, and a collective consciousness among its citizens. The military regime has rated less highly the abstract concepts of individual freedom, liberty, voluntary expression and organization. This is not to suggest that in February 1958 all U.A.R. citizens ought to have been immediately let loose on the ramparts of freedom, but that the Egyptian junta has so far considered the members of the political community in the U.A.R. to be in need of "training" for responsible citizenship, before it could trust them with individual freedom and liberty in the modern political sense of these terms.

Political Power in the U.A.R.

Power in the United Arab Republic has thus far been concentrated rather than dispersed. Although it could be argued that there was never really a diffusion of power in Egypt or Syria in the past, it should be recognized that traditional social institutions on various levels did exert some control over their members. With the break-up, first gradual and then rapid, of many traditional arrangements under the impact of foreign influences as well as of the modernization programs of native military leadership, power has tended to accumulate in the hands of the agents of change, the innovators. The corrosion of older, relatively stable, rural social structures by new methods of controlled irrigation, centrally devised and supervised national cooperatives, and other schemes represents, according to many observers of the Middle Eastern scene today, a combination of political, social, and economic change. The question is how purposive and conscious this change has been, and what bearing it has on the relation of the power structure in the U.A.R. to the ruling group of army officers.

As an example of traditional groupings in the U.A.R. one could cite Egypt's religious hierarchy, starting at the institution of al-Azhar, whose influence filtered down all the way to the village through its mosques and religious magistrates, or *qadis*. There are also the various religious orders and village, town, and city neighborhood saint cults. In Syria the groupings arise from the tribes, family alliances, and sectarian and religious minorities.[2] For a long time (1516–1918, at least in Syria) the Ottoman governors in Syria and the kaleidoscope of vassal satraps and dynasties in Egypt represented an autocratic ruling class with which were allied religious leaders, a bureaucracy, and a military caste. During the first half of the present century, early political groups expressed the interests and aspirations of a very small percentage of the population: landowners and monarchs in Egypt and Syria, rich merchants in Syria. Power was concentrated in the hands of these groups. Not until the Second World War did the impact of a slow social and economic development give rise to new groups, mainly white-collar and labor, as distinguished from the mass of peasant farmers. Alongside these, a native military establishment also emerged.

In order to analyze the relative significance of the Army Officer Corps in the power structure of the U.A.R. it is necessary to examine the nature of the state. The preceding discussion referred to the novelty of the idea of a secular state among Arab-Islamic communities. The state in the Arab environment was always a weak institution, weaker than other social establishments such as the family, the religious community, and the ruling class. Private interest was always paramount over public interest. In fact, the idea of the public interest was lacking, apart from the notion of the religious welfare of the community of believers. In the West practically all members of a political community organized in a state are committed to pay allegiance to that state, regardless of their particular interests. In the Arab countries, however, the modern state is still seeking the predictable allegiance of the majority of its citizens.

The prominent role of army officers in revolutionary movements in the modern Middle East does not derive solely from the army's access to physical force. Its nationalist orientation has been of crucial significance. The army in these countries was one of the first institutions to be exposed to Western ideas and techniques. The influence of British training in the army of Egypt, for example, rendered it the most disciplined national institution. Later, with the achievement of greater independence, the army also became one of the most representative institutions, as army officers were recruited from a cross-section of the population. With the passing of years the bulk of the Army Officer Corps lost all identification with the ruling class and members of the civilian power elite. The majority of younger army officers were now closer in sentiment and aspirations to the so-called nationalists among the intelligentsia and working classes. Whereas Ataturk was already a member of the governing class in the Ottoman military caste and a Pasha (General) when he embarked on the struggle for national regeneration in 1919, President Nasser and his Free Officers were not in 1952 members of the governing class in Egypt, represented by the monarchy, landowners, and old-guard politicians. Worse still, the Free Officers in Egypt were by 1952 politically alienated from and opposed to the governing class.

To the new group of middle and lower class Egyptians, whom Daniel Lerner in *The Passing of Traditional Society* refers to as "transitionals," the career of an army officer meant, first, economic security. To many of these men it also meant belonging to an institution which reflected national independence and sovereign power. By the end of the Second World War members of this new group of officers clearly outnumbered the traditional aristocrats in the Army Officer Corps.

When, moreover, the Egyptian army, like other armies in the Middle East, was exposed to the modernizing influences of technology, the beneficiaries were members of this nationalist-motivated group. More modernization also produced a stronger feeling of professionalism among them and consequently cohesiveness.

For a long time, as indicated previously, the function of the army was confined to protecting the existing regime and maintaining internal order and security. It is obvious, however, from the account of the Free Officers in Chapter 3 that certain members of the new officer class had different views of their proper role. As a result of improved systematic training, especially in Staff College, and of their combat experience in Palestine, they came to appreciate at least what their role was not: continuing to be the loyal arm of the Crown and of a regime oblivious to what they as army officers felt was the national interest. The politicalization of these officers before and during their army careers helped to provide them with a new role, not at all inconsistent with historical precedents and cultural norms: that of leading a revolution and of governing.

In Western society, the army officer, together with the politician, bureaucrat, and intellectual, has often formed an integral part of the ruling class or political elite. The same may be said of Turkey at the end of World War I. In Arab society, on the other hand, although historically the army officer did constitute an important part of the ruling class, in the last forty years he did not belong to that class usually associated with status, power, and property. The army officer in contemporary Arab society had no influence on political or social establishments. One illustration of the army's ineffective relationship with the political power structure was the fact that its recommendations about the general unpreparedness of the armed forces were disregarded by the King and the Government in Egypt on the eve of the Arab-Israeli war in Palestine in 1948.

In the nineteenth century, however, the army officer became an object as well as an agent of change. But the latter role remained latent during the more recent history of the armies of independent Arab states. Whereas Muhammad Ali, Viceroy of Egypt during the first half of the nineteenth century, made the army the instrument of modernization and change, the British who occupied Egypt in 1882 modernized the army itself more thoroughly. While the country was under British control, however, the incipient native military establishment was rigidly controlled and therefore confined to its police function. But the moment British control ended and general British influence receded from Egyptian national politics, the function of the army officer, now recruited largely from the rising native urban and semi-urban classes, became uncertain.

If the function of any army is to train, prepare, and organize for war or the possibility of war, for defense of the nation against invaders and the maintenance of national security, there should be little scope left for its participation in domestic power struggles. Why, then, does an army seek or feel compelled to participate actively in such power struggles? One possible explanation is that put forward by Lucian Pye in *Armies in the Process of Political Modernization*. Mr. Pye argues that the army "is a modern-type institution in disorganized traditional societies" and that there is a "role the army can play in shaping attitudes toward modernity in other spheres of society."[3] What this assertion implies in the case of the U.A.R. is that there is disorganization of the traditional society; that the society aspires to become modern; and that the army can shape workable attitudes toward modernity. At the same time, Mr. Pye's proposition assumes (1) that an army regime is interested, once it accedes to political power, in modernizing the disintegrating traditional society, and (2) that there is a necessary and essential relationship between a military coup d'état and a revolution. If the society desires to become modern, why does it acquiesce in the leadership of a military power elite that is also highly authoritarian in its outlook? Without generalizing for all so-called underdeveloped countries, the case of Egypt and the U.A.R. is interesting.

For a long time in Egypt a monarch made decisions with the acquiescence and assistance of a small ruling class. So long as Britain was in Egypt, the monarch's choice of decisions was limited by the presence of British troops. Later, specifically between 1947 and 1952, the ruling class in Egypt could count on an efficient British-trained military establishment to sanction its policies whenever they met with popular resistance. What is interesting, however, is that the maintenance of an army even as small as Egypt's, say in 1950 (about 75,000 officers and men), was utterly out of proportion to the industrial resources of the country. This military establishment had to secure its supplies almost entirely from abroad, at great expense to the state. Much was contributed toward its maintenance by the postwar military aid programs of the powers, especially Britain. But economic development, industrialization, and social reform lagged behind to the point of contributing to the unpopularity of the existing ruling class and its eventual overthrow in 1952. The rise, then, of a few effectively organized groups that could challenge the authority of the established ruling class finally led to the breakdown of the traditional decision-making process. At the same time the principal beneficiary, in terms of political power, of the policy of maintaining a well-trained and equipped army was the army itself and militant revolutionary groups such as the Free Officers within it.

Under these circumstances a conspiracy of a new group among the army officers flourished. This group, led by Nasser, realized from the beginning that there was no need to provide new justifications for power. Its understanding of the traditional acquiescence of the masses was reassuring. Yet, in contrast to the old ruling class, this new power group was willing to make one crucial concession: to subsume, indeed champion, the aspirations of the small but vociferous rising urban groups in the political, economic, and social fields. In this respect, Nasser differs from a Shishakli, a Zaim, or a Bakr Sidki in the Middle East, and from a Trujillo, a Jiminez, and other Latin-American military *caudillos*. As the nucleus of the new power elite Nasser and his Free Officers Executive represented the highly-trained, politically motivated, nationalistically oriented, petty bourgeois revolutionary, in contrast to the old guard. Conveniently for the Nasser-led movement, the motivation of the Free Officers for status and national achievement coincided with that of the rising new social and economic classes in civilian society. Both groups were "outs" in relation to the ruling class; both sought to become "ins" or at least to influence the ruling class.

What is interesting about Nasser as a conspirator, however, is his refusal to permit any arrangement with civilian groups of similar political orientation before the coup. The Free Officers thus acceded to power without the active support of a single civilian group in Egyptian society, although the prolonged (1947–52) political agitation of some groups—the Muslim Brethren, the Socialists, the Communists—against established authority contributed to the weakening of the old regime. Whereas Ataturk, for example, in Anatolia recruited and organized local committees of national resistance throughout the countryside before his successful take-over, Nasser did nothing of the sort beyond his secret recruitment of followers in the army.[4] There was practically no working relationship between the army Free Officers movement and a civilian base prior to the 1952 coup, other than a passive common sentiment of resentment against the existing regime.

The overthrow of the monarchy in July 1952, therefore, brought to power in Egypt a clearly military ruling class whose position was buttressed only by the threat of military force. It is doubtful whether the masses would have reacted at all differently if another non-military power elite had displaced the regime. The Free Officers were aware of this public apathy, and it was important for them only as it helped to insure that no rival *military* power group could emerge to challenge their authority. For the average Egyptian in July 1952 the Free Officers and their leader, Gamal Abdel Nasser, represented merely another ruler. But for the politically conscious Egyptian, Nasser and the Free Officers may very well have represented another ruler *with a difference*. The question, though, was whom did this new army power elite represent? This has been a difficult question to answer, because the Free Officers junta proceeded to control not only key government posts but also the various levels of administration, the economy, and education.

Did the accession to power of an army group reflect the aspirations of the larger forces of political unrest in the country or was it the mere satisfaction of ambition on the part of a few army officers? Some have argued that the Free Officers junta which came to power in Egypt in 1952 represented, or was the instrument of, a new *class* that sought political status and power, but for a long time was unable to achieve either; that this army group was the strongest element in the ranks of this new class.[5] But not all groups within this so-called new class (granted that it really existed in 1952) of intellectuals, professionals, and workers were agreed that the Nasser-led junta represented them. For example, not all writers, teachers, lawyers, and civilian engineers have willingly accepted army leadership or the pre-eminence of army officers in positions of power and political responsibility. The question, therefore, is whether the Army Officer Corps represented the best leadership for the social, economic, and political advancement of this new class, or whether its role as leader of the class that desired to effect organized change toward a more modern society was acceptable to members of that class. These questions are difficult to answer. Syrian political leaders, for example, were reluctant, immediately after Union with Egypt in February 1958, to hail army leadership as the panacea for all Arab political ills. This was especially the view of the intellectual cadre in Baath leadership.

The so-called intellectual core in the Baath hierarchy doubted the wisdom and efficacy of the National Union scheme to replace traditional party politics. They were also irked at their political displacement by what they considered inexperienced leadership. They resented the reluctance of the military regime to appreciate the fact that without the Baath, Union between Syria and Egypt never would have materialized. Intellectuals in Egypt, at least, while they rationalized the role of a highly disciplined and cohesive Army Officer Corps in expressing the interests of a "shapeless" mass which has existed as the "public" for some four thousand years, have, so far, been dubious of extending this role to the total control of all change in the future. They have recognized the fluidity of the situation in the country and the need for an experimental period of formative efforts. They have claimed that they are willing to accept a transition period during which the government must "think for the people" until the people learn how to do so responsibly on their own. This, the intellectuals hope, will come to pass after the public matures politically in the practical schools of the National Union scheme, national cooperatives, local councils, and the military service. Professionals and intellectuals in Egyptian society have further insisted that they are willing to defer to military leadership in this task because it has been able to provide, for the first time in the country's modern history, the psychological motivation of independence, dignity, and opportunity for constructive action. For this reason, many intellectuals have argued that they would be willing to be recruited into the service of the army power elite on its restrictive terms. This represents briefly the position of the majority of intellectuals and professionals in Egypt.

There is a smaller, more radical group among the Egyptian and Syrian educated classes who have insisted that the new power elite has not been using the intellectuals to the greatest advantage. The members of this group feel, and to some extent rightly, that young intellectuals today have greater popularity and command a larger following among the reading public than their predecessors of a generation ago. This, they contend entitles them to a larger share in the shaping of things to come, which in turn would help to recruit wider popular support for a basically army-dominated ruling class. Although they admit that the military regime has so far been preoccupied with the paramount problem of security and that of identifying and responding to public needs and demands, this group of intellectuals has been concerned over whether the regime will continue to be unresponsive to them after such issues are somehow resolved. This group feels that, without permitting wider participation especially from the literate and skilled classes in society, the junta now ruling the U.A.R. will merely continue to concentrate power in its own hands.

Again, such groups as students and academics generally have secretly deplored the fact that they were never permitted to mature into a political pressure group. Students in the Arab countries have always been a vociferous if not forceful group in mass politics. Today, moreover, they feel that before the revolution of 1952 it was the student organizations that really paved the way in making the public aware of the hollowness of the political parties, the King's usurpation of power, and other inadequacies of the old regime. They therefore believe they had the makings of a genuine social-political-economic pressure group, a leavening force of change. Recently, their scope of action has been greatly limited by state-created and state-controlled organizations. Also, among professionals, executives, engineers, and bureaucrats, there was initially some resentment when army officers were appointed in supervisory positions over them without displaying any relevant qualifications other than an army commission.

Such sources of friction as have been described are inevitable when an army group comes to power in a society in which there is already a sensitive and articulate intellectual and professional group, regardless of the extent of its cohesiveness or level of its organization. The expectations of the articulate groups are such that they are apt to resent their exclusion from positions of real authority. Consequently, it is not strange that the response of the intellectual and professional classes in the U.A.R. to army leadership has not always been unequivocal. Despite these undercurrents a close working relationship between the so-called new class and the army ruling group has been achieved for the first time. The army group seems to have deliberately utilized the services of qualified members of the professional class in the conduct of the state and the shaping of its institutions. How much responsibility in the making of decisions the military core of the ruling authority permits or will permit in the future to members of this class is another matter.

Despite the elaborate cabinet system in the U.A.R., the intricate array of committees and commissions, ultimate responsibility and power still rest in 1960 with President Nasser and the small coterie of original Free Officers closest to him. On the other hand, any civilian members of the Cabinet, however able and anxious to increase their share in power, have not been able to find easy access to civilian support. The National Union scheme of 1958–60 was strictly the creation and adjunct of the original army movement. Cabinet members have therefore been dependent for their continued participation in government on the sufferance of their Free Officer mentors. Gradually, their interests may well become so closely identified with those of the army officers in power that they will be ready to defend the *status quo* against attack from other quarters. Economic planning, industrialization, and the wider development of the media of communication may strengthen the alliance between economists, industrialists, investors, professional classes, those working in the various media of communication, and possibly labor, on the one hand, and the originally military regime on the other. In this sense, the Nasser forces may, if they are still in power during the coming decade, eventually create a class in U.A.R. society, other than the army, which they can rightfully claim that they represent.

So far, the power structure in Egypt still follows the lines of the alliances made when the conspiracy against the pre-1952 regime was still within the army. President Nasser has so far depended heavily for the formulation and execution of policy on a very few key ex-army officers, who were members of the original Free Officers Executive in 1949 and 1952. Among these have been his personal and close friend Abdel Hakim Amer, Commander-in-Chief, Armed Forces, and governor of Syria from December 1959 to the spring of 1960, and Abdel Latif al-Boghdadi, Vice-President of the Republic and Minister of Planning. Undoubtedly, Boghdadi represents theoretically the interests of the air force, if one can speak of air force interests separately from those of the army and other branches of the services. Kamal al-Din Husein, Central Minister of Education, and supervisor-general of the implementation of the National Union scheme in Egypt, has been a member of the inner circle who continues to exert much influence as supreme commander of the National Guard, a force estimated at between 60,000 and 100,000. Zakariyya Muhieddin, Central Minister of Interior, another member of the original junta, has been indispensable in decision-making because he has directed the extensive security apparatus of the state. Observers of the present Egyptian power elite would disagree about the position of ex-colonel Anwar es-Sadat, Secretary-General of the Islamic Congress and National Union.[6] Undoubtedly, his past connections with conservative religious elements and his access to the press—as one-time director-general of *Dar al-Tahrir*, the government publishing agency—have always afforded him some leeway with the President and his inner councils. Husein Shafei, a steady member of the original junta, has served as Central Minister of Social Affairs and Labor. He may be generally considered as representing the Cavalry-Armor Corps in the army. The Sabri brothers, ex-air force pilots, are also still members of the inner circle. Ali Sabri, as Minister for Presidential Affairs, has served as close adviser, confidant, and trouble-shooter for the President. His brother, Hasan Dhu' l-Fiqar Sabri, as Deputy Minister of Foreign Affairs, has supplied the liaison between the foreign office and the inner circle. A trained lawyer-diplomat, Dr. Mahmoud Fawzi, Minister for Foreign Affairs, has represented the interests of the elite in international councils abroad.

There has been an outer rim to the core of the Free Officers power elite whose members have shared significantly in the formulation of public policy by virtue of their personal relationship with the President. General Ibrahim, Minister of State for Defence, Colonel Kamal Rifaat (currently self-styled theoretician on socialism and Minister of State), Colonel Abdel Kader Hatim (President of the Egyptian Political Science Society, Chief Censor and Deputy Minister for Presidential Affairs), Colonel Tuaima (Minister of *Waqfs*), and others have been at one time or another influential in their performance of specific tasks for the President. To these should be added the Free Officers who have held portfolios in the Regional Cabinet for Egypt, the Southern Region of the Republic: Sarwat Ukasha, Abbas Radwan, General Nasser, Tawfiq Abdel Fattah, Fathi Rizq, and others. Furthermore, the appointment of Free Officers to key administrative and diplomatic posts, such as postmaster-general, director of Egyptian state railways, special ambassadors and consuls, personal advisors to the President (e.g., Colonel Mahmoud Riyad), directors of nationalized foreign concerns and firms, have provided the present leadership of the U.A.R. not only with assured control of policy but quite logically with a smooth system of communication among members of a group with similar training and understanding.

But the utilization of civilian professional and qualified personnel in advisory capacities and responsible administrative posts may eventually affect the composition as well as the mentality of the present elite. It has been evident so far that President Nasser has not been too anxious to continue drawing on the Army Officer Corps in recruiting executive personnel. Indeed, he has presumably been anxious to replace this source by a closer alliance with civilian groups among the professional and intellectual classes. His success in this respect will depend largely on his ability to concede a wider area of initiative to non-military members of the emerging ruling class. So long as he can rightfully claim certain achievements in behalf of his original constituency, the armed forces, so long as he can satisfy their reasonable expectations, President Nasser will not be jeopardizing his position by courting more closely potential civilian leadership.

In Syria, Northern Region of the Republic, on the other hand, recruitment to high offices of state has been crucial ever since the Baath, the party which helped bring about Union, was discredited in December 1959. It will be recalled that the resignation of Akram Hourani, Salah Bitar, Khalil Kallas, Abd al-Ghani Qannut, Mustafa Hamdoun, and Riyad al-Malki from the Central as well as Syrian Executive Cabinet, between September and December 1959, left at least five portfolios vacant. The resigning ministers were all Baathists. On the last day of his visit to Syria in the spring of 1960 President Nasser filled the five vacancies and appointed, for the first time since Union, a Minister of *Waqfs* for the Syrian Region and one for Supply. Seven new ministers, then, joined the Syrian Executive Cabinet in March 1960. Nasser's choice of personnel has left no doubt that active collaboration with the Baath has come to an end.

Of the seven new ministers, four were army officers. It should be noted that with the resignation or dismissal of four pro-Baathist officers by December 1959 the Syrian Cabinet was left with one officer, Tu'mah al-Awdat Allah (Municipal and Rural Affairs). In March 1960, four more new officers were added in key ministries of the Northern Region: Social Affairs and Labor, Agrarian Reform, Supply, and the newly created Ministry for Presidential Affairs. These were to be held by Colonel Akram Dairi, Colonel Ahmad Hneidi, Colonel Jamal Sufi, and Colonel Gadu Izz al-Din. All of these officers were 1947 graduates of the Syrian Military Academy; all attended Staff College in France and saw action in the Palestine War of 1948–49. The four held responsible positions in the First Army of the U.A.R., which implies that they were carefully selected at the recommendation of Commander-in-Chief Abdel Hakim Amer. Colonel Dairi was Chief of the *Deuxième Bureau* (Military Intelligence), First Army, and Director of Training and Organization. Colonel Hneidi was Commanding Officer, Armored Brigade, First Army, a staff officer in the Combined Chiefs of Staff office in Cairo prior to Union, and later Director General, Office of the Commander-in-Chief, Armed Forces, Damascus. Colonel Jamal Sufi was, until his appointment to the Cabinet, Commanding Officer, Coastal Guard Command, Syria. Colonel Gadu Izz al-Din was Commanding Officer, Southern Sector, First Army (on the Syrian-Israeli border). The three new civilians on the reconstituted Syrian Council of Ministers of March 1960 were civil servants and foreign service officers.

What is interesting is that no Syrians have until this writing been appointed to replace Hourani and Bitar on the U.A.R. Central Cabinet.[7] It is also significant that President Nasser had allegedly met with the Nationalist party leader Sabri Assali before making the March 1960 appointments. While President Nasser had been anxious to get Assali's cooperation since the break with the Baathists, it was doubtful whether Assali would ever agree to any rapprochement.[8] It is also evident that from the original group which agitated for and achieved Union with Egypt, only Colonel Abdel Hamid Serraj managed to survive and continue as head of the powerful ministry of interior.

The Chances of an Opposition

People usually ask: Has there been any opposition to President Nasser's regime? They rarely ask: Why has President Nasser's regime been seemingly acceptable to the country, at least in Egypt? No doubt there have been complaints about the regime ever since it assumed office; opposition is another matter. From the jokes circulating about the regime in 1958 and 1959 alone, one can glean a certain sophisticated reserve on the part of the public toward its claims. Yet the majority of Egyptians seem to have accepted President Nasser's regime as the most promising political development during the present century. Outside the professional groups mentioned in this chapter there has been little objection to the Army Officer Corps as the leader of the regeneration of Egyptian society. Regardless of the world forces and Big-Power political interests which brought the Arab countries into the forefront of world politics in the last decade, to the average Egyptian President Nasser has appeared as his first modern ruler to be taken seriously by the Great Powers.

Many traditional factors help to explain the ready acceptance of President Nasser and his ruling class of army officers by the average Egyptian in the 1950's, apart from what some may describe as practical advantages. In the Egyptian-Islamic tradition the emphasis on personal qualifications of the ruler was the sole important proposition of constitutional theory. Most Islamic constitutional lawyers, including such eminent figures as Mawardi and Ibn Khaldun, when they spoke of political leadership emphasized specific personal qualifications of the ruler. This emphasis was closely connected throughout Islamic history with military ability and prominence. There was rarely any serious discussion of any checks to be placed upon the ruler. Thus the ruler came to be accepted as the lawmaker, dispenser of justice, and chief executive. When he combined with these qualities that of military leadership, his position was still stronger. President Nasser appeared in 1952 and 1958 to satisfy both these requirements in the eyes of his public.

In the absence of highly organized and articulate group interests, especially in the rural areas, representation of the public interest was usually left to small but articulate urban groups, landed oligarchs, and bureaucrats. Most Egyptians since 1952 have claimed that the military power elite has been able to express the national and sectional interests of rural and urban, professional and agricultural, labor and business groups. They have claimed further that this elite has subsumed all these interests and aspirations in the personal leadership of Nasser and the Army movement which he led successfully against the old regime. At the same time, the techniques used by this elite for communication with the various groups have not all been modern or alien to the masses. Along with highly developed mass media, the army officers in power have retained the use of certain traditional techniques, such as the old-style court of the ruler held to hear complaints. Such were the various rallies and meetings between the leaders of the junta in the early days of the regime and those of the National Union under Kamal al-Din Husein and Kamal Rifaat as late as 1960.[9] Where there was practically no incentive for political organization before the military regime came to power, there was some organization afterward even though it was state-inspired and directed. Where the villager previously left the representation of his interests to the landlord-oligarch or religious leader (ulema), under Nasser he presumably expresses his interests through local and national organizations in which he aspires to participate actively.

Does the military group which now governs the U.A.R. represent the public interest? How does the public make its demands known to the rulers? It is difficult to give direct answers to either of these questions. Most Egyptians insist that the regime has represented the public interest. This, Egyptians contend, has been reflected in its policy of independence, industrialization, economic development, and agrarian reform. Most Egyptians, however, cannot say how the U.A.R. public makes its demands known to the ruling class. Some have argued that President Nasser simply knows the demands of the public; others have insisted that in a "period of transition" it does not matter whether there are mechanisms for making public demands known to the ruler. In 1958 Egyptians liked to refer to the Suez crisis of 1956 as an example of President Nasser's representing the public interest. They described at the time the aim of England, France, and Israel to destroy President Nasser's regime as short-sighted because it would have made no difference in Egyptian attitudes toward the West.

One is left with the impression that a charismatic leader is more important in Arab politics than the mechanisms, checks and balances that loom large in Western political theory, because the type of leadership has always been more important in Arab societies than the type of political institutions. The old concepts of *Ra'is* (Chief) and *Za'im* (Leader) in tribal and other institutions can until this day command a great deal of status and respect. The tradition of centralized authority in Egypt especially breeds charismatic qualities in the ruler, whoever he may be, who alone can meet the expectations of his subjects. The remoteness and unlimited authority of the ruler has been so pronounced in Egypt that it is reflected in the richness of Egyptian folklore. Awe and fear of authority as well as political submissiveness are enshrined in daily sayings in current usage: "Your governor is your lord," "Fortunate is the one who has a *naqib* [representative of families descended from the Prophet] for an uncle." "If you are saddled with a tyrant, humor him." "The reward of serving the Turks faithfully is a belting." The relation of subject to ruler could not be better expressed.

More important is the proposition that in the pre-World War II period, and as far back as the nineteenth century, the military caste, or elite, was associated with the ruler but not necessarily with the national aspirations of "out" groups. By the 1950's the military establishment in many Middle Eastern countries came to be significantly identified with the spirit and aims of nationalism, which it has constantly invoked whenever it has assumed a position of political leadership. The Army Officer Corps in Egypt, Syria, and Iraq has, within the past decade, destroyed the political power of those groups which the public identified with tyranny, rid the country of foreign occupation, and embarked upon some measure of social and economic reform. There has thus developed a closer affinity in nationalist aspirations as well as interests between the new power elite of army officers and the rising dissatisfied groups in society.[10]

Egyptians, moreover, have recently argued that when colonialism arrived in Egypt and Syria there was already a Western-educated class of citizens who aspired to participate in politics as part of their commitment to become modern. Foreign control, however, thwarted the initial efforts and frustrated the aspirations of this incipient class. Among its members, they contend further, one must include the army officers, who were just as committed to modernization through industrialization, economic and social reform, and the creation of more secular institutions.[11] Although one can still include the religious leader, the landowner, and the bureaucrat in any pyramid of power or ruling class in the U.A.R. today, it is obvious that these groups are no longer at the apex of the pyramid. They continue to exert a degree of influence in U.A.R. society, but the revolutionary army officers, together with their allies among the more radical Nationalist professional groups, who are also perhaps more class-conscious, have moved to the apex. Whether the alliance of the military with these professionals will prove too radical in its policies for the seemingly conservative army power elite remains to be seen. Meanwhile, the search for an organization in depth to link military rulers with the masses has continued. One cannot overlook the possibility that if such an organization in depth were ever to materialize it might provide the basis for more differentiated associations of interest.

Another reason for the acceptance of the military regime by the Egyptian people during the past eight years is more intangible but no less cogent. It pertains to the internal moral and social crisis that Egyptian as well as Arab society elsewhere has experienced since independence. Is there anything for an Egyptian to defend? Why should he, if there is? Closely connected with this has been the psychological issue of security. In what may perhaps be the highest achievement in modern playwriting by a contemporary Arab author, Yusuf Idris in *The Critical Moment* (*Al-lahza al-hariga*) (Cairo, 1958) begins with a brilliant exposition of the average Egyptian's concern with economic security in terms of a minor position in the government; his fear of military service; his alienation from any feeling of identity with the state; his plain cowardice. Thus, in the play, the son addresses his mother:

You people have taught us cowardice, fear. You permitted the world to ride us like horses, and defeat us. Mothers abroad carry their own rifles in defense of their countries. . . . You here want to break our spirits. You live in humiliation and wish us humiliated too.

In spite of the staggering economic odds, this generation, represented by Idris, has until recently expected army leadership to face this crisis squarely, if not resolve it. Having been humiliated themselves as army officers in battle, members of the military ruling class appeared initially sensitive to this need.

In Egypt since 1955, the chief vehicle for vigorous and responsible citizenship training has been the rigidly enforced military service law. Until the promulgation of the Military Draft Law in 1955, military service was not an experience shared by every able-bodied male Egyptian. Indeed, until 1947 there was no uniform military draft law. Even then payment of *badaliyya,* or a fee of up to £E20, waived actual service for many Egyptians. Only those who could not afford it among peasants and the poorer urban classes usually served. Under Law 505/1955, the military regime instituted a more uniform draft law which did away with the old payment in lieu of service. Consequently, there have recently been military draftees who were university graduates, serving eighteen to thirty-six months in the armed forces, National Guard, or the police forces. On the other hand, the need for technical and special skills in the armed forces tended to place secondary school and university graduates in a favorable position. Holders of university and technical degrees began to receive direct commissions, together with a variety of benefits introduced by the regime to attract better people into the services.

In a few years the Nasser regime has managed to create a new attitude among youth toward military service. The author can still remember ten years back when a middle or upper-class youth viewed military service as strictly the job of the illiterate and impoverished *fellah,* or peasant. By 1959, however, he was beginning to take the service in his stride and, to some extent, accept it as a national duty. The possible future of such changes in attitude could be significant for education, citizenship, and politics.

Because there has recently been an influx of better educated draftees into the Armed Forces, the regime has had to improve the standards of the military academies from which come the career officers. In recruiting cadets, Egyptian authorities have continued to discriminate against members of the old aristocracy in favor of small-town and village middle-class elements. But they have continued to honor an old unwritten rule of favoring sons of career officers. At the same time, the Nasser government has raised salaries and increased fringe benefits in order to make a military career more attractive. It has expanded facilities in Abbasieh and Heliopolis by introducing a more comfortable and dignified standard of living for the cadets.

As to why young men in the U.A.R. today go into the military academy, high-ranking army officers have listed three principal motivations in this order: security, prestige, and tradition. One of the Undersecretaries of War in 1959 seemed to accept the author's suggestion of additional motivations, based on contacts with a variety of young officers: (1) special privileges and increased pay under the present army-supported regime, (2) expanded job opportunities for an army officer or ex-officer on resignation of his commission. Recognizing that they form the major base of the support for the Nasser regime, young Egyptian and Syrian cadets are likely to view an army officer's career as leading to more powerful positions in government and to more prestige in society.

At the same time, Egyptian and Syrian youth have identified the army with a tradition, brief as it may be, of leadership in the nationalist cause and the movement for social change. In contrast to the traditional lack of civic spirit among civilians, the army officer today can claim a share in the leadership which aims to harness natural and human resources for purposeful change. It is enough for an intensely nationalist Egyptian or Syrian youth that the army officer has recently been associated with the forces of advancement.

The core of the Nasser-led Free Officers in power today exert total power, and influence all the institutions of the U.A.R. This does not mean that the military power elite has replaced all existing institutions at all levels of society by new ones of its own design. Its power is limited more by exogenous forces, the influence of power politics and Middle Eastern power rivalries, than by indigenous forces. The military regime's articulation of public desires and aspirations has so heightened public expectations, however, that very soon indigenous forces may also limit the power of its leaders, or at least influence the use of this power. So far, though, these rulers decree laws, and are answerable for their actions and behavior only to their own peculiar code, inspired and supervised by President Nasser. And yet so long as they propose to transform society from a backward traditional one to a modern industrialized and economically viable one, army officers in power manage to capture the imagination of the masses. It is no use deploring the authoritarian methods used by the military regime, for they are indigenous to the society. President Nasser was perhaps both shrewd and sincere when he reminded U.A.R. citizens that the democracy of the West with its intricate institutions is based on a political philosophy peculiar to the West. He has constantly emphasized the idea that whatever political system may emerge in the U.A.R., it must be conditioned by local circumstances, "our existential situation" (*min waqi'ina*), as he called it—preferably what *he* defines as "local circumstances." It is possible that President Nasser has read Barbara Ward's remark, "Liberal, humane society in the West has not entirely abandoned its metaphysical beliefs. But the institutions of liberal society have been transplanted to Asia with no links to any great religious tradition."[12]

Some will argue that there has been more Nasserite propaganda through the controlled mass media of the U.A.R. than actual planning for economic and other development. Even if this were true, there has been more substantial communication with the public about such issues than there was during the pre-1952 regimes. This in itself may constitute some systematic plan for "political socialization."[13] Even the elite-oriented torrent of ideological discussion in the press, pamphlets, cheaply priced popular books and magazines in the past eight years has been in itself a new preoccupation for most Egyptians. It would be indeed strange if a military ruler were eventually to provide the proper climate as well as training for political debate.[14]

It is not enough, therefore, or is actually misleading, to speak only of the present military ruling class, for there are other potential ruling *groups*. The commitment of the ruling army officers to modernize U.A.R. society through industrialization, education, universal military training, and general economic and social reform and development should logically encourage the emergence of new groups demanding status, economic benefits, and power. Industrialization, if not monopolized by the state, might create a class, even though small, of industrialists, highly skilled technicians, engineers, managers, and executives, a larger class of industrial workers, and a more purposeful intelligentsia. Agrarian and social reform in rural communities may give rise to a group of scientifically oriented farmers who not only own small tracts of land but manage them on modern lines. The political tasks the Free Officer leaders have chosen to perform since 1952 permit speculation along these lines.

The future proliferation in the U.A.R. of such groups as described above, however, does not necessarily mean the achievement of a stable political system. In Syria, for instance, there was a great advance in education, commerce, business and managerial skills, but very little toward the establishment of a stable state. The traditional religious and tribal leadership, the highly personal type of leadership in the early political groupings of the independence period, and the more recent populistic-charismatic type of army leadership reflected in a series of army coups d'état (1949–54) have not been conducive to collective social endeavor in Syria and the other Arab countries, or to the crystallization of a generally accepted and understood concept of public authority. It is this gap between personalized leadership and publicly sustained authority which President Nasser and his colleagues must bridge if their revolution is to have a lasting and beneficent effect on U.A.R. society.

Traditional Islam, it should be pointed out, provided in the past a religious hierarchy, an extensive bureaucracy, and to some extent an integrated political community. In 1960 the impact of outside forces as well as indigenous attempts at secular change and reform have produced disparate levels of political orientation and behavior. Earlier attempts by Arab leaders to modernize their societies did not succeed in breaking down the traditional ethic and institutions. On the contrary, these unsuccessful experiments, especially in the 1930's, led to such strong fundamentalist movements as that of the Muslim Brethren. The forceful pace, since 1952, of the military regime in the U.A.R. toward eventual industrialization may break down the older ethic. What is not clear is whether it will lead to more stable secular institutions.[15] The author doubts the adequacy of a developmental theory with empirical content to provide the basis of a stable modern polity in the U.A.R. without the commitment of both leaders and followers to certain values that are commonly associated with a secular political system.

Undoubtedly the basis of political legitimacy in Egypt and the U.A.R. has changed as the religious base has been undermined, though not completely rejected. Legitimacy is gradually becoming contingent on some representative character and some positive performance by the ruling class. The army regime in the U.A.R. is still in a formative stage, and criteria by which the public may judge it are not yet clear. But it can be said that its achievements in education, economy, and social reform have so far been meager, and that members of the political community have reached no agreement on fundamental principles, practical goals, or the means to achieve them.

The new army rulers have been careful to avoid the indiscriminate borrowing of foreign political institutions, the extreme formalism of which has been tempered to Middle Eastern conditions as these rulers see them. The highly personalized conception of the ruler *qua* hero is still very much in evidence. The regular reader of any U.A.R. newspaper is constantly reminded of the age-old Arab-Islamic relationship between subject and ruler when he finds the press abounding with resolutions by associations, trade unions, schools, university faculties, and student organizations, passed to greet the "leader-hero" (*al-zaim al-batal*), who in 1960 happens to be Gamal Abdel Nasser, and to record their undying allegiance (*Bay'a*) to him on this or that occasion. This highly personalized adulation for President Nasser has by no means been palatable to all Egyptians or Syrians. Some of the politically more articulate U.A.R. citizens have already sensed grave danger in the fact that the whole population depends on the actions and thought—perhaps whim—of one man. These elements will not be satisfied until some broad principles of policy emerge.

The loyalty, however, of the Army Officer Corps in the

United Arab Republic has been so far to President Nasser. In spite of his efforts to divest his presidential office of military overtones, Nasser's political clientele still consists largely of army officers. Their experience with the Muslim Brethren, for example, soon after the coup (1952–54) strengthened the Free Officers' reliance on army officers for the maintenance and security of their regime. Thus President Nasser has continued to let the military group be the supervisor of all political organization and the *avant-garde* of centrally instituted change. Economic planning, political organization for the masses, education, social affairs and labor, national guidance, and military training are all aspects of national life which have largely, if not solely, been controlled by members of President Nasser's Free Officers Corps.

To sum up, in July 1952 the army appeared to be everything to all men. It consolidated its power partly by sharing the common Egyptian feeling that things were bad and it was time for a change, and partly because it sympathized with the desire of politically conscious but suppressed groups for modernization. In this general sense, all radical and nationalist elements in Egypt were at that time willing to be loyal to the army-led regime.

Similar expectations in Syria centered around the Baath party and its followers. Union with Egypt in February 1958 meant defeat of the local Communist party and destruction of conservative political groups seeking political accommodation with monarchist Iraq; it meant the triumph of the Baath and its Pan-Arab socialist program. The Baath mistakenly counted on the certainty of its own natural political pre-eminence in a United Arab Republic. This gross miscalculation cost the Baath its political life in the U.A.R. twenty-two months after Union with Egypt. The Baath, which helped certain elements in the Syrian army into political importance, lost out to them as soon as they came under more direct Egyptian military control toward the end of 1959.

9. The Army in Politics: Conclusions

THE OLD ORDER is dying rapidly in the Arab countries of the Middle East. It has not been completely replaced, and only foolish prophecy would dare describe what the new order will be. The internal power struggle in these countries revolves around the question: Who will control and direct the forging of the new order? As Robert Stephens put it:

. . . The political evolution of the Middle Eastern states also forms part of a bigger historical development: the adjustment of Islamic society and other old established non-European civilizations to the impact of the scientific techniques and political and moral concepts of the Western world. This process has been going on for several decades at a varying pace and is now going forward faster than ever before. Consequently, the whole Islamic world from Morocco to Indonesia is in the throes of one of the deepest crises in its history.[1]

The military establishment in many Muslim countries—Turkey, Pakistan, Indonesia, the Sudan, Egypt, and Iraq—has recently taken the initiative to claim a pre-eminent role in this revolution against the old order. Nasser, the Free Officers, Nasserism if you will, is one of the contenders, perhaps the strongest, among the Arabic-speaking countries, for the leadership of the revolution of modernization. "For some reason," said Gamal Abdel Nasser earlier in his political career,

238

it seems to me that within the Arab circle there is a role, wandering aimlessly in search of a hero. And I do not know why it seems to me that this role exhausted by its wanderings, has at last settled down, tired and weary, near the borders of our country and is beckoning to us to move, to take up its lines, to put on its costume, since no one else is qualified to play it.[2]

It is not only Egypt to which he refers as the one "qualified to play" this role, but more specifically to the army elite, because elsewhere he has said:

The army is the shield [*dar*'] of Egypt. . . . It carries the responsibility of a heavy and difficult duty . . . the task represented in its defense of the nation against all external foes . . . the defense of the nation against internal exploitation, and domination.[3]

Many students of the Arab world have contended that Nasser and the Free Officers began their regime with no fixed ideas about a political system. This may be to some extent a valid contention. It is nevertheless misleading if one overlooks the vague yet moving idea in the minds of these officers of a powerful regenerated Arab socialist militarist state. President Nasser has unrelentingly reminded his U.A.R. and other Arab audiences:

We want to build a new society, to change the known reactionary and opportunist society we were used to. . . . We want a society which aims at cooperation, work, and productivity. . . . We want to build a cooperative society; not an exploitative one . . . [a society] for the welfare of the group.[4]

Francis Bertier, another commentator on the Nasser regime, has argued that "The officers of the junta had no acquaintance whatsoever with the practical aspects of political life; only theoretical notions expounded by the Wafd and leftist press in Egypt; recollections of political demonstrations during their student days before the war."[5] This view is somewhat exaggerated. The survival and relative stability of the regime from 1952 to date is evidence that the members of the Free Officers Executive at least were politically shrewd and highly practical.

For a group of conspiring army officers to make the "right" or popular political commitments of independence (*istiqlal*), industrialization (*tasni'*), and Arab nationalism (*al-qawmiyya al-arabiyya*) reflects more than haphazard choice.

Mr. Albert Hourani, one of the ablest students of the Middle East, has remarked aptly that the new regimes in that region "rest on a combination of army officers, officials who have mastered the technique of modern administration, and educated nationalists."[6] Another writer has suggested that at present, "the army remains the only instrument of popular aspiration that is capable of bringing about social democracy."[7] By accepting this role of innovators, developers, and guardians of the national conscience during the 1950's the Army Officer Corps in Egypt, Iraq, Pakistan, and elsewhere in Asia has introduced an image of the future to which the masses who seek emancipation must aspire. But in doing this, the Army Officer Corps has endangered its chances of continuing to rule without some proof of effective performance toward these professed goals. President Nasser has claimed:

Our ultimate aim is to provide Egypt with a truly democratic and representative government, not the type of parliamentary dictatorship which the Palace and corrupt "pasha" class imposed on the people. . . . We want to make sure that in the future senators and deputies will serve all the Egyptians rather than a few.[8]

Meanwhile the military rulers have demanded that the people sacrifice personal freedom during a transition period until conditions for a truly representative and equitable political system—industrialization, economic and social reform, higher standards of living—can be achieved. So far, the ruling Free Officers have partially legitimated their centralized authority and power by the use of plebiscites, or as Mr. Lerner put it, by the use of mass communication media to arrive at consensus without the active participation of the people.[9]

Two propositions emerge from the foregoing discussion: (1) The army has recently emerged as the most progressive element in Arab society today, as the Army Officer Corps appears to be the most willing among Arab groups to seek empirically rational solutions to outstanding problems—to resolve situations on the basis of fact. (2) The Army Officer Corps has appeared as the group most inclined to push Arab society into the modern age by its serious commitment to secular policies and institutions. In the opinion of the leading and most colorful Egyptian journalist:

The regime will not countenance or encourage the use of religion in the old conservative way for political gain. . . . Yet the regime accepts the cultural value of religion and its significance as the moral basis of society. The regime, however, is definitely committed to a secular concept of national identity, loyalty, and legitimacy. It must nevertheless use religion [defer to it] in order to retain contact with the masses, until the desired standards of education and economic improvement are achieved.

Although this is not a totally unequivocal statement, the same journalist asserted:

The Anglo-French attack on Suez in 1956, with its aim to overthrow President Nasser, was hopeless. Even if President Nasser were the worst dictator, people would have stood by him because of past recollections of British and French rule, and because he is to them the most progressive ruler modern Egyptians have known.[10]

It is also clear that members of the military power elite in the U.A.R. as well as in Iraq and Pakistan (but according to all reports, not the Sudan) have viewed their role in society as a progressive one.[11] A cursory examination of military publications in Egypt alone is enough to convey the intensity of this self-assumed role. *The Armed Forces (Al-quwwat al-musallaha)*, published by the Department of Public Affairs, Armed Forces, *The Army Magazine (Magallat al-gaish)* published by the army in Abbasia Barracks, and the *Military Magazine (Al-majalla al-askariyya)* published in Damascus GHQ, as well as Air Force and other specialized military pub-

lications, are full of articles on nationalism, responsible citizenship, and national goals.

Not only has the Army Officer Corps in the U.A.R. been
conscious of its progressive role in the political and economic
evolution of the Arab world, but it has proposed to impose
change on the members of a society who have long lacked
organization and civic spirit. It has sought to create a new
society, more or less by command from the top. This seems a
bold and at times immature attitude. Yet, after viewing the
record of "representative systems" hastily transplanted into
the Arab countries during the inter-war period, one cannot
fairly deny the army leaders the benefit of the doubt. Unfortunately, too much was expected previously from representative
governments in the Middle East once they had been formed at
the peak of nationalist agitation. There was every reason for
these governments to fail, because representative institutions
were mere transplantations without the necessary social or
economic base. It was obvious to honest observers that these
representative institutions were mere forms at best, and at
worst means for the usurpation of authority. Such systems in
the Arab states did not expand the political experience or
participation of the public, nor did they provide any organizational strength in the political structure of their societies.

As was noted in Chapter 4, the army in 1952 was the only
national institution in Egypt able to provide order in a
politically disorganized society. It is proposed here, then, that
the Army Officer Corps was at that time the only group in
Egyptian society, with the exception perhaps of the Muslim
Brethren, that had sufficient organizational strength, discipline,
and highly motivated leadership (the conspiratorial leadership
of Nasser) to conduct the affairs of the state. The members of
the national Officer Corps as individuals, and the army itself
as an organizational structure, appeared in Egypt then as the
group best equipped to resolve political chaos. The small
group of the Free Officers Executive subsequently showed that
they could acquire enough organizational strength, unity of

purpose, and enough popular support to counterbalance all other groups in the political arena.

The organizational ability of the Officer Corps in the U.A.R. is a matter of record. They have been able to create and lead mass organizations, to establish a disciplined hierarchy and a dependable chain of command. All these are commendable attributes in any Arab political community. What has not been readily apparent so far is the ability of the new leadership to act as a dynamic social force capable of leading Arab society in reform and development.

The leaders of the military regime in the U.A.R. have claimed that the Officer Corps constitutes the nucleus of a constructive force which would spearhead national regeneration and development. So far, in Egypt at least, this assumed position of leadership has been tolerated and in many respects accepted. Egyptians, but not necessarily Syrians, have realized that a return to the old civilian instrumentalities of representative government would be both impractical and undesirable. Moreover, the failure of parliamentary systems before the military came to power has indicated to them that genuine representative government in the Arab countries is not yet feasible. It is this realization which today presents the politically sophisticated members of the Arab community with a choice between two alternatives: the regimented political tutelage of a military power elite with the hope of future development in political integration and possibly freer institutions; or the probability of political instability, disintegration, and confusion. Many educated Egyptians have felt (publicly at least) that this period of transition is a fair risk to take, even though there is no guarantee that it will ever end.

At the same time Nasser forces have not been unaware of the necessity of a strong, broadly based organization which would provide continuity and stability to any new order they may establish in the U.A.R. They have recognized that the lack of organizational depth rendered ephemeral all previous parliamentary regimes in the Arab world and led to their downfall. No one will deny, however, the difficulty of building such an organization, for it is the central problem of contemporary Arab politics. Lacking a tradition of and an infrastructure for representative government, the U.A.R. and other Arab states have suffered from an institutional weakness which cannot be remedied easily. More difficult for any Arab government to master will be the process of social communication that is essential to the proper functioning of representative government. On the other hand, the Nasser-led power elite in the U.A.R. may choose to continue to forcefully mobilize the masses as it appears to be doing at present.

The Free Officers in the U.A.R. must also find a constituency for their modernizing "New Deal." Despite the Army Officer Corps' vanguard position as a professional class providing political leadership for a guided revolution aiming at long-term change, the power elite within the Corps will have to create a social class on which to center its organizational strength. Recruitment into the ruling class, as was noted elsewhere, has so far been largely confined to the Army Officer Corps; and attempts to allow intellectuals, for example, into its inner circle have often been unhappy.[12] The ultimate question for the army in politics, therefore, is whether the army junta will be able to consolidate its power through the army alone. Ataturk, we are told, divorced the army from politics by the establishment of the Republican People's party.[13] Recent studies, however, show that the political significance of army officers in the Turkish National Assembly had never been really diminished and that, in fact, it has been increased lately.[14] President Nasser, on the other hand, has been trying to create a civilian political instrument to replace the army. His chances of success in Egypt may be greater than in Syria.

A commonly held view has been that the National Union experiment in the U.A.R. is in effect the creation of a revolutionary chief, President Nasser. The Baathists outside the U.A.R. especially have charged that the National Union has so far been nothing more than an expression of President

Nasser's ideology.[15] This narrow conception of the attempt to create a civilian political instrument implies, of course, rigid control by the military cadre, a consequence of which is to deprive the nation of the services of many moderate and conservative elements. It is not at all clear, however, that the moderates and conservatives in the U.A.R. can provide the beginnings of a political organizational structure for society, because the Arabs have traditionally viewed the state as an entity completely separate from themselves:

The truth of the matter is that we [the Arabs] have inherited from the past a feeling that the state is separated from us; that it is imposed upon us; and that we have no influence upon it or interest in it; . . . the simple individual in our Arab society feels that the state is a powerful and distant thing and that he must accept its rulings without hesitation, pay taxes without argument, and not ask anything in return . . . that he has a duty toward it, but no rights forthcoming from it.[16]

Considering the past failure of experiments in representative government, and the lack of an economic and social base for institutional reform, the army elite thus appear to have chosen the revolutionary method of imposed change. The Army Officer Corps was a usable agent in this policy and to a great extent continues to be. To deplore this situation is unrealistic. Yet in contrast to older regimes, that of President Nasser has perceived and communicated to the public a desirable future in terms of what the public good is, or ought to be. To get public agreement on the nature of this public good by the well-tried methods of Western political processes is impossible in the Arab countries. But to activate change toward achieving such a consensus in the future, some would agree, is in itself important.

Ishaq al-Huseini, a prominent literary critic and contemporary Arab thinker, deplored in *Azamat al-fikr al-arabi* (The Crisis in Arab Thought) the uncertainty, confusion, and haphazardness of Arab thought and national endeavor. Huseini's work represents the quandary of the intellectuals, who never really came to grips with the impact of modern thought and science on their society. For a long time there was no relation between the concerns of the Arab intellectual and practical problems of Arab society. The new power elite of army officers, with its commitment to such political tasks as economic development, modernization, and systematic politicalization of town and country, may for the first time provide the basis for some degree of political integration and, consequently, of consensus.

So far, however, no one can claim that these weaknesses and deficiencies in the political system have been or will be overcome by political revolutions led by the military. We may be justified in hypothesizing that the army in Egypt since July 1952 has achieved a political revolution from the top by a swift seizure and consolidation of power, quickly followed by the elimination of all possible opposition. Its accession to power was not accompanied by extensive persuasion, negotiation, or political compromise, which might have ensured a political climate of voluntary discipline and support. There was, to be sure, dissatisfaction and unrest among the masses below, but they were not permitted to develop into a mass revolutionary movement. Instead, the junta chose to regiment a mass following under a plan of its own choice.

For similar reasons formalism in U.A.R. politics may be disturbing. But it is inevitable until a stable social structure emerges to buttress the political system, whatever it may be. D. W. Brogan in *The Free State* argues that "Integration of national life is usually the result of the operation of free institutions, not regimentation." It is doubtful whether this was ever true in the Arab countries in the past. Before 1952 there was no real opposition to the established political system. In Iraq, on the other hand, opponents of the regime were usually jailed. There was thus no alternative government; violence or military take-over were the only real alternatives. Under these circumstances political disintegration under the impact of internal unrest and external pressure was probable, for the performance of the old political aristocracy was not such as to provide political organization and stability. Fundamentalist militant mass movements and radical leftist revolutionary groups might have conceivably benefited from such political chaos and unrest. The army power elite, at least in Egypt, has proved a stabilizing group with enough national motivation to effect some permanent political change and make a beginning in economic and social change. At the same time, its cohesiveness and nationalist orientation have diminished the chance that leftist and fundamentalist groups may attain power.

Guy J. Pauker, a prominent student of Southeast Asia, and especially of the role of the military in politics in the new countries there (Indonesia, Burma), admonishes judiciously:

Our liberal tradition makes it repugnant to contemplate regimes controlled by military elements rather than by the civilian instrumentalities of representative government, but in Southeast Asia today the choice is not between two equally real alternatives. Recent developments indicate that the hope for genuinely representative government is premature. The choice rather is between some form of tutelage that would leave the future open for development in a democratic direction, or political disintegration, economic stagnation, and social confusion that would lead the peoples of Southeast Asia toward communism. Contemporary history gives strong evidence that totalitarianism can be destroyed only by warfare, whereas military regimes do not preclude developments in the direction of constitutional democracy.[17]

Lacking proper political organization and being unable to break through the old political structure, the civilian professional and commercial groups in Egypt and elsewhere in the Arab countries were superseded by the military. Faced with a variety of political, social, and economic problems, these new groups not only disagreed with the old leaders but were themselves unable to agree on the fundamentals of a political and social system, let alone the means to effect change. The army officer class, on the other hand, could claim to have been the first agent of change and innovation in the area since the early nineteenth century. This claim found increased support in the gradual waning of civilian authority in the Middle East following the break-up of the Ottoman Empire in 1918. The frequent collapse of regimes in the modern period (1935–60) therefore left no civilian alternatives for succession.

The recurrence of military coups d'état, and the instances in which former army officers have acquired the role of political leadership, assuming presidencies of republics and, in some cases, imperial thrones, clearly indicate the significance of the role of the military in the modern political life and development of some Middle Eastern countries. Besides conducting two military coups in Turkey (1908, 1909), Kemal Ataturk, an army officer, founded the present Turkish Republic. Reza Pahlevi, a colonel in the Persian Army, founded the Pahlevi dynasty in 1925. There have been eight coups d'état in Iraq so far, seven between 1936 and 1941, and one in July 1958. Neighboring Syria has had five coups between 1949 and 1954, Egypt two (1881, 1952), the Sudan one (1958), and Pakistan one (1958). In Lebanon the army had occasion to act as a caretaker in a period of political crisis (September 1952), and its former chief of staff is, at this writing, President of the Republic. Elements in the Jordanian army were implicated in the abortive attempt to overthrow King Husein in 1957, which was followed by a purge of politically suspect officers.

This presentation has stressed the abuse of the complex processes of representative government by unscrupulous political leaders, the absence of genuine political opposition, and the general lack of voluntary organized political expression. A pattern of latent underground conspiratorial opposition therefore emerged in many of these countries, which tended to produce violent change instead of a peaceful transfer of authority. Violence has not been due, as many believe, to the mere corruption of certain regimes. There is some corruption in all governments. It has been rather the result of the inability of these governments to formulate public policies in response to new demands. It has also been due to the lack of legal checks and balances by which public restraint of power could be peacefully exercised.

Whatever many Egyptians or Syrians may think of President Nasser and his ruling elite of army officers, they still feel that he has been able to discern what people want and act accordingly. On the surface, people claim they want freedom from foreign control; they want industrialization, regardless of whether this is brought about in what Westerners would call a democratic or an authoritarian way. If the very maintenance of the state is a major task of any ruler in these countries, one cannot fairly expect that political performance be judged by the democratic standards of political discussion and compromise.

Moreover, the struggle for power in the Middle East has been confined for many centuries to a small group of traditional elites, namely, ruling dynasties, religious hierarchies, and big landowners. These groups ruled while the masses placidly followed. There was rarely a conscious and deliberate attempt on the part of the rulers to extend political participation to a large section of the population. The consequent lack of public political experience invited two patterns of development: (1) expression of political disaffection through mass movements—usually inchoate or badly organized—rather than through highly organized interest groups; or (2) political change by violent and extra-legal means. Often those who introduced, or purported to introduce, political change have been army officers: Ataturk in Turkey, Reza Shah in Iran, Bakr Sidki in Iraq, Zaim and Shishakli in Syria.

Voluntary political association, however, is perhaps a uniquely Western notion. It is difficult to come by in the Middle East considering the region's cultural and traditional diversity, let alone its social and political heterogeneity. Agreement on the fundamentals for a more cohesive political culture, therefore, is apt to be imposed from above. Thus political behavior in Arab societies for a long time did not encompass well-organized interests which sought, through rational means, to influence the political process and public policy.

The more recent impact of Western technology, culture, and rule created two conflicting political trends: (1) resentment toward the West for its ascendancy and control, and (2) a desire to emulate the West's techniques and methods as quickly as possible. The inability of a public subscribing to an old, but different, established cultural tradition to assimilate Western ideas and institutions left the role of political leadership in a rapidly changing society to those who could subscribe to and capitalize on both of these trends simultaneously. The resulting dilemma and frustration of political leadership also led to a general discrediting of liberal constitutional ideas and forms in most of the Middle Eastern countries today. Instead there seems to be a popular inclination toward strong and efficient rule. Under these circumstances the Army Officer Corps has become a major source of leadership.

In their enthusiasm to achieve political as well as intellectual independence from the outside world, especially the West, the Arab countries have identified army leadership with the potential renaissance of past Islamic military power. At the same time, the army so far has been the only group in the Arab countries possessing the kind of organization and discipline required for quick and systematic action. When the cadre of political leadership in the army appeared to come from a younger age group, belonging to the nationalist generation, it was easily identified with the aspiring masses. The Army Officer Corps has thus easily assumed national leadership for reform and, together with other emerging professional and educational groups, it has become the new power elite. In Egypt the army regime has, moreover, a good record at least in the field of independence from foreign control: the Sudan agreement in 1953, the British evacuation agreement in 1954, and the arms deal with the Soviet bloc in 1955. It has also survived the concerted attack of Britain, France, and Israel in

1956, has continued to block the Suez Canal against Israeli shipping, and has managed to hang on to the Syrian Region of the Republic in the face of inimical Iraq.

As the new power elite, the Officer Corps considers itself the key factor in the forging of the new order in the U.A.R. This was made quite clear between December 1959 and March 1960, when the Free Officers regime did not tolerate continued rivalry from a well-organized and highly motivated political party in Syria, the Baath. But the military regime in Cairo has also been flexible in its policy. Although the popularity of President Nasser's government among the rest of the Arabs was not in 1960 as great as it was in 1955 and 1956, he has shown a willingness to adapt his policy toward the other Arab states sufficiently to avoid serious conflict. This was apparent especially after the rift between the U.A.R. and Iraq in 1959. The U.A.R. for a while appeared more flexible in its attitude toward Jordan, the North African states, and the West. The same flexibility has also prompted the army rulers in the U.A.R. to look more closely at their home policy in connection with development and reform.

At home the U.A.R. rulers have been faced with the problem of economic survival. They are not unaware of the potential danger of a population that multiplies at the rate of 500,000 per year, and continues to harbor some ten million unemployed citizens. Confronted by the eternal lack of enough cultivable land, incipient industrialization, and unfavorable trade conditions, the U.A.R. government realizes that it cannot hope to fulfill its public promises without outside help. To seek this outside aid at a time of tension between East and West is to invite problems, political and otherwise, at least as serious as those at home.

In the past, Middle Eastern rulers were primarily interested in building strong dynasties. This was true of the Ottomans in Turkey and of Muhammad Ali in Egypt. Hence they inevitably neglected the internal problems of societies over which they ruled, which led to social and economic unrest. Today, on the other hand, the military strong men who rule some Middle Eastern states have at least publicly disavowed dynastic ambitions. On the contrary, they claim that they will seek to build up the strength of their total societies by regenerating and developing their various resources. So far, at least in the U.A.R., President Nasser and his Free Officers have not been challenged in their assumed leadership of the reconstruction and development of Egypt and Syria. Whether they are well equipped for the task is another matter. It was indicated earlier in this study that in many respects they may be better equipped than other groups. But how much better, only time will tell.

There are indications, however, that the military leadership itself realizes that it is not self-sufficient for the task ahead. Recently, the U.A.R. rulers have been preoccupied with the problem of motivation for their citizens. They have felt that politically, as well as socially, Egypt at least will never be again what it was before 1952. Hence President Nasser's motto, "The new generation is the future, and the future is the new generation." For this reason, President Nasser formed in 1960 a Committee on National Education, whose task was to "create a new generation of youth, who understand the stage through which their nation is presently passing." To aid this Committee, the President also created a society of so-called savants or thinkers. The composition of the Committee is interesting. Among the members of this first committee of sixteen were such army officers as Kamal Rifaat, Salah Dasuqi, Hasan Saati (a leading Egyptian sociologist), and others. There were engineers (Samir Fahmi), religious conservatives (Abdullah al-Arabi), and powerful advocates of Egyptianization in arts and letters (Said al-Arian). Questioned on the program of the Committee, Salah Dasuqi explained that it was not established to evolve any political doctrine or theory. Rather it aimed to study existing principles in the U.A.R. as enunciated by President Nasser in his speeches. The primary function of the Committee was to discuss these principles and ideas of the President and present them in simplified fashion to the new generation. This was necessary, according to Dasuqi, so that the new generation would understand fully what the state stands for, what it is that the new generation must defend, and why. He also asserted that the Committee would serve as a guidance agency, not a propaganda bureau. Among the interests of the Committee was that of urging the younger generation to acquire practical education rather than the traditional theoretical training of the past.

Although nothing may come of these experiments in creating new attitudes of thought and behavior among the citizens of the U.A.R., they are still significant in themselves because they are novel to the Arab environment. One danger inherent in this type of guided intellectual and social activity, however, is the compulsion—due to fear or to hope of ingratiation—on the part of those involved to perpetuate the glorification of the leader, a practice which has been common to Arab societies in the past. Although one feels that there has been wider discussion of public issues in the U.A.R. today—through press, radio, and books—one also suspects that much of it has tended to create and perpetuate what Daniel Lerner has called the "Nasser syndrome." Much of this type of activity on the part of the rulers may have been directed at those among the intellectual and professional classes who could not be ignored, who had somehow to be convinced.

Recently, for example, the U.A.R. government decided to introduce television services into Egypt and Syria. It is not surprising that a ruling group so conscious of the importance of mass media should attach great importance to television. The low rate of literacy emphasizes the importance of a medium which is more impressive than the printed word and more easily understood by the average man. Nor is it surprising that the government has been willing to pay far higher wages to those trained in the manipulation of this medium than it would pay to many of its professionally trained citizens in other fields (economists, engineers, teachers). The regime's wider Arab policy interests have added to the significance of television. On the other hand, such a medium might help intensify the expectations of the audience—poor or rich, literate or illiterate—and increase the pressure on the rulers to perform effectively. It is therefore unfair to interpret the use of television as an instrument of further regimentation and control alone. It is certainly that, but it may also serve to promote the political integration of the community, diversify its interests and desires, and multiply its demands on the ruling class.

Although the press in the U.A.R. has so far been strictly censored and controlled (since May 1960 nationalized), its airing of general welfare problems may have a long-range effect. It was not common in Egypt in the recent past to discuss openly the problems of the Egyptian village. By 1960 the regime permitted—perhaps for reasons of its own—a leading weekly to write at length about "The Oppressed Village," exposing the myriad problems faced by the eighteen million rural Egyptians living in some 5,000 villages, from endemic disease, lack of electricity and drinking water to schools and sanitary conditions. This type of public discussion, controlled though it may be, can in the long run have far-reaching effects.[18] One of its most significant consequences has been the growing attitude among Egyptians that it is not merely "big" project plans that matter, but small ones as well. Many feel, for instance, that the doubling of the national income in Egypt will be meaningless without a rise in the income of individual citizens, especially the villagers. And they feel now more strongly than ever that "modern advancement" cannot be fruitfully concentrated in a few cities. Its dispersal throughout the population is necessary for survival.

Contrary to the situation in some countries of Southeast Asia (Indonesia and Burma), the army as a national institution in Egypt did not develop as a result of a nationalist war for independence. It was originally created by the dynasty or monarch ruling the country and developed to serve the ruler. The army in Egypt and Syria, however, had acquired by the end of World War II the necessary nationalist composition and orientation—a characteristic further sharpened by the Palestine debacle in 1948–49. In Iraq, the army came to power in July 1958 when the ability of the civilian politicians allied with the throne to make decisions was undermined. But the rise of the military to power in all these countries was made easier by its recent alignment and identification with the prevailing national interest, regardless of how vague or uncrystallized that may have been at the time. Yet, as Michael Howard said: "In states where no orderly tradition of power and obedience has yet been established military force is the final and sometimes the only arbiter in government."[19]

Does the army's seizure of power in Egypt in 1952 and the extension of its authority over Syria in 1958 imply, then, a mandate from the people of these two countries to rule? This question cannot be answered with a categorical negative on the basis of our Western concepts of legitimacy and representativeness. Together with the Army Officer Corps, the President of the U.A.R. has gradually permitted a narrow section of society—some members of the group of professionals and intellectuals, the bureaucracy, and religious leaders—to share in government, thus satisfying the only possibly articulate source of enlightened criticism. With the backing of some privileged members of these groups, President Nasser has been able to rule the passive masses, whose relative inertia made it easy to coerce them. It is not a particularly dangerous situation, for the idea of public restraint of power is still undeveloped among the Arab masses. In fact, it is less dangerous than the probable alternative of political chaos, for although the Islamic idea of an authority higher than temporal power exists, it does not yet have a social counterpart.

Consequently, the distribution of power still largely depends on the control of the means of violence, that is, the army, the politically capable elite of professionals, the bureaucracy, intellectuals and, in the Arab countries, religious leaders. In Iraq, until recently, there was a contest for power between an army-supported regime and an opposition supported by the People's Militia. In Egypt, there was initially some inter-service conflict between the army and the air force, while in 1958 a National Union popular mass organization to "plan interests" was being devised. In Jordan, a ten-year-old Palestine refugee group has been trying (with some outside help) to check the power of a monarch who has been ruling with the support of an army whose officers and ranks are of predominantly tribal stock. In the absence of any system of legal checks and balances, such conflicts must be fought out by extra-legal means.

In trying to telescope developments of many decades, sometimes centuries, into a short period, most army-based regimes in the Middle East as well as in other underdeveloped areas have tended to concentrate power in one man, or in an elite, without realizing the importance of developing stable political institutions. Faced with serious economic and social problems from overpopulation to the dire need of raising living standards, they have preferred to postpone political freedom indefinitely. Meanwhile, these regimes have not failed to support their total control of power with all the techniques available for manipulating the masses. Although, as was noted earlier, the military regime in the U.A.R. is making serious efforts to develop more broadly based political institutions, the crucial problem of agreeing on some idea of national identity, a concept of uniform loyalty, and a peaceful (non-violent) basis for legitimate power remains unresolved. As a leading Egyptian historian put it to the author recently, "It is immaterial whether the Corps of Army Officers constitutes a distinct ruling elite or not. The masses must somehow adjust. They never understood the significance of even incipient representative institutions."

Those of us who have recently visited and observed some of the Arab countries may argue that military regimes have infused into these societies a new sense of order and national pride, made more purposeful by extensive plans for economic development and internal reform. At the same time, close study of the structure and organization of these governments fails as yet to provide satisfactory answers to such questions as public responsibility and power, or to indicate more permanent characteristics of a stable political system. The ruler or "chief" continues to exercise almost unlimited authority, as in Iraq and Egypt. This, on the other hand, may be due to the relatively recent accession of the military to power in these countries.

That the U.A.R., or Egypt and Syria, will never be the same again as far as the political system or balance is concerned, no one can seriously doubt. This much of a revolution has occurred. But the claim of the army officers to be leading a revolution that will change the Arab political community and society has yet to be proved. In fairness to the present regime in the U.A.R., one must withhold final judgment until many more years have passed.

The present regime in the U.A.R. is, after eight years in power in Egypt and two in Syria, still largely army-supported. The increased number of army officers in the Cabinet, diplomatic corps, administration, and other executive positions, as well as in the National Union, supports this statement. The regime, though, has been urgently trying to broaden the base of its support through such devices as the National Union, National Cooperative unions, education, and military service. The method followed in these institutional devices continues to be one of absolute control and direction from the highest authority. It carries therefore the seeds of its own possible failure, because the rigid supervision of these institutional devices can cause revulsion and a recurrence of "silent conspiracy." A similar situation prevailed in Iraq before the July 14, 1958, army coup, in Jordan after 1951, and in Syria after 1949. The army leaders of the U.A.R. regime have mean-

while transformed themselves into a political interest group—
one could well agree with Michel Aflaq, one of the Baath
leaders, and say a political party—which has specific interests
it is now trying to foster and translate into public policy. In
doing so, the army leaders may well create the conditions for
a stable political system. On the other hand, they may pave
the way for future upheaval. It would be unwise, at this
time, to attempt any final assessment of the role of the military
in Arab politics, or to project current analyses into the future.

A final hypothesis about the phenomenon of the army in
politics in the Middle East is in order because it may be also
applicable to Pakistan and Southeast Asia. The politically
conscious members of Arab societies have felt during the past
ten to fifteen years the need for change. Old political systems
and politicians had been given a chance and failed. Gradually
the politically minded Arabs came to view the Corps of Army
Officers—the army in general—as the most modern, least traditional, and most cohesive institution. The army, at the same
time, acquired a similar image of itself. The public, therefore,
expected it to perform more efficiently than the previous
regimes. Considering the situation between Israel and the
Arab countries, the public felt, moreover, that in a time of
military threat the army would be the most competent group
to lead and defend Arab society. Members of the Army Officer
Corps, on the other hand, shared the intensified public feeling
of nationalism and desire for change and modernization. At
the same time, their acquisition of a political role was not repugnant to the Islamic environment. The competence of the
army officers in dealing with the leaders of the previous regimes, their versatility in communicating with the public, and
their apparent seriousness of purpose helped them further to
impress the public favorably.[20]

While the author cannot agree with the *Economist* that
"politics are dead in the Southern Region of the United Arab
Republic," or that "nothing seems to be happening," he must
endorse that paper's recent appraisal of President Nasser:

His inspirational method is not that of a hot-gospeller sweeping souls to revolutionary salvation. Over the years he has unrelentingly hammered his purpose into the minds of the people: Egypt must march boldly into the modern world. It is noticeable in little things that the message has got through.[21]

But even if among the "has-beens" of Egyptian politics there are those who still hope for the collapse of President Nasser and his regime, they are today perhaps resigned to the idea that both the man and his regime are firmly established. While at one point President Nasser appeared inclined to temper his revolutionary drive by relaxing some of the more stringent revolutionary controls, there are indications now that the movement toward a highly authoritarian system has gathered momentum.

As we have seen, the accession of the military to political power in Egypt was not a particularly revolutionary phenomenon in the annals of that country. National or foreign armies, especially when serving as arms of a ruling monarch or class, have always influenced and sanctioned the making of policy. The events of 1952 did not introduce a drastic change as regards the relationship between the average Egyptian and the decision-making process. It has also been suggested that this development was not alien to the Islamic tradition in the Arab countries. It may not be wrong, therefore, to conclude that citizens of the U.A.R. should settle for an improvement within the existing order. And since the existing order has shown a greater proclivity toward social improvement than any other previous order in Egypt or Syria, the hope might not be in vain.

Postscript

MIDDLE EASTERN politics are in a state of furious evolution, and all generalizations about their emerging patterns must be tentative and subject to constant revision in the light of events. Nevertheless, the author, writing this postscript early in 1961, does not feel compelled to modify the major findings of his analysis, first made in 1959–60. But as events progress it is becoming more apparent that the theoretical relationship between nationalism and constitutionalism in the Middle East after World War I has been rejected, and one cannot expect that the achievement of national self-determination by the so-called new states will have a democratizing effect upon their political life. Constitutionalism gives way to the cult of leadership, and the assertion of an independent nationalism tends to have little bearing on the development of any particular kind of political institutions.

While most Arabs in general, and Egyptians in particular, expected all good things to flow from nationalism and independence, they were never clear as to whether this meant good things at home or abroad. At present no one seems to hail enthusiastically any political development at home that spells a difference in the relationship of the subject to the ruler. The Arab is told that nationalism means dignity, freedom from foreign control, and sacrifice on his part to unite all Arabs under one banner. Unfortunately, whether his ruler is modern or archaic, he still finds it hard to determine whether nationalism has any other solid content for his benefit at home: expanded social and economic welfare, freedom of thought and expression, or a feeling that at last he is a subject, not merely an object, of politics.

Bibliographical Note

THE FOLLOWING bibliographical note does not mention or discuss all the sources consulted in the course of preparing this study. It is rather an attempt to comment on English works relevant to the study of the military regime in Egypt and the U.A.R., and to present certain Arabic publications, but by no means all, that are also relevant to both the U.A.R. regime and the general problem of Arab nationalism and unity.

It would be difficult to compile a complete list of all the sources of information on which this study is based. Much of the information and data essential to the preparation of the study have been gathered from personal interviews and reports in the Egyptian press from 1952 to 1960. Here one should mention *al-Ahram, al-Gumhuriyya,* and *Akhbar el-Yom,* three leading Cairo dailies, all of which came under strict censorship by the military regime and, since May 1960, have been the products of the nationalized press. The weekly *Rose el-Youssef* and its companion *Sabah al-khair,* edited and published by an imaginative staff under the direction of its personable and adaptable editor, Ihsan Abdel Quddus* (who is

---

* Mr. Ihsan Abdel Quddus finally achieved in 1961 a public position in the new regime as member of the Permanent (Standing) Committee on National Guidance of the National Union. He will probably prove more accommodating still as a junior member of the new ruling class.

sometimes outdone by the brilliant cartoonist, George al-Bahgouri), enjoy the highest circulation of any weekly publication in the U.A.R. Magazine publications of the Armed Forces have been revealing in the overdose of nationalist preaching that they indulge in. Among these *al-quwwat al-musallaha* (Armed Forces) is the most interesting and popular.

Prolific publishing in Cairo since the army coup in July 1952, by both the Department of Information and the Ministry of National Guidance and Culture, makes it impossible for any one person to keep abreast of all that is being written, whether good or bad. For example, there is a variety of "series" booklets, pamphlets, and popular brochures. Among these "Ikhtarna lak" (We Chose for You) and "Kutub siyasiyya" (Political Books) are interesting. The first series has already provided the public in the U.A.R. with cheap editions of President Nasser's public utterances, while the second provides readable information on Arab and international political issues generally. Two other series, "Kitab al-shaab" (Book of the People) and "Iqra" (Read!) are perhaps more educational insofar as they make available in abbreviated and inexpensive form works of general historical and national interest.

There is no general work specifically dealing with the modern Egyptian army. The story of the rise of a modern military establishment in Egypt must therefore be constructed from reports available in general histories of the reign of Muhammad Ali and his successors, as well as the later reorganization of that army under British control between 1882 and 1936. Among the most recent general works on Egypt which devote at least one chapter to the nineteenth century, Tom Little, *Egypt* (New York: Frederick A. Praeger, Inc., 1958) though hastily written, is dependable and balanced. In contrast, Muhammad Rifaat Bey, *The Awakening of Modern Egypt* (London: Longmans, Green & Co., Ltd., 1947) is rather a panegyric of the Muhammad Ali dynasty but nevertheless represents an Egyptian point of view. A different type of general work written over thirty years ago with the sympathy of an

expatriate Englishman enjoying the oasis weather of Heliopolis is Lieutenant Colonel P. G. Elgood, *The Transit of
Egypt* (London: Edward Arnold & Co., 1928). The section on
Muhammad Ali and the successor Khedives in the nineteenth
century, however, is more detailed and superior to both Little
and Rifaat. An earlier work by an Englishman who came to
serve Britain's mission in Egypt faithfully during the closing
decades of the nineteenth century is Viscount Milner, *England
in Egypt* (London: Edward Arnold & Co., 11th ed., 1904), first
published in 1892. The book deals with the aftermath of the
Orabi Revolt and is characterized by the tone of one who
came to help "restore order." Nevertheless, it is an outspoken
work which shows intimate knowledge of the problems of
Egypt in 1882.

A recent monograph by Professor Morroe Berger, *The Military Elite and Social Change* (Princeton University: Center for
International Studies, 1960, mimeographed) in many respects
breaks new ground in the study of the military establishment
in Egypt and its role in social change. The early part of the
monograph dealing with the Napoleonic impact upon Egypt
and Muhammad Ali's reign is a first-rate analysis.

For the period 1885–1923, Lord Cromer, *Modern Egypt*
(London: Macmillan & Co., Ltd., 2 vols., 1908), Lord Lloyd,
Egypt Since Cromer (London: Macmillan & Co., Ltd., 2 vols.,
1933–34), and Lord Wavell, *Allenby in Egypt* (London:
George G. Harrap & Co., Ltd., 1943) are indispensable. They
can be supplemented by George Young, *Egypt, A Survey of
Historical Forces* (London: Ernest Benn, Ltd., 1930), Sir
Auckland Colvin, *The Making of Modern Egypt* (London:
Seeley & Co., Ltd., 2d ed., 1906), and Sidney Low, *Egypt in
Transition* (London: Smith, Elder & Co., 1914). An interesting
general work covering part of the nineteenth century and
especially the period beginning with the British occupation is
Sir Valentine Chirol, *The Egyptian Problem* (London: Mac-
millan & Co., Ltd., 1920).

More detailed information on nineteenth-century Egypt may

be found in the works of the Egyptian historian Abder Rahman Rafii. These should be classified into three major categories: histories of monarchs or rulers, histories of nationalist leaders or heroes, and histories of the national movement in Egypt. In this connection his most relevant works are *Asr Muhammad Ali* (The Age of Muhammad Ali) (Cairo: al-Nahda al-misriyya, 3d printing, 1951), first published in 1930; *Asr Ismail* (The Age of Ismail) (Cairo: al-Nahda al-misriyya, 2 vols., 2d printing, 1948), first published in 1932; *al Thawra al-urabiyya wa al-ihtilal al-inglizi* (The Orabi Revolt and the British Occupation) (Cairo: al-Nahda al-misriyya, 2d printing, 1949), first published in 1937; and *Mustafa Kamel, baeth al-haraka al-wataniyya* (Mustafa Kamel, Leader of the National Movement) (Cairo: al-Nahda al-misriyya, 3d printing, 1950), first published in 1939. All of these contain fairly comprehensive coverage, detailed information, as well as generally valid material on the growth of the Egyptian military establishment in the nineteenth century. While as a detached historian Rafii may leave much to be desired, his access to archives in Cairo and especially the Abdin Palace papers lends his series of historical volumes on modern Egypt the advantage of detail.

Whereas readers interested in the early evolution of the modern nationalist movement in Egypt can avail themselves of Fritz Steppat, *Nationalismus und Islam bei Mustafa Kamil* (Leiden: E. J. Brill for *Die Welt des Islams,* Vol. IV, No. 4, 1956), no comparable work on Orabi and the first intervention of the Egyptian army in domestic politics exists. W. S. Blunt, *Secret History of the English Occupation of Egypt* (New York: Alfred A. Knopf, Inc., 1922), is a partisan apologia for Orabi by one who was directly involved in his cause. The same can be said of Alexander M. Broadley, *How We Defended Orabi and His Friends* (London: Chapman and Hall, Ltd., 1884). A rather flimsy article by Desmond Stewart, "The Revolution that Failed," *Middle East Forum,* Vol. 33, No. 7, pp. 12–16, cannot be taken too seriously. Indeed, this writer has seen no single work on the army in Egypt, even in Arabic. A recent

doctoral thesis by Nazir Hassan Saadawi resulted in two published works: *Tarikh misr al-harbi fi ayyam Salah al-Din*
(Military History of Egypt under Saladin) (Cairo: al-Nahda
al-misriyya, 1957), and *Jaish misr* (The Army of Egypt) (Cairo:
al-Nahda al-misriyya, 1958). Although most revealing when
one considers the popularity of Saladin among Egyptians these
days (Saladin according to these two works did not consider
Egyptians proper material for his army), both these books
deal with a period in Egyptian history which does not add
much to our understanding of the modern military establishment or its political role.

Perhaps the ablest analysis of Egyptian politics from independence to 1950 has been Marcel Colombe, *L'Evolution de
l'Egypte* (Paris: Editions G. P. Maisonneuve et Cie., 1951). A
comparable survey of the Egyptian economy of importance to
the student of Egyptian politics during the period 1923–50 is
that of Charles Issawi, *Egypt at Mid-Century* (London: Oxford
University Press, 1954). There is, however, no general analysis
of the politics of the Egyptian parliamentary period in English comparable to that of M. Colombe. With the exception of
Jacob Landau, *Parties and Parliaments in Egypt (1866–1924)*
(Tel Aviv: Israel Publishing House, for Israel Oriental Society, 1953), treating early and incipient experiments in
representative government during the nineteenth century, we
have no specialized study of parties and parliaments in Egypt
after independence. There are studies of certain political
groups such as J. Heyworth-Dunne, *Religious and Political
Trends in Modern Egypt* (Washington, D.C., privately published, 1950), and Ishaq al-Husaini, *The Moslem Brethren*
(Beirut: Khayyat College Bookshop, 1956). For information on
the parliamentary period, 1923–52, English readers usually
depend on contemporary press files, but particularly the exhaustive *Surveys of International Affairs,* published by the
Royal Institute of International Affairs, London, and especially the sections of those Surveys prepared by George Kirk.

On the early constitutional developments of independence

the reader may find useful Sir William G. Hayter, *Recent Constitutional Developments in Egypt* (Cambridge University Press, 1924), and Major E. W. Polson Newman, *Great Britain in Egypt* (London: Cassell & Co., Ltd., 1928). A very good recent and general work with fair perspective is John Marlowe, *A History of Modern Egypt and Anglo-Egyptian Relations, 1800–1953* (New York: Frederick A. Praeger, Inc., 1954). The same unfortunately cannot be said of another contemporary, namely, Desmond Stewart, *Young Egypt* (London: Allan Wingate, 1958). A well-written but not too critical pamphlet, John S. Badeau, *Emergence of Modern Egypt* (New York: Foreign Policy Association Headline Series, 1953) seems to be the only brochure in English of its kind. More interesting, however, are the broadcasts of Professor Shafiq Ghorbal, *Formation of Egypt,* available to the writer in the Arabic translation, *Takwin misr* (Cairo: al-Nahda al-misriyya for the Ministry of National Guidance, 1957).

It appears that the evolution of national ideas and the movement for Egyptian nationalism during the latter part of the nineteenth century until the 1930's are better represented in published studies. The classic by Charles C. Adams, *Islam and Modernism in Egypt* (London: Oxford University Press, 1933), is a thorough presentation of the movement for Islamic reform led by Shaikh Muhammad Abdouh. The recent *Intellectual Origins of Egyptian Nationalism* by J. M. Ahmed (London: Oxford University Press, for the Royal Institute of International Affairs, 1960) is perhaps the best short study in English of its kind. But here again Egyptian publications, especially by Abder Rahman Rafii, offer more or less complete coverage of the national movement, including minute details about internal politics from 1919 to 1952. Whereas Rafii, *Tarikh al-haraka al-qawmiyya wa tatawwur nizam al-hukm fi misr* (The History of the National Movement and the Evolution of the Political System in Egypt) (Cairo: al-Nahda al-misriyya, 3 vols., 1929, 5th ed., 1955), traced the national movement from the Napoleonic invasion until Orabi, his later work, *Fi aaqab al-thawra al-misriyya* (Aftermath of the Egyptian Revolution) (Cairo: al-Nahda al-misriyya, 3 vols., 1949) is an indispensable detailed narrative of Egyptian national history and politics from the Anglo-Egyptian negotiations in 1921 to the return of the Wafd to power in 1950–51. Another work by Rafii in two volumes, *Thawrat sanat 1919* (The 1919 Revolution) (Cairo: al-Nahda al-misriyya, 1944) constitutes a survey of Egypt during the First World War, the causes of the 1919 revolution together with detailed materials on the politics of that revolution. More recent but of questionable quality is Shuhdi Attiya al-Shafei, *Tatawwur al-haraka al-wataniyya al-misriyya, 1882–1956* (The Evolution of the Egyptian National Movement, 1882–1956) (Cairo: al-Dar al-misriyya, 1956).

More essential to the study of crucial issues in pre-coup politics is Rafii's fair analysis in *Muqaddamat thawrat thalatha wa ishrin yulio 1952* (Cairo: al-Nahda al-misriyya, 1957). This, in a way, supplements the third and last volume of his *Fi aaqab al-thawra al-misriyya*. A remarkably complete record of Egyptian politics covering this period is to be found in Muhammad Husein Haikal, *Mudhakkirat fi al-siyasa al-misriyya* (Memoirs on Egyptian Politics) (2 vols., Cairo: al-Nahda al-misriyya and Matbaat misr, 1951, 1953). In using them one must bear in mind that the writer was a member and later head of the Liberal Constitutional party, and president of the Egyptian Senate as recently as 1950. Many passages, therefore, as well as the over-all presentation, are colored by the writer's political convictions, his partisan involvement in Egyptian politics, and his attempt to justify his political conduct and behavior. This does not imply that the Memoirs are not a dependable source of information on party and parliamentary politics in Egypt from 1923 to 1952. On the contrary, they are most informative and lively. Another active Egyptian politician and past Prime Minister has left a more brief volume of memoirs, namely, the late Ismail Sidky. His *Mudhakkirati* (My Memoirs) (Cairo: Dar al-Hilal, 1950) are especially important for the 1930–35 suspension of the Constitution in Egypt as well as for the 1945–46 period.

A less exhaustive yet revealing treatment of specific aspects of Egyptian politics in the 1930's is Mahmud Azmi, *Al-ayyam al-mi'a* (The Hundred Days) (Cairo: al-Nahda al-misriyya, n.d.), a study of the Ali Maher Government from January 30 to May 6, 1936. The most valuable part of this presentation is the reproduction of some of Ali Maher's official correspondence and decrees while in office.

While many things have been written on ex-King Farouq and his involvement in Egyptian politics, Ahmad Baha al-Din, *Farouq . . . malikan* (Farouq . . . King) (Cairo: Rose el-Youssef, 1952), is interesting and well written, albeit a scathing attack on the deposed monarch's interference in politics and especially his political entourage. In literature, Muhammad Farid Abu Hadid, *Ana al-shaab* (Cairo: Maaref Press, 1958) is an imaginative and vivid protest against the "police methods" of the Farouq regime, a humorous and fairly accurate portrayal of provincial politics in Egypt.

Members of the Free Officers junta that carried out the July 1952 coup d'état in Cairo were hardly known to the Egyptian public, let alone the outside world. Nasser, the Salem Brothers, Zakariyya Muhieddin, and the others were perhaps familiar outside Egypt only to their individual British instructors (by 1952 most of them back in England) in Staff College, although Anwar es-Sadat must have been quite well known to British Security officers in Egypt during World War II. Apart from brief press reports by various foreign correspondents in the Middle East on some of the junta members, there were no published accounts of the beginnings of their organization— whatever its proportions before the coup—its members and activities. In 1952 the first book-length account of the coup appeared in Cairo. Originally written by Rashed al-Barawi (a young economist) in Arabic under the title *Haqiqat al-inqilab al-akhir fi misr* (Cairo: al-Nahda al-misriyya, 1952), and hastily translated into English under the title *The Military Coup in*

Egypt (Cairo: Renaissance Bookshop, 1952), it purported to be an analysis of the upheaval and included spotty data on the Free Officers. In 1955, ex-President Muhammad Naguib's statement, *Egypt's Destiny; A Personal Statement* (New York: Doubleday and Co., Inc., 1955) appeared almost simultaneously with Gamal Abdel Nasser's *Egypt's Liberation: A Philosophy of the Revolution* (Washington, D.C.: Public Affairs Press, 1955). Here were the personal statements of two leaders during the first two years of the army's accession to political power. Whereas Naguib's statement was, in many respects, an apologia for his conduct and all too brief political career as titular head of the Free Officers regime, Nasser's work was an attempted though not too successful manifesto.

It was not until 1957 that a member of the Free Officer organization came forward with more intimate details of the conspiracy. Anwar es-Sadat's *Revolt on the Nile* (London: Allan Wingate, 1957) is a bold, although many argue not too accurate, account of the beginnings of the conspiracy, its organization, and success. What is more interesting, however, is the autobiographical account of the author's checkered career as a conspirator. It should also be noted that the English edition is presumably a translation of es-Sadat, *Qissat al-thawra kamila,* published in Cairo by Dar al-Hilal in 1956. Yet the Arabic version is largely directed at the Egyptian public with a view to (1) discrediting Naguib, (2) justifying the army leadership of the revolution, (3) finding a new definition for democracy. The interesting theory is also developed by es-Sadat in the Arabic volume that the junta represented the "Egyptian revolution," not the "Egyptian government."

In 1956 the journalists Jean and Simonne Lacouture published their *L'Egypte en Mouvement* (Paris: Editions du Seuil, 1956), translated into English by Francis Scarfe in 1958 as *Egypt in Transition* (London: Methuen & Co., Ltd.), with revisions and additions by the authors incorporating the events leading up to the Union between Syria and Egypt in

February 1958. This is perhaps the best general work on the coming of the army to power in Egypt, written critically but not unsympathetically, with imaginative organization of the material, and a fine sense for the historical nexus of Egyptian social and political life. Tom Little, *Egypt* (New York: Frederick A. Praeger, Inc., 1958) covers practically the same ground, contains excellent detail on the junta, to which the author, a veteran newspaperman in the Middle East, apparently had access, but suffers from having been hastily written. Moreover, the book is written as part of the Benn Nations of the Modern World Series in London, without any chapter headings or proper bibliography, in spite of the long list of books at the beginning.

A third work on the Free Officers regime, *Nasser's New Egypt* (New York: Frederick A. Praeger, Inc., for the University of Pennsylvania Foreign Policy Research Institute Series, No. 8, 1960) by Keith Wheelock is one of the most detailed and critical presentations of the regime in Egypt. Unfortunately, the author is limited in his presentation by the interests of the sponsor and consequently does not devote much space to the conspiracy. His chapter on the Entrenchment of the Military Regime is all too brief. The rest of his discussion is scholarly and balanced. More unfortunate is the organization of the material in a problematic scheme without any attempt to link the findings to any over-all evaluation of the military regime. The book must be admired for its painstaking detail, but some might deplore the fact that such detail may become historically obsolete in a very short time. Nevertheless, Mr. Wheelock's is a discerning analysis, marred only by poor style.

More recently three books on President Nasser of the U.A.R. have appeared in English, purporting to be biographical sketches or portraits of his rise to power: C. Wilton Wynn, *Nasser of Egypt: The Search for Dignity* (Cambridge, Mass.: Arlington Books, 1959), Robert St. John, *The Boss* (New York: McGraw-Hill Book Co., 1960), and Joachim Joesten, *Nasser:*

Rise to Power (London: Odhams Press Ltd., 1960). The first two of these may be taken seriously; the third will excite no one except those who have already made up their minds about the intrinsic cussedness of President Nasser. Mr. Wynn, a veteran American correspondent in the Middle East, with apparent access to President Nasser, argues the theme that a Nasser was inevitable in the Arab world since his rise is associated by all Arabs with the search for dignity. He seems to admonish Western leaders to resign themselves to this phenomenon. Mr. St. John's is a fairly accurate account of Nasser's background (for instance, St. John is one of the few writers who mentions the fact that President Nasser was *not* born in Beni Merr as popular legend has it), an able description of his political shrewdness and his mastery of political intrigue without attaching undue mystery to these qualifications for political survival in the Middle East. St. John, like Wheelock and Wynn, had access to Nasser and other members of the Egyptian power elite, and produced a balanced and critical analysis of his subject. He is moreover successful in keeping the attention of the reader upon the main character of his narrative in the early part of the book, and only later does he subtly launch his own analysis of his biographical subject. This is, indeed, a most readable book. Unfortunately, the same cannot be said of Mr. Joesten's volume. First, it is not "the first biography of President Nasser to be published in English" as the author claims. Second, gross factual errors, not mere oversights, in the narrative render suspect the research the author may have conducted before writing.

What is interesting is the fact that there are no comparably good books in Arabic on the military regime in Egypt; still sloppier is published information on the background of the leading Free Officers. Popular books published during the first two or three years of the regime are laden with repetition and embellishment, but give little factual information. Here one should mention Hasan Marei and Amin Afifi Abd al-Ela,

Thawrat shaab (A Peoples Revolution) (Cairo: Anglo-Egyptian Press, 1952). The authors try to trace briefly the modern Egyptian revolution for political emancipation from the revolt led by Omar Makram during the Napoleonic sojourn in Egypt, ending with a discussion of the proposed "new society" for Egypt under the army-led movement. A popular pamphlet in the series, "Kutub siyasiyya" (Political Books) of the Department of Information in Cairo, penned by Abdel Moneim Shamis in 1954 under the title *al-Zaim al-thair* (The Rebel Leader), is an unsatisfactory short biography of President Nasser. A sort of Who's Who in the Revolution, *Qamus al-thawra al-misriyya* (Dictionary of the Egyptian Revolution) (Cairo: Anglo-Egyptian Press, 1954) by Ahmad Atiyyat Allah contains entries on most of the junta members, new terminology of the RCC, and many on Sudanese affairs. But the entries on junta members are not consistent in the arrangement of data; nor is the data complete for all of them. It does contain an appendix, however, of principal events since the July 1952 revolution through January 1954. A book by Abbas Muhammad al-Tayyib, *Batal al-thawra al-qaid Muhammad Naguib* (Hero of the Revolution, the Leader Muhammad Naguib) (Cairo: Ataya Press, 1953) purports to be a history of the Free Officer movement and its reform program during the first year, but it cannot be considered an appraisal of the regime at such an early stage. The same may be said of Muhammad Amin Hassuna, *Gumhuriyyat Misr fi amiha al-awwal* (The Republic of Egypt in its First Year) (Cairo: Department of Public Affairs, Armed Forces, 1954), for it is merely a publicity record of the year 1953–54.

One of the more impressive Arabic publications on the first year of the military regime is Fawzi al-Wakil, *Hadhihi al-thawra* (This Revolution) (Cairo: al-Ahram, 1953), published under the auspices of the Department of Public Information of the Armed Forces for distribution to members of the military establishment. This publication is most valuable for the record of statements and speeches by members of the junta

during the difficult first year of establishing communication
with the people.* Just as impressive for its attempt to reach
the Egyptian public is *Mahkamat al-thawra* (Court of the
Revolution) (3 vols., Cairo: Misr Press, 1953/54), a verbatim
record of the early trials of dissident labor (Kaf al-Dawar,
1952), politicians of the old regime, and defecting army officers, prepared by Major Amin Hassan Kamel with a publicity-
conscious introduction.

In contrast to the scarcity of detailed and dependable information on the Free Officers and the actual politics of the
regime so far, there is a variety of Arabic sources on such
themes as "the revolution," "the new society," Arabism, "the
new ideology," "the meaning of the new social revolution,"
the National Union, and related subjects. It is not possible to
comment upon or even list all of these publications. Many of
them are inevitably emotional panegyrics of dubious scholarly
merit; others are too general and repetitious in content to
offer useful analysis.

More serious and responsible is Ishaq Musa al-Huseini,
Azamat al-fikr al-arabi (The Crisis in Arab Thought) (Beirut:
1954), in which the author attempts a detached identification
of shortcomings in modern Arab thought with their obvious
consequences for the problem of national identification. Less
cogent, but more ambitious, is the booklet by Mustafa al-
Saharti, *Idiolojiyya arabiyya jadida* (A New Arab Ideology)
(Cairo: al-Baath al-jadid, 1957), in which the author attempts
a general application of mainly Western sociological theory
and concepts to the problems of an Arab public philosophy.
Another popular publication, Ibrahim Gumaa, *al-Imlaq al-
jadid al-Qawmiyya al-arabiyya* (Arab Nationalism, the New
Element) (Cairo: Dar al-fikr al-arabi, 1958) tends to present
Arab nationalism as the panacea for the solution of Arab
problems. Gumaa argues the usual bases for Arab unity (lan-

---

* The Department of Information in Cairo has been following up with
similar publications under the general title, The Republic in Five Years,
Eight Years, etc.

guage, history, culture, etc.), from which he proceeds to suggest that the new element of Arab nationalism constitutes a universal Arab belief which is presently in doubt because of the many battles it must fight (against Israel, imperialism).

With the exception of Huseini's brief but clear analysis, neither of the other two statements are comparable to the more serious and thoughtful work of mainly Syrian writers on the Arab search for a new "philosophy" and political formula. Among these one might single out the following: Walid al-Qamhawi, *al-Nakba wa al-bina'* (The Catastrophe and Reconstruction: Toward the Resurrection of the Arab Nation) (Beirut, 1956); Abdel Latif Sharara, *Ruh al-uruba* (The Spirit of Arabism) (Saida: al-maktaba al-asriyya, 1947), and *Fi al-qawmiyya al-arabiyya* (Beirut: Ouweidat, 1947); Michel Aflaq, *Maarakat al-masir al-wahid* (Battle of the Single Destiny) (Beirut: Dar al-adab, 1958); the well-written and massive, albeit in parts questionable, volume *Maalem al-hayat al-arabiyya al-jadida* (Essentials of the New Arab Life) (Beirut: Dar al-ilm lil-malayeen, 1956, 1959) by Munif al-Razzaz; and Muhammad Izzat Darwaza, *al-Wahda al-arabiyya* (Arab Unity) (Beirut: al-Maktab al-tijari, 1957).

Many of the works above listed follow to a great extent the ideal of a secular Arab nationalism originally proposed, and almost worked into the ground, by the venerable Abu Khaldun Sati' al-Husri in his better-known works *Ara' wa ahadith fi al-wataniyya wa al-qawmiyya* (Opinions and Talks on Patriotism and Nationalism) (Cairo: Risala Press, 1944); *Muhadarat fi nushu' al-fikra al-wataniyya* (Lectures on the Formation of the Idea of Nationalism) (Cairo: Risala Press, 1951; Beirut: Dar al-ilm lil-malayeen, 1956); *Ara' wa ahadith fi al-qawmiyya al-arabiyya* (Views and Talks on Arab Nationalism) (Beirut, 1956); *al-Uruba awwalan* (Arabism First) (Beirut, 1955); *al-Uruba baina duatiha wa muaridiha* (Arabism Between Its Advocates and Opponents) (Cairo, 1954); *Difa' an al-uruba* (In Defense of Arabism) (Beirut, 1956).

Inasmuch as Arab nationalism and Arab unity are relatively

new causes or variables in the politics of any Egyptian ruling class, there has been relatively scanty writing on this subject by Egyptians. A Hilal Monthly Book Selection, *Qissat al-wahda al-arabiyya* (Story of Arab Unity) (December 1957) by Anwar es-Sadat is an attempt to justify the relationship between Egyptian *wataniyya* (or local nationalism) and Arab national-ism, and to show that the only obstacle to Arab unity is Western imperialism. Another obviously propagandistic book, *Uruba wa din* (Arabism and Religion) by Ahmad Hasan al-Baquri, Minister of *Waqfs* for the first six years of the regime until his dismissal in 1959, was also published by Dar al-Hilal (n.d.). In it Baquri tries to emphasize the Islamic foundations of Arabism and the advantages of such a foundation.*

A similar lack of publications on the proposed "new phi-losophy" of the Revolution in Egypt obtains outside the Col-lected Speeches of President Nasser and some magazine ar-ticles. Anwar es-Sadat again has tried in a pamphlet, *Maana al-ittihad al-qawmi* (The Meaning of the National Union) (Cairo: S.O.P. Press, 1958), to discredit party politics and de-fine the new "democracy" under the National Union scheme, which is here presented as the means by which the public can assume the political responsibilities of citizenship. There has been some doubt in Arab circles whether this pamphlet was actually penned by es-Sadat or ghost-written. The bulk of the published material on the goals of the new political power elite, the meaning of "Nasserism" if you will, is to be found in the speeches of the President as published by the Depart-ment of Information in Cairo and especially the volume, *Thawratuna al-ijtimaiyya* (Our Social Revolution) (Cairo: Department of Information, Collected Speeches of President Nasser, 1959). An extension of the Presidential ideology into Syria also appeared in the published speeches of Gamal Abdel Nasser in the Northern Region, *Khutab al-rais Gamal Abdel Nasser fi al-id al-awwal lil-gumhuriyya al-arabiyya al-mut-*

---

* There were reports in January 1961 that President Nasser was con-sidering the appointment of religious attachés to all U.A.R. diplomatic missions.

tahida (The Speeches of President Gamal Abdel Nasser on the First Anniversary of the U.A.R.) (Cairo: Department of Information, "Kutub siyasiyya" series, Parts I and II, March 1959).

There are as yet no published appraisals of the U.A.R. by Egyptians, but there are fairly complimentary works by outsiders, namely, Lebanese writers whom one can describe vaguely as Arabists. Dr. George Hanna (allegedly a Communist) is one of the most prolific among these, and two of his works are worthy of mention: *Maana al-thawra* (Meaning of the Revolution) (Beirut: Dar Beirut, 1957), a leftist interpretation, largely pro-Nasser, of the Egyptian revolution as having wide significance for all Arabs in their struggle against Western imperialism; and *Khawatir hawl al-jumhuriyya al-arabiyya al-muttahida* (Random Observations on the U.A.R.), a heavily pro-U.A.R. sort of diary on events in the Arab world. In a combined volume of articles on Arab unity, *Risalat al-ittihad* (The Message of Unity) (Dar al-Hayat Press, Beirut, 1954) Sati' al-Husri, Kamel Mruwwa, and Akram Zuaitar argue unity as a political necessity among Arabs, especially in countering the Israeli threat, but are not particularly recommending an Egyptian-controlled union.

A popular record of the formation of the U.A.R. by Tahir Abu Fasha, *al-jumhuriyya al-arabiyya al-muttahida* (The U.A.R.) (Cairo: 1958) is an uncritical review of the events of February 1958 in Cairo dealing with the announcement of the new united Republic.

Needless to say, there are no published works in Arabic on the role of the army or military in politics other than the statements made early during the assumption of power by the junta members. There is much writing in Egypt on the popularization of the New Order, but no seriously critical analyses of problems involved in the development of a political system. In 1955 Professor Majid Khadduri published his often quoted article, "The Army Officer: His Role in Middle Eastern Politics," in S. N. Fisher, ed., *Social Forces in the Middle East* (Ithaca, N.Y.: Cornell University Press, 1955), a brilliant gen-

eral analysis of the involvement of the army in politics deriving largely from the author's extensive and rather definitive
work on modern Iraqi politics in *Independent Iraq* (London:
Oxford University Press, 1951). A second revised edition of this
work has appeared recently, but the present writer has not
been able to read it before going to press. A very good article,
not as extensive in coverage, by Alford Carleton, "The Syrian
Coups d'Etat," *The Middle East Journal,* Vol. IV (January
1950), pp. 1–12, attempted an explanation of events in Syria,
especially the quick succession of military coups between the
end of March and December 1949. A thoughtful presentation
of the Egyptian coup and the role of the military in politics
appeared in T.R.L., "Egypt Since the Coup d'Etat of 1952,"
World Today (April 1954), pp. 140–49.

Perhaps the most consistently superior analyses on the Egyptian military regime and the U.A.R. generally have been ap-
pearing in the French journal, *L'Orient,* edited by M. Marcel
Colombe, especially the articles by the editor and his associates Simon Jarjy and François Bertier. There is unfortunately
nothing in the United States to compare to this journal in
quality and usefulness for the student of U.A.R. politics. An
attempt to assess the Nasser regime by the *Middle East Forum,*
published by the Alumni Association of the American University of Beirut, Special Issue on "Nasserism," Vol. XXXIV,
No. 4 (April 1959), represents the views of many contributors,
both Western and Arab. A more serious and scholarly effort
was made by the participants in a Seminar on the Egyptian
Regime held at St. Antony's College, Oxford, in the summer
of 1957. (See Unpublished Papers of the Seminar on the Egyptian Regime, 1957.)

Regarding Syrian politics before Union with Egypt, some
published works by Arab writers deserve consideration. While
the students of Syrian politics can profitably use such English
works as the excellent essay, *Syria and Lebanon, A Political
Essay* (London: Oxford University Press, for the Royal Institute of International Affairs, London, 1947) by Albert Hourani, the poorer but more up-to-date *Syria and Lebanon* (New

York: Frederick A. Praeger, Inc., 1957) by Nicola Ziadeh, or Stephen Longrigg, *Syria and Lebanon under the Mandate* (London: Oxford University Press, 1958), or the more popular, but less cogent, analyses in Professor Philip Hitti, *History of Syria* (New York: The Macmillan Co., 1951), there are some interesting partisan works by Syrians on the post-World-War-II Syrian political situation. Zaki al-Arsuzi, *Mashakiluna al-qawmiyya wa mawqif al-ahzab minha* (Our National Problems and the Attitude of the Political Parties Toward Them) (Damascus: Dar al-yaqza, 1956), albeit somewhat partisan, is a bold confrontation of political parties with the responsibility of power and its social and economic requisites. A more fundamental questioning of the whole political system in Syria, even though somewhat idealistic, is to be found in Adnan al-Atasi, *Azamat al-hukm fi Suriya* (The Crisis of Government in Syria) (Homs: Al-maitam al-islami Press, 1954). Indeed, Atasi's work is one of the rare attempts by an Arab to suggest a possible theory for a viable political system. A general work of historical use on Syria is Najib al-Armanazi, *Muhadarat an Suriya min al-ihtilal hatta al-jala'* (Lectures on Syria from Occupation to Evacuation, or 1920–1946) (Cairo: Arab League Institute of Higher Arab Studies, 1954). Then there are such brief works of dubious value as Fathalla Mikhail, *Min dhikriyyat hukumat al-Zaim Husni al-Zaim* (Memories of the Zaim Government) (Cairo: Dar al-Maaref, 1952), and the highly partisan, pro-Fertile-Crescent-scheme, anti-military-coup tirade by Salim Taha al-Takriti, *Asrar al-inqilab al-askari al-akhir fi Suriya* (Secrets of the Latest Military Coup in Syria) (Baghdad: al-Basri, 1950).

It appears as if contemporary Egyptian non-fiction writers cannot, will not, or are not permitted to produce work that can compare in quality with the works of such older authors as the late Ahmad Amin. Both in his autobiography, *Hayati* (My Life) (Cairo: al-Adab Press, 1952) and his later *al-Sharq wa al-gharb* (Cairo: Lajnat al-ta'lif wa al-nashr, 1955), Ahmad Amin raised such fundamental problems confronting Egyptian society as the usefulness of Western norms in developing local institutions, educational values, and public responsibility.

In contrast to non-fiction writing, young writers of fiction have made a definite advance over their predecessors of the old school, when one considers the works of such authors as Dr. Yusuf Idris, especially his collection of short stories, *Hadithat Sharaf* (A Matter of Honor) (Beirut, 1957) and his play *al-Lahza al-hariga* (The Critical Moment) (Cairo, 1958).

A wider interest on the part of American students of politics in the role of the military in politics elsewhere in the Middle East has been apparent lately. Professor Dankwart A. Rustow, "The Army and the Founding of the Turkish Republic," *World Politics,* Vol. XI, No. 4 (July 1959), pp. 513–52, is a painstaking and systematic attempt to gauge this role. A more popular but brilliant analysis of the latest intervention of the military in Turkish politics (May 1960) and the breakdown of party politics is Fred Frye, "Arms and the Man in Turkish Politics," *Land Reborn,* Vol. XI, No. 2 (August 1960), pp. 3–14.

Reference has already been made to Professor Berger's monograph which traces the role of the military in Egypt, especially in its modern variety as the agent of social change. The construction of a theoretical scheme to explain or at least interpret the phenomenon of the role of the military in so-called underdeveloped countries was essayed at a Special Conference sponsored by and held at the Rand Corporation, California, in 1959. A number of unpublished papers were presented.

Perhaps one of the ablest assessments of the Middle Eastern political scene that takes into serious account the phenomenon of the military is the very recent contribution by George Kirk to *The Year Book of World Affairs, 1960* (London: Stevens & Sons, Ltd., for the London Institute of World Affairs, 1960), pp. 142–75, under the title, "The Middle Eastern Scene." Mr. Kirk will probably concern himself at still greater length with this problem in his forthcoming general survey, *Contemporary Arab Politics,* to be published by Praeger in 1961.

Notes

Introduction

1. "Tabaatuna al-ruhiyya baad al-maaraka" ("Spiritual Consequences of the Battle"), *al-Hilal* (March 1957), pp. 6–11.

Chapter 1

1. It is interesting to note that the leader of the movement, Colonel Salim, was later a staunch supporter of Mustafa Kamil (d. 1908), leader of the nationalist movement in Egypt and head of the National party at the turn of the century.

2. See text of Khedive Tewfiq's order to Sherif Pasha entrusting him with the formation of the Cabinet, reported in *al-Waqai' al-misriyya* (The Egyptian Gazette), July 5, 1879, and quoted in Abder Rahman Rafii, *al-Thawra al-urabiyya wa al-ihtilal al-inglizi* (The Orabi Revolt and the British Occupation) (2d ed., Cairo: al-Nahda al-misriyya, 1949), pp. 24–26.

3. The *firman*, or decree, of August 7, 1879, issued by the Ottoman Sultan to the Khedive Tewfiq confirming him in office, included among its clauses a provision to the effect that the strength of the Egyptian army should be limited to 18,000 men in peacetime. This was a serious limitation in contrast to the earlier *firman*, of 1873, which had not placed any limitation upon the number of Egyptian armed forces.

4. New York: Alfred A. Knopf, 1922, passim.

5. "The Revolution that Failed," *Middle East Forum*, XXXIII, No. 7, pp. 12–16.

Chapter 2

1. See *Mudhakkirat fi al-siyasa al-misriyya* (Memoirs on Egyptian Politics) (Cairo: Matbaat Misr, 1953), Vol. II, p. 19. (Henceforward cited as *Haikal*.)

2. Cairo: al-Nahda al-misriyya, 1957.

3. Cairo: Rose el-Youssef, 1952.

4. *Haikal*, II, p. 332.

5. Faluja is the name of the beleaguered fortress in the Sinai defended by an Egyptian battalion against persistent Israeli attacks during the Arab-Israeli war in Palestine, 1948–49.

6. See *Fi a'aqab al-thawra al-misriyya* (Aftermath of the Egyptian Revolution) (Cairo: al-Nahda al-misriyya, 1951), Vol. III, pp. 295–327.

7. Text of the letter is reproduced in Abder Rahman Rafii, *Muqaddamat thawrat thalatha wa ishrin yulio 1952* (Cairo: al-Nahda al-misriyya, 1957), pp. 208–10, and *Haikal*, II, pp. 358–60.

8. See *Haikal*, II, p. 354.

9. One cannot say with certainty who was responsible for the burning of Cairo on January 26, 1952. Even the Revolutionary Court of 1953–54 could not, or was not willing to, identify the instigators and leaders of the riots. It would be too eclectic to assign guilt to everyone: the Wafd Government at the time, extremist groups, and the Palace. Even Abder Rahman Rafii in *Muqaddamat thawrat thalatha wa ishrin yulio 1952* avoids definite accusations. Other writers—Tom Little, the Lacoutures, and George Kirk—are inclined to pinpoint guilt on the Communists and Muslim Brethren. In the absence of conclusive evidence—official or otherwise—the present writer prefers to avoid positive statements on the responsibility for the disturbances.

Chapter 3

1. Reports have appeared from time to time indicating the dependence of the military regime in Egypt since 1952 upon German advisers in military training and the operation of mass media. What is interesting about these reports is the allegation that German personnel in the service of the U.A.R. Government were of Nazi background. In a recent political biography of U.A.R. President Nasser, Robert St. John, *The Boss: The Story of Gamal Abdel Nasser* (New York: McGraw-Hill Book Co., 1960), intimates that key German personnel in Egypt adopted, on Presidential orders, Egyptian names. Another recent work, *Behind the Egyptian Sphinx: Prelude to World War III?* (Philadelphia and New York: Chilton Co., 1960), by Irving Sedar and Harold Greenberg, suggests an exaggerated and somewhat implausible—but nevertheless in the view of the authors diabolical—alliance between a rising Germany and a Nasser-dominated U.A.R.

2. See Bibliographical Essay.

3. In S. N. Fisher (ed.), *Social Forces in the Middle East* (Ithaca: Cornell University Press, 1955), pp. 162–83. See also Majid Khadduri, *Independent Iraq* (Oxford University Press, 1951), especially pp. 71–182.

4. Cairo: al-Nahda al-misriyya, 1952.

5. In his "Qissat al-thawra" ("The Story of the Revolution") published in the press on July 22, 1953, and reproduced in *Khutab al-rais Gamal Abdel Nasser* (Speeches of President Gamal Abdel Nasser) (henceforward cited as *Khutab al-rais*) (Cairo: Department of Information, "Ikhtarna lak" Series, n.d.), I, pp. 54–68.

Chapter 4

1. For instance the *bay'a*, or oath of allegiance, to President Naguib in 1953, the text of which may be found in Fawzi al-Wakil, *Hadhihi al-thawra* (This Revolution: A Record of the First Year) (Cairo: al-Ahram, 1953), p. 317; the general *bay'a* to President Nasser on national occasions. See my "Recent Developments in Islam," in *Tensions in the Middle East*, edited by P. W. Thayer (Baltimore: The Johns Hopkins Press, 1958), pp. 165–80.

2. See especially the discussion in Chapters 5 and 7.

3. See *Hadhihi al-thawra*, p. 209.

4. Actually only fifteen parties applied for recognition under the Reorganization of Parties Order in October 1952: the Wafd, Liberal Constitutional, Kutla, Saadist, National, Socialist, Labor, Muslim Brethren, Fallahin, National Feminist, Daughters of the Nile, Fallah Socialist, New Democratic, New Socialist, and Nile Democrat.

5. For text of the mass oath and President Naguib's statement, see *Hadhihi al-thawra*, p. 307.

6. Cairo: Anglo-Egyptian Press, n.d., p. 37.

7. See *Survey of International Affairs* (Oxford University Press, for the Royal Institute of International Affairs, London, 1955), p. 201.

8. This was indicated by the early removal of Colonel Rashad Mehanna from the Regency Council in October 1952.

9. It was reported in December 1960 that General Naguib was released from house arrest.

10. See especially President Nasser's attacks on the Muslim Brethren in his famous speech at a Labor Congress sponsored by the Liberation Rally in Cairo on October 29, 1954, in *Khutab al-rais*, III (1956).

11. See especially section on Executive Structure in Chapter 6, and general discussion in Part III.

Chapter 5

1. The Liberation Rally referred to earlier was primarily a device by President Nasser to clear out elements subversive to the regime from existing organizations among workers and students. It cannot therefore be considered as a serious attempt on the part of the regime at some representation formula.

2. A stimulating and imaginative discussion on this problem is to be found in Seymour M. Lipset, *Political Man* (New York: Doubleday & Co., 1960), especially Part I, pp. 45–178. Other aspects of this problem are treated in a novel theoretical attempt in Gabriel A. Almond and James S. Coleman, eds., *The Politics of Developing Areas* (Princeton: Princeton University Press, 1960). Daniel Lerner, *The Passing of Traditional Society* (Glencoe, Ill.: The Free Press, 1958) theorizes on some of these issues in the Middle East, but his historical justifications in many instances are tenuous.

3. The Assembly, however, must be credited with its criticism of the Liberation Province agricultural project initiated at great cost by the regime in 1955 as a model experiment in desert land reclamation. Financial malpractice and malodorous handling by the head of the project, Major Magdi Hasanein, a Free Officer, caused the government to relieve him of his post and institute an investigation of the whole project. On this particular point, see the excellent comments in Keith Wheelock, *Nasser's New Egypt* (New York: Frederick A. Praeger, 1960), pp. 67–68, 94–99.

4. This procedure was not unusual since the Ministry of Interior as a rule supervised all elections.

5. Actually met on July 22, 1960.

6. The President would appoint a Higher Advisory Committee representing all the appropriate ministries. These committees would advise local and municipal councils. All towns with a population of 15,000 and over would have municipal councils, consisting of seventeen members: a governor as chairman of the council, six representing government departments, and ten elected. Those elected, who should not be over thirty-five years of age, should be able to read and write, and would have to pay a minimum annual income tax of £E20, as well as have a minimum monthly salary of £E20.

It should be pointed out that although these local government schemes are still in the formative stage they nevertheless smack of being adjuncts of a central administration, controlled through the governor, who is appointed by the Central Executive. It will be interesting, therefore, to observe the value of these schemes, all presently under the supervision of a new Ministry of Local Administration headed by Kamal al-Din Husein, in training local citizens in the art of representative institutions and self-government.

7. Formation of the National Union presented no serious problems in Egypt, where President Nasser's army control was complete. In Syria, however, the formation of a National Union rendered the army-Baath diumvirate meaningless.

8. Khalil Kallas, another Baathist, who had served as Executive Minister

of Economy for the Syrian Region, resigned a few weeks later in January 1960. Hamdoun and Qannut, it will be recalled, were leading Baathist-sympathizer army officers in the coup against Shishakli in 1954 and in the movement for Union with Egypt in 1957–58.

9. Rumors of disaffection among Syrian army officers led Amer to address troops in Homs on October 29, warning them against dissension. Complaints from Aleppo and northern farmers about distribution of seed and grain elicited an immediate response. Amer made such items available under a crash emergency program. The apparent urgency of complaints about the economic situation was further evidenced by Amer's immediate steps to assure a sufficient supply of foodstuffs and to reduce prices of staple commodities. At the same time Amer made a token distribution of land to small groups of peasant farmers.

10. Cambridge, Mass.: Harvard University Press, p. 1.

11. He has so far written some fifty books, only two of which in this writer's view can be seriously considered as worth-while literature, namely, *Ard al-nifaq* (Land of the Double-Cross), prize publication, "The Silver Book" of the Short Story Club (Cairo: al-Sharika al-arabiyya lil-tibaa wa al-nashr, 1958), and *al-Saqamat* (Disgusting Sights), prize publication, "The Golden Book" of the Short Story Club (Cairo: Rose el-Youssef, 1956).

12. Generally, the purpose of the Council is to encourage writers to carry the national message in their work in an effort to develop a body of national literature and lore. See text of Law No. 4/1956 establishing the Higher Council of Arts and Letters, together with Note from President Nasser and accompanying Internal Organization Chart, issued by the Office of the President (*Qanun insha' al-majlis wa al-laiha al-dakhiliyya*).

13. Playwrights rarely receive more than £E50 for a play accepted by the National Theater.

14. The revival of Egyptian folklore and folk art has engendered some interest especially through the writings of Zakariyya al-Haggawi in *al-Risala al-gadida* (The New Message), monthly literary publication issued under the auspices of the Higher Council of Arts and Letters. See especially the 1956 volume.

15. See the excellent paper by M. T. Audsley, "Labor and Social Affairs in Egypt," *Middle Eastern Affairs*, No. One, St. Antony's Papers, No. 4 (New York: Frederick A. Praeger, 1959), pp. 95–106.

16. See the study by Harbison and Ibrahim, *Human Resources for Egyptian Enterprise* (New York: The Macmillan Co., 1959).

17. For instance, the Economic Organization (*al-muassasa al-iqtisadiyya*) established by the government in 1956. It is the major investment agency of the government. Its first director, Squadron Leader Hasan Ibrahim, a Free Officer and member of the RCC, was removed from office in October

1959. The Central Minister of the Economy, Abdel Moneim al-Kaisouni, then took over direction of the Organization.

18. The latest report listed forty-one trade and labor unions in the Syrian Region.

19. For the legislation establishing the National Planning Committee of the Presidency of the Republic, see Committee on National Planning, "Essays on Economic Planning (4)—Documents on the Formation of the Committee on National Planning," (Arabic) (Cairo: Amiriyya Press, 1957). For a general treatment of the concept of economic planning, see "General Principles of Planning," by Dr. Ibrahim Hilmi Abder Rahman, Committee on National Planning Publications, No. 5 (Arabic) (Cairo, 1957). See also the official report of the Ministry of Industry on industrialization, "Industry in the Revolution and the Five Year Plan" (Arabic) (Cairo, July 1957). On special problems of planning and the politics surrounding them within Egypt, see Keith Wheelock, *op. cit.*, especially pp. 137–72.

20. The Industrial Bank established in 1955 with an initial capital of £E1.5 million was presumably to be the major source of government-guaranteed loans for industry.

21. Although the U.A.R. government has been aware of the need to extend communications, power, and public services for a wider geographical distribution of industrial centers, not until January 1960 did it announce its program to establish thirty-seven industrial centers in Egypt. Their geographical distribution would be as follows: Damietta, Rashid, Bilbis, Helwan, al-Wasti, Abu Qurqas, Sohag, Aswan, Port Said, Ismailia, Benha, al-Masara, al-Fayyoum, Nag' Hamadi, Damanhour, Tanta, Giza, Abu Za'bal, Beni Sueif, Dairut, Qena, Edfu, Malwi, Mansura, Turah, al-Hawamdiya, Beni Mazar, Asiout. This would constitute a more even distribution of industry, alleviate population pressure in the Delta region, and disperse enterprises away from Cairo, Alexandria, Kafr al-Dawar, Mehalla el-Kubra, Suez, and Komombo.

22. "The Concentration and Dispersion of Charisma: Their Bearing on Economic Policy in Underdeveloped Countries," *World Politics*, XI, No. 1, pp. 1–19.

23. See *Thawratuna al-ijtimaiyya* (Our Social Revolution) (Cairo: Department of Information Special Issue, "Ikhtarna lak" Series: Collected Speeches of President Nasser before the General Congresses of the Cooperative Unions, 1959).

Chapter 6

1. See Michel Aflaq, *Maarakat al-masir al-wahid* (Battle of the Single Destiny) (Beirut: Dar al-adab, 1958).

2. New York: Frederick A. Praeger, 1959.

3. See *Constitution of the Arab Socialist Baath Party* (Arabic). See also

Fikratuna (Our Idea) (Arabic) by Michel Aflaq and others (Baath Party Cultural Office, 1948).

4. See *Hawl al-qawmiyya wa al-ishtirakiyya* (On Nationalism and Socialism) by Michel Aflaq, Akram Hourani, Munif al-Razzaz, and Adnan al-Atasi (Beirut, 1957).

5. *Memoirs of Muhammad Kurd Ali: A Selection* (Washington, D.C.: American Council of Learned Societies, 1954), pp. 205–07. The Memoirs were first published in four volumes in Damascus, 1948–51, under the title *Mudhakkirat*.

6. Lest the impression is given that the leadership of these new groups was devoid of rich landowners, one has only to refer to Khaled Azm's or Sabri Assali's opulent wealth. What is interesting is that the new leaders came primarily from the North: both Hourani and Assali, for example, were Deputies from Homs and Hama. Nor were these new leaders political novices. Both Khaled Azm and Hourani, for instance, had been cabinet members during the Shishakli regime.

7. The cleavages between the competitors were so sharp as to make the continued "political existence" of Khaled Azm after union with Egypt problematic at best, and dangerous at worst.

8. An Economic Union agreement with Egypt was actually signed on September 3, 1957.

9. Note that both camps tended to seek a following in the Army Officer Corps.

10. This was especially the view of Baathist leaders in 1958 and 1959 outside Syria. One of these, an editor and publisher of a leading Baathist paper in Beirut, cast serious doubts on the potential of the National Union scheme in the U.A.R.

11. Michel Aflaq, for example, or Munif al-Razzaz, a prominent Baathist writer. Aflaq left Syria early in 1960, probably for Lebanon.

12. A gigantic task is involved here of transferring traditional loyalty from the tribal chief to a central government. To legitimize its authority, the government in Cairo or Damascus must further respond to demands of tribesmen long fulfilled by their chiefs and gradually assimilate this nomadic and semi-nomadic community into the fabric of the state. Whether this can be done by transforming tribes into sedentary agricultural communities or industrial labor groups remains to be seen. The difficulties are staggering when one considers the fierce atomism and independence of tribesmen, their limited sense of loyalty, and their existence long based on the ability to wage war across boundaries, and to settle disputes within the context of their tribal customary law and practice.

13. It will be recalled that between 1955 and 1958 the regime in Cairo had temporarily relaxed its suppression of left-wing groups and persons in Egypt, and that the Communists had decided to go along with the

regime, especially after the September 1955 arms deal with the Soviet bloc. It will also be recalled that the Syrian Communist party had originally supported a federal union plan between Egypt and Syria before it was outmaneuvered by the Baath-army group into a plan of complete union. Khaled Bakdash, Secretary-General of the Communist party, thus left Syria as soon as the U.A.R. was announced, but the party continued to function underground and soon thereafter from neighboring Iraq.

14. Interestingly enough, the campaign was led by three leading leftist journalists (one of them jailed for six months in 1954–55 by President Nasser for views expressed). These were Ihsan Abdel Quddus, of *Rose el-Youssef,* and Ahmad Baha al-Din and Salah Abdel Sabur of *Sabah al-Khair.*

15. A still more interesting aspect of the early battle between the U.A.R. and the Communist parties in Syria and Iraq affecting Union can be observed if one reviews the position of members of the Egyptian Communist party as of January 1, 1959. It appears that after the arms deal with the Soviet bloc in September 1955, President Nasser decided to bring back gradually "into things" some of the left-wing or even Communist groups who were willing to accept (1) the official outlawing of the party in Egypt, and (2) the new relationship with the Soviet Union, without a compensating relaxation of control by the Egyptian Government over the party's activities. President Nasser felt he could do this and still keep an eye on "his" Communists.

The establishment of the newspaper *al-Misa* in 1956 to employ Major Khaled Muhieddin as editor-in-chief is a case in point. Before being ousted from the Revolution Command Council in 1954, Khaled Muhieddin had apparently been quite frank about his political orientation. But he was involved in the March–April 1954 conspiracy to undermine Nasser's position of leadership among the Free Officers in the army. President Nasser, who in those days was bent on a more balanced type of political strategy, decided that Khaled had not outlived his usefulness. In the meantime, the President wished to show the public that he believed at least in the freedom of the press—even one representing the extreme left point of view. And so it was that *al-Misa* began publication. More important, however, was Nasser's shrewd utilization of Khaled for information regarding the activities of the Egyptian extreme left in general, both among civilians as well as the Armed Forces.

16. Egyptians were assigned the key ministries such as War, Planning, Interior, Foreign Affairs, Education, Presidential Affairs, Municipal and Rural Affairs, Economy, and Industry.

17. The Egyptian Deputy was Hasan Dhu'l-Fiqar Sabri, an Air Force flight officer, member of the Free Officers movement, who crashed in a stolen plane when he was trying to pilot General Aziz al-Masri to the

German lines in 1941. He was the brother of another Air Force officer, Ali Sabry, Minister for Presidential Affairs and close adviser to the President. The Syrian Deputy was Farid Zein al-Din, career diplomat, previously Ambassador to Washington, and until his cabinet appointment in October 1958, U.A.R. Ambassador to Bonn.

18. The new National Assembly of the U.A.R. met finally in July 1960. See further discussion of the July 1959 elections in the section of Chapter 5 above dealing with the National Union.

19. Resigned along with other leading Baathists in December 1959.

Chapter 7

1. It will be recalled that the struggle between the Free Officers and the Supreme Council of the Muslim Brethren had been going on since August 1952, when the latter organization insisted upon a share in government. By the autumn of 1954, the Free Officers in power were well on their way to outlawing the Brethren after they had been implicated in the Naguib-Nasser controversy of February–March 1954, on the side of General Naguib.

2. See press interview with Anwar es-Sadat, Secretary-General of the Islamic Congress, in *al-Ahram*, July 6, 1956.

3. See discussion of the political significance of the bond of Islam in P. J. Vatikiotis, "Recent Developments in Islam," in *Tensions in the Middle East*, edited by P. W. Thayer (Baltimore: The Johns Hopkins Press, 1958), pp. 165–80.

4. Princeton University Press, 1957.

5. See P. J. Vatikiotis, *The Fatimid Theory of the State* (Lahore: Orientalia Publishers, 1957).

6. See, for example, Abder Rahman al-Bazzaz, "Islam and Arab Nationalism," *Die Welt des Islams* (1954), Parts 3–4, pp. 210–18, where he asserts that "Arab nationalism devoid of the spirit of Islam is like a body without a soul." But compare this view with Sati' al-Husri, *Al-uruba awwalan* (Arabism First) (Beirut, 1955), which presents a case for a secular nationalism.

7. See the excellent study by Hamed Ammar, *Growing Up in an Egyptian Village* (London: Routledge & Kegan Paul, Ltd., 1954), especially pp. 214–37.

8. Cambridge, Mass.: Arlington Books, 1959, p. 205.

9. Note especially the efforts of the Ministry of National Guidance and Culture to dignify holy feasts, such as the Prophet's Birthday (*mulid en-nabi*), by curbing the mass celebrations of *tariqas*. See a special report to the press by former minister Fathi Radwan in *al-Ahram*, September 25, 1958.

10. *Al-Ahram*, September 27, 1959.

11. Cf. his *Arab Awakening* (London: Hamish Hamilton, 1938).

12. See his *Maarakat al-masir al-wahid,* especially pp. 72–110.

13. In the Special Issue of *al-Hilal* magazine, January 1957.

14. Reported in *al-Ahram,* March 10, 1957.

15. See especially the volume by Muhammad Izzat Darwaza, *al-Wahda al-arabiyya* (Arab Unity) (Beirut: al-Maktab al-tijari, 1957).

16. Personal interview with the Senior Editor of *al-Gumhuriyya,* official newspaper of the regime.

17. It will be recalled that the Baath party in Syria was instrumental in bringing about Union between Damascus and Cairo. One of their fundamental party objectives was Arab unity. After a brief participation in both the Central Government of the U.A.R. and the Executive Cabinet for the Syrian Region (February 1958–December 1959), most of the Baathist leaders in these positions either resigned or were ousted from office, so that by July 1960 the Central Government of the U.A.R. had come under almost completely Egyptian leadership.

18. If Arabism, for example, includes among its fundamental beliefs the granting of the franchise to the people and the establishment of some form of popular representation, present-day army rulers must make token concessions in this direction. The claim to representative legitimacy becomes just as competitive among competing military regimes as that of leadership of Arabism. Thus, in 1959, the announcement by General Abdel Karim Qassem of his intention to restore party politics in Iraq in January 1960 prompted President Nasser of the U.A.R. in the summer of 1959 to advance the date of the general elections for the National Union, originally scheduled for November, to July 1959.

Chapter 8

1. See, for example, John C. Campbell, *Defense of the Middle East* (New York: Harper & Brothers, 1958), pp. 70–72.

2. Such religious minority groups as the Druzes, Alawites, and others.

3. Cambridge, Mass.: Center for International Studies, Massachusetts Institute of Technology (mimeographed), 1959.

4. In addition to the general description of recruiting methods into the Free Officers movement available in such published accounts as Anwar es-Sadat, *Revolt on the Nile* (London: Wingate, 1957), and Gamal Abdel Nasser, *Egypt's Liberation* (Washington, D.C.: Public Affairs Press, 1955), President Nasser declared in his *Palestine War Memoirs:* "I grew restless at H.Q. and went out on a tour of our positions in order to ascertain the mood of the officers. I will not deny that I was really trying to enlist some of them in our Free Officers Organization. In my conversations with the officers I did not come directly to the point. I did not want to distract their minds from their immediate environment, nor to divert their attention from the enemy who was lying in wait for them. My method at that

time aimed at two things. First, to win the confidence of those I met and secondly to strengthen my personal relationships with them as much as possible. I was sure—and this has been amply justified by my experience—that trust and personal friendship were certain to turn into something deeper when the opportune moment arose. When I look around me today I see many faces in the Free Officers Organization which I met for the first time in the trenches during that strange period of our lives which we spent in Palestine." (Mimeographed MS. translation by Professor Walid al-Khalidi of the American University of Beirut, p. 32.)

5. See Manfred Halpern, *Middle Eastern Armies as the Vanguard and Chief Political Instrument of the New Middle Class,* The Rand Corporation, California (mimeographed), 1959. It should be noted that this paper is rather involved with "jargon" about "theories of middle class" and was written before the writer had ever seen the Middle East.

6. Anwar es-Sadat became President of the first National Assembly of the U.A.R., which met in July 1960.

7. On September 21, 1960, President Nasser appointed Nur al-Din Kahhale Vice-President of the Republic and Central Minister of Planning. Abdul Hamid Serraj moved up to the chairmanship of the Syrian Executive Council of Ministers, a post held previously by Kahhale. But Serraj continued to serve as both Syrian Minister of the Interior and Minister of State.

The reshuffling of the cabinets in the U.A.R., however, supports the thesis that President Nasser is concentrating more power and responsibility in the hands of a few trusted aides. Kamal al-Din Husein, for example, besides holding the portfolio of the Central Ministry of Education, was appointed Chairman of the Executive Council of Ministers for Egypt, replacing Nur al-Din Tarraf, who was appointed Central Minister of Health, replacing the Syrian Bashir al-Azmah. Husein was also appointed Minister for Local Government in Egypt. In addition he continued as Supervisor-General of the National Union in Egypt. Serraj in Syria, besides replacing Kahhale as Chairman of the Council of Ministers, was also appointed a Minister of State in addition to his portfolio of the Interior for Syria. (*Ahram,* September 21, 1960.)

8. It is interesting to note that recently Ma'mun al-Kuzbari, one of the Populist party leaders, was assigned to work on the unification of legislation between the two Regions of the Republic.

9. See *al-Ahram* issues of March 1960, especially March 16, 1960.

10. "The Middle East and the Crisis of 1956," *Middle Eastern Affairs,* No. One, St. Antony's Papers, No. 4 (New York: Frederick A. Praeger, 1959), p. 31.

11. Other examples of army leadership in this commitment are the cases of Turkey under Ataturk, Pakistan under Ayyub Khan, Iraq under

Qassem, Indonesia under Soekarno-Nasution, but not so obviously the Sudan under General Abboud.

12. *Interplay of East and West* (New York: W. H. Norton & Co., 1957), p. 132.

13. See *The Politics of Developing Areas,* edited by Gabriel A. Almond and James S. Coleman (Princeton University Press, 1960).

14. For instance, such popular series as "Ikhtarna lak" (We Chose for You), the various military journals, *Kitab al-Hilal* (Book Selection of Dar al-Hilal), and others.

15. Some American students of comparative government have recently been interested in constructing and arguing a "developmental theory" of politics in the non-Western societies, including those in the Middle East and Arab states. By "developmental" they seem to imply generally the ultimate development of democratic institutions or at least the development of institutions oriented toward democratic goals. Such factors as industrialization, the raising of living standards, achievement of literacy, social and economic mobility, are often invoked as essential to this developmental theory. Lately, however, the absence of any inevitable link between these factors and the necessary or ultimate achievement of a greater democratization of society and institutions in these states has impelled many of these scholars to suspect the validity of such a theory. They are unavoidably beginning to consider the question of basic commitments to democratic goals on the part of the leadership and society in new states as distinguished from the implementation of programs that meet theoretically the prerequisites of a democratic establishment. The hopeful aspect of this reorientation is, in many respects, inevitable when one considers (1) the limitations of applying a concept of nationalism as a democratizing force to the Middle Eastern states, and (2) the unfortunate fact that we actually know very little about the content of Middle Eastern nationalism or nationalisms, if indeed there is content. Two interesting analyses of aspects of this question may be found in Edward Shils, *op. cit.,* and Rupert Emerson, *From Empire to Nations* (Cambridge, Mass.: Harvard University Press, 1960).

Chapter 9

1. "Political and Social Development," *Political Quarterly* (Special Issue on the Middle East), XXVIII, No. 2 (April–June 1957), p. 109.

2. *Egypt's Liberation* (Washington, D.C.: Public Affairs Press, 1955), pp. 87–88.

3. *Khutab al-rais,* III, p. 682.

4. *Our Social Revolution,* pp. 48, 49, 50.

5. "Les Forces Sociales à l'Oeuvre dans le Nationalisme Egyptien," *Orient,* II, No. 5 (1958), p. 82.

6. "The Decline of the West in the Middle East," *International Affairs,* XXIX, No. 2 (April 1953), p. 180.

7. Jean Vigneau, "The Ideology of the Egyptian Revolution," in *The Middle East in Transition,* Walter Z. Laqueur, ed. (New York: Frederick A. Praeger, 1958), p. 144.

8. "The Egyptian Revolution," *Foreign Affairs,* XXXIII, No. 2 (January 1955), p. 208.

9. See *The Passing of Traditional Society* (Glencoe, Ill.: The Free Press, 1958).

10. Personal interview with Ihsan Abdel Quddus, October 1958. Cf. my discussion in Chapter 7.

11. See Ayyub Khan, "Pakistan Perspective," *Foreign Affairs,* 38 (July 1960), pp. 547–56.

12. As late as March 1959 the regime was still restricting the freedom and activity of leading writers in Egypt.

13. See Dankwart A. Rustow, "The Army and the Founding of the Turkish Republic," *World Politics,* XI (July 1959), No. 4, pp. 513–52.

14. This view is based on information supplied by Professor Fred W. Frye of M.I.T., who had conducted an extensive survey of the National Assembly membership in Turkey.

15. Chibli Isam in *al-Sahafa,* Baathist newspaper in Beirut, February 28, 1958. See also *al-Akhbar* of Beirut, June 7, 1959. Similar remarks were made to the writer by Jibran Majdalani, editor of *al-Sahafa,* in a personal interview in February 1959.

16. Munif al-Razzaz, *Maalem al-hayat al-arabiyya al-jadida* (Fundamentals of the New Arab Life) (Beirut: Dar al-ilm lil-malayeen, 1956, 3d ed. 1959).

17. "Southeast Asia as a Problem Area in the Next Decade," *World Politics,* XI, No. 3 (April 1959), p. 343.

18. The Press was nationalized in the U.A.R. (or as the favorite phrase of *Rose el-Youssef* put it, "organized") in May 1960.

19. *Soldiers and Governments,* edited by Michael Howard (London: Eyre & Spottiswoode, 1957; Bloomington, Ind.: Indiana University Press, 1959), p. 12.

20. For example, where the civilian bureaucracy has failed to provide efficient administrative continuity, the army has stepped in. The control of political power by the army has not, on the other hand, necessarily implied a displacement of civil bureaucracies. These have survived and continue to function in many instances. So far, in the U.A.R., for instance, army infiltration into the bureaucracy has reflected additional political control in the various functions of the state.

21. April 23, 1960, pp. 341–44.

Index

Abbas, Pasha, Viceroy of Egypt, 8
Abd al-Raziq, Ali, 26
Abdel Hadi, Ibrahim, 35, 60, 62
Abdel Nasser, Gamel, 32, 45, 56, 61,
  65, 68, 79, 82, 120, 137–138, 140,
  181, 218, 222, 227, 233, 236, 238,
  249, 255, 259, 269, 270, 276, 283n,
  288n; early career, 47–50; and
  Wafd, 50; political activity, 50–51;
  first cabinet, 83, 92; as policy
  maker for RCC, 84; attempt on
  his life, 93, 192; and RCC, 94; and
  mass national organization, 102–
  104, 139; views on economic planning, 136; and Baghdad Pact, 160;
  attack on Communist party, 172–
  174; attitude to Islam, 193–194,
  195–196, 198; as a conspirator, 218
Abdel Quddus, Ihsan, 32, 62, 93,
  183, 262, 288n
Abdou, Sheikh Muhammad, 11
Abdullah, King of Jordan, 33
Abu Hadid, Muhammad Farid, 32,
  269
Abul Fath, 62, 93
al-Afghani, Jamal al-Din, 10; pan-
  Islamic agitation, 10–11

Afifi, Hafiz, 39, 66
Aflaq, Michel, 143–145, 147, 153,
  168, 200, 207, 258, 275
Agrarian Reform Law, 75–76, 98;
  in Syria, 171
Amer, Abdel Hakim, 45, 47, 61, 79,
  105, 223, 226; National Union Su-
  pervisor for Syria, 108; Governor
  of Syria, 113, 119–120
Amer, Husein Sirry, 64–66
Ammar, Abbas, 81
Amr, Abdel Fattah, 39
Andrawus, Elias, 34, 39
Anglo-Egyptian Agreement, 1954, 98
Anglo-Egyptian Treaty of 1936, 23,
  39, 45
Antonius, George, 200
Arabism, 190, 197, 198, 200, 201, 203,
  204, 205, 207–208, 209, 274, 290n;
  and Islam, 205–206
Arab-Israeli War, see Palestine War
Arab League, 141, 159, 160, 161
Arab Liberation Party, 151
Arab nationalism, see Arabism
Army Officer Corps, 30, 86, 124, 198,
  205, 214, 219, 228–230, 236–237,
  244, 245, 248, 250–251, 255, 256;

295

Army Officer Corps (*cont.*)
and political groups, 121–122; and
the Baath, 147–148; in Syria, 150;
as political interest group, 169;
and Arabism, 190; and power
structure, 213–217; as leader of
Egyptian society, 227; as mod-
ernizer, 240–243
Army Officers Club, 62–64
Arts, Letters, and Social Sciences,
Higher Council on, 111, 126–128,
285n
Ashmawi, 77, 87, 89
Assali, Sabri, 149, 151, 154, 155,
287n; first government of, 159,
185–186
Aswan Dam, 137
Aswan Officers School, 5, 6
Ataturk, 214, 218, 244, 248, 249
Azhar University, 192, 197, 200, 213
Azm, Khaled, 154, 156, 159, 287n

Baath, 107, 114–119, 123, 143, 149,
150, 155, 168–170, 176, 205, 219,
237, 290n; and National Union,
118, 119, 220, 287n; platform, 144–
145; and Arab unity, 145–146;
and Syrian Parliament, 146; and
Army Officer Corps, 147–148; and
Baghdad Pact, 157
Baghdad Pact, 98, 157, 159
Baha al-Din, Ahmad, 32, 33, 38
Bakdash, Khaled, 149, 155, 288n
al-Banna, Hasan, 29, 51, 188; assassination of, 35
al-Baquri, Sheikh Hasan, 78, 276
Barakat, Bahieddin, 76
al-Barawi, Rashed, 59, 71, 269
Barudi, Mahmud Sami Pasha, 13,
16, 17, 18
al-Bitar, Salah, 153, 162, 182, 225,
226
al-Bizri, General Afif, 159, 162

al-Boghdadi, Abdel Latif, 45, 47, 51,
61, 79, 105, 136, 173, 174, 223; in
Palestine War, 52–53

Combined Centers (*al-wahdat al-
mugamm'a*), *see* National Union
Committee of Union and Progress,
67
Committee on National Education,
252–253
Communist party, 40, 56, 88, 91,
123, 129, 147, 175; in Syria, 151,
155, 163, 172–174, 287n, 288n
Constitutional Liberals, 24, 35, 37,
268
Consultative Assembly, 7–9, 10, 11,
12, 13–14

Economic Organization (*al-mu'as-
sasa al-iqtisadiyya*), 285n
Egypt, military tradition, 3, 4, 44;
conquests of, 4; army, 4 (*see also*
Egyptian Army); early representative government, 8–10, 11, 13;
British financial control, 11–14;
1882 Constitution, 18; British occupation, 19; British protectorate,
21; British Declaration, February
1922, 22; 1923 Constitution, 23–24,
42; early political parties, 24; Parliament, 25, 28, 33–34; national
thought, 26–27; politics 1946–
1952, 29–31; labor unrest, 31; radical writers, 31–32; and Palestine
War, 33; Communist party, 56,
287n, 288n; 1956 Constitution, 98–
99, 175; and democratic government, 98–102; local government
schemes, 108–110; educational policy, 128–131; social and economic
development, 132–138; trade and
labor unions, 134–135; and Iraq,
158–159; traditional policy in

Egypt, military tradition (*cont.*)
Syria, 160–161; Arab policy, 200–202; intellectuals, 220–221, 222; power structure, 223

Egyptian Army, 4, 217, 254, 255; under Muhammad Ali, 3–7, 216; under Mamelukes, 5; conscription, 6; under Saladin, 7; and British occupation, 7; under Abbas Pasha, 8; under Said Pasha, 8; early Army Officers School under Ismail, 8–9; national demands, 14–16; British control, 21; Officers Corps, 30; and King Farouq, 41–42; Sirdar, 44; *badaliyya*, 44; Anglo-Egyptian Treaty, 45; Wafd policy, 45; Staff College, 47; as political leader, 125; and Arabism, 190; and modernization, 215–217; *see also* Egypt

Faluja, 282n

al-Farghali, Sheikh Muhammad, 88, 93

Farouq, King, 22; and parliament, 25, 33–34; absolute rule, 35–37; and the press, 36–42; and opposition parties, 37; and Wafd, 37–40; and Army, 41–42; deposition of, 75

Fawzi, Mahmoud, 224

Feisal, King of Iraq, 157

Free Officers, 45–46, 97, 181, 214–215, 217, 219, 233, 239, 244, 252, 274; education, 46–47; early activities, 53–60, 66–68; Executive Committee, 60–61, 68, 71, 96; and Army Officers Club elections, 63–64; and the Wafd, 64–65; and political groups, 77–80; 86–89, 95; and Muslim Brethren, 77–78, 86–87, 92–94, 289n; February–March 1954 crisis, 89–92; 1956 Constitution, 103; political ideologies, 122–124; and Arab nationalism, 146–147, 202, 203–204, 208; and Islam, 193–194; recruitment, 290n

Fuad, King of Egypt, 24, 25

Galal, Fuad, 81

Green Shirts, *see* Misr al-Fatat

Gumaa, Abdel Salam Fahmi, 39

Haidar, General Muhammad, 39, 64–66

Haikal, Muhammad Husein, 31, 33, 37, 38, 73, 268

al-Hakim, Tawfiq, 127

Hamdoun, Mustafa, 115, 118, 154, 156, 160

Hicks, General, 44

Hilali, Nagib, 40, 66

Hilmi, Abdel Al, 16, 18, 20

Hinnawi, 151, 152, 161

Hodeibi, *see* Hudeibi

Hourani, Akram, 115–119, 143, 144, 147, 152, 153, 155, 170, 173, 182, 186, 225, 226

Hudeibi, 77, 87–88

Husein, Abdel Nasser, 47

Husein, Ahmad, 24, 34, 37, 93, 102

Husein, Kamal al-Din, 45, 47, 61, 79, 80, 83, 93, 109, 223, 228, 284n, 291n; *fedayeen* activities, 53; National Union supervisor, 107, 108, 109, 111, 113, 129; Minister of Education, 127

Husein, Sherif of Mecca, 205, 208

Husein, Taha, 26, 32, 127

al-Huseini, Ishaq, 245–246, 274, 275

Ibrahim, Hasan, 45, 61, 64, 74, 92

Idris, Yusuf, 32, 128, 231, 280

Ikhwan, *see* Muslim Brethren

Iraq, 251, 256, 257; Free Officers, 203, 204, 208

Islamic Congress, 51, 52; aims, 191–192

Ismail, Khedive of Egypt, 3; Army Officer schools, 8–9; and representative government, 8–10, 13; financial difficulties, 10; deposition of, 12

Jamali, Fadhil, 185, 186
al-Jaza'iri, Salim, 205

Kafr al-Dawar uprising, 79–80
Kahhale, Nur al-Din, 116, 291n
al-Kaisouni, Abdel Moneim, 286n
Kamil, Mustafa, 21, 281n
Kassem, General, 167, 174, 290n, 292n
Khadduri, Majid, 58
Khalid, Khalid Muhammad, 31
Kuwwatli, Shukri, 140, 143, 154, 156, 161

Labor Affairs, Supreme Advisory Council for, 133
League of Arab States, see Arab League
Legislative Assembly, see Consultative Assembly
Liberal Constitutionals, see Constitutional Liberals
Liberation Province, 284n
Liberation Rally, 82–84, 86–87, 91, 93, 111, 283n
Little, Tom, 67, 71

Mahdawi, Colonel, 185
Maher, Ahmad, 24, 30, 34, 40
Maher, Ali, 40, 66, 74, 76, 269
al-Malki, Riyad, 116, 225
Mameluke, 3, 4, 5, 6
al-Masri, General Aziz, 51, 56, 205
Mehanna, Rashad, 64, 80, 94
Military Academy, 45, 46, 50, 57, 58

Military service, 7, 14, 98, 231–233
Ministry of Education, 127–129, 137
Misr al-Fatat (Green Shirts), 34, 37, 51, 56, 59, 93, 102
al-Misri, 62
Montreux Convention, 1937, 26
Muhammad Ali, Viceroy of Egypt, 3–7, 22, 161, 216, 251
Muhieddin, Khaled, 45, 53, 61, 62, 94, 288n
Muhieddin, Zakariyya, 45, 47, 105, 173, 174, 223, 269
Muslim Brethren, 29, 51, 53, 59, 64, 88, 95, 102, 123, 142, 146, 191, 192, 242, 283n; in Egyptian politics, 29–30, 32; terrorism, 34–35; and Free Officers, 73; and Liberation Rally, 86–87; political agitation, 87–88
Muslim Brotherhood, see Muslim Brethren

Nafuri, Colonel, 115
Naguib, General Muhammad, 46, 63, 66, 68, 71, 79, 82, 87–89, 90, 93, 270, 283n; cabinet, 76, 81, 84; and political parties, 76–80; conflict with Nasser, 89–93
Nahhas, Mustafa, 39, 77
National Assembly, 105–107, 108, 113, 175, 181, 289n
National Cooperatives Union, 138–139, 257
National Party, 13, 14, 35, 37
National Planning Committee, 136–138, 286n
National Union, 51, 122, 139, 169, 184, 222, 228, 244–245, 256, 284n; device for populist support, 101–102; formation, 103–106; purpose, 104, 107; 1957 elections, 105–106; executive committee, 105, 110, 111, 113; organization and develop-

National Union (*cont.*)
ment, 107–112; and local government, 108–110; General Congress, 108, 110; Secretariat, 110, 112; membership, 112; 1959 elections, 112; Advisory Committee for Syria, 119; political implications, 120–124; educational policy, 128–131; Combined Centers, 131, 139; social and economic development, 132–138; trade and labor unions, 134–135
Nubar Pasha, 11, 12
Nuqrashi, Mahmoud, 30, 32, 34

Orabi, Ahmad Pasha, 18–21, 68; *see also* Orabi Revolt
Orabi Revolt, 11, 14–18, 20, 21
Osman, Amin Pasha, 34, 52

Palestine War, 29, 32, 33, 51, 54, 57, 59, 60, 64, 147, 149, 215
Peoples Party, 24
Peoples Party in Syria, *see* Shaab Party
Pioneers, *see Ruwwad*
President Nasser, *see* Abdel Nasser, Gamal
Production, Permanent Council for National, 98, 134

Qannut, Colonel, 115, 118
Qassem, Abdel Karim, *see* General Kassem
qawmiyya, 124
Qawuqji, Fawzi, 52–53

al-Rafii, Abder Rahman, 7, 16, 33, 37, 267–268, 282n
al-Razzaz, Munif, 147, 206, 275
Revolutionary Command Council (RCC), 53, 94, 97, 175, 181, 191, 218, 242; composition of, 74; and

political parties, 76–77, 92; popular campaign, 78–80; and labor unrest, 78–80; and Army Officer Corps, 80–81; rule by decree, 98
Revolutionary Council, *see* Revolutionary Command Council
Rifaat, Kamal, 224, 228
Rifqi, Osman Pasha, 15, 16
Riyad, Pasha, 14, 15, 16, 17
Rose el-Youssef, 62, 93, 104, 113, 262
Ruwwad (Pioneers), 81

Saadist party, 24, 37
Sabri, Ali, 45, 127, 223
Sabri, Hasan Dhu'l-Fiqar, 46, 224, 288n, 289n
es-Sadat, Anwar, 32, 45, 47, 51, 56, 61, 62, 80, 223, 269, 270, 291n; revolutionary activity, 51–52; National Union Secretary-General, 103, 104; Islamic Congress Secretary General, 191
Safawi, Nawab, 88
al-Said, Nuri, 157, 158, 159, 205, 208
Said Pasha, Viceroy of Egypt, 3, 19; military service policy, 8, 9
Saladin, 4, 7, 22
Salem, Gamal, 45, 61, 67, 74, 92
Salem, Salah, 45, 58, 60, 61, 62, 74, 84, 85, 92
Salim, Latif Bey, 12, 281n
Serag al-Din, Fuad, 38
Serraj, Colonel Abdel Hamid, 108, 115, 118–119, 154, 156, 160, 162, 170, 175, 226, 291n
Shaab Party, 118, 157
Shafei, Husein, 45, 74, 80, 88, 92, 109, 223
Sherif Pasha, 13–15, 17, 18, 20, 281n
Sherine, Ismail, 66
Shikan, battle of, 44
Shishakli, Adib, 118, 146, 151, 153, 154, 162, 218, 249, 285n

Sibai, Yusuf, 111, 127

Sidki, Bakr, 58, 218, 249

Sidky, Ismail, 24, 30, 50, 268

Sirry, Husein, coalition cabinet, 35–36, 40, 66

Socialist party, see Misr al-Fatat

Society of Free Officers, see Free Officers

Stack, Sir Lee Pasha, Sirdar, Egyptian Army, 45

Staff College, 47, 51, 57–58, 60

Students, General Federation of U.A.R., 129, 130

Sudan, 6

Suez Canal, 38–39, 65, 90, 97

Suleiman Pasha, al-Faransawi, 5

Syria, 7, 225; political party activity, 107, 151–153; National Union, 107–108, 112–116, 120, 172; dissolution of political parties, 114; emergency high commission, 115, 173; political difficulties, 116–120; union with Egypt, 143–144, 161, 163, 167; Republic, 148; Communist party, 151, 163; union with Iraq schemes, 151, 152; and Baghdad Pact, 157; political experience, 163–166; northern region of U.A.R., 167

Syrian Army, 148–149, 255; and political parties, 149–150; purge by Shishakli, 153; in politics, 155–156

Tahawi, Ibrahim, 110

tariqas, 197

Tewfiq, Khedive of Egypt, 3, 12, 13, 14, 19, 44; military service law of 1880, 15, 281n; constitution of 1882, 18

Thabit, Karim, 34, 37

Tuaimah, Abdallah, 93, 110, 224

Ukasha, Sarwat, 46, 224

United Arab Republic, 257; educational problems, 128–131; industrialization, 134; Central Planning Committee, 136–137; formation of, 140–142; October 1958 government, 171–175, 178; provisional constitution 1958, 176; elections 1959, 180–181, 183; cabinet system, 181–193; political power in, 212, 213–217; political groups, 234–235

Voice of the Arabs, 161

Wafd, 22, 23, 24, 28, 32, 35, 36, 77, 82, 95, 102; as a mass party, 24–25; and Palace, 24–25, 37–40; leadership, 26; abrogation of Anglo-Egyptian Treaty, 39; Military Academy, 45

Young Egypt, see Misr al-Fatat

Yunes, Ahmad al-Haj, 119

Zaghloul, Saad, 21, 22; political ascendancy, 23–24

Zaim, 146, 149, 150, 218, 249

Zaki, General Salim, 24